COLUMBIA COLLEGE
973R595L   C1   V0
THE RISE AND FALL OF ANTI-AMERICANISM

973 R595L

Amerique dans les tetes.

The rise and fall of anti-
 Americanism

D1787249

261-2500

ENTERED NOV 21 1990

THE RISE AND FALL OF ANTI-AMERICANISM

The Rise and Fall of Anti-Americanism

A Century of French Perception

Edited by

Denis Lacorne
Senior Fellow, CERI
Fondation Nationale des Sciences Politiques

Jacques Rupnik
Senior Fellow, CERI
Fondation Nationale des Sciences Politiques

Marie-France Toinet
Senior Fellow, CERI
Fondation Nationale des Sciences Politiques

Translated by

Gerry Turner

St. Martin's Press   New York

© Hachette 1986. First published as *L'Amérique dans les Têtes: Un Siècle de Fascinations et d'Aversions*

Translation © Gerry Turner 1990

All rights reserved. For information, write:
Scholarly and Reference Division,
St. Martin's Press, Inc., 175 Fifth Avenue,
New York, N.Y. 10010

First published in the United States of America in 1990

Printed in Hong Kong

Library of Congress Cataloging-in-Publication Data
Amérique dans les têtes. English.
The Rise and Fall of Anti-Americanism: a Century of French Perception/edited by Denis Lacorne, Jacques Rupnik, Marie-France Toinet; translated by Gerry Turner.
   p. cm.
Translation of: L'Amérique dans les têtes.
Includes bibliographical references.
ISBN 0–312–04206–X
1. United States – Foreign public opinion, French – Congresses.
2. Public opinion – France – History – 20th century – Congresses.
I. Lacorne, Denis. II. Rupnik, Jacques. III. Toinet, Marie-France.
IV. Title.
E183.8.F8A6413   1990
973–dc20   89–29381
                                                                   CIP

```
973 R595L
Amerique dans les tetes.
The rise and fall of anti-
    Americanism
```

Contents

Acknowledgements	vii
Notes on the Contributors	viii
Foreword *Theodore Zeldin*	x
Introduction: France Bewitched by America *Denis Lacorne and Jacques Rupnik*	1

PART I THE ORIGINS OF ANTI-AMERICANISM: HISTORY AND HYSTERIA

1	The Pathology of Anti-Americanism *Theodore Zeldin*	35
2	From Baudelaire to Duhamel: An Unlikely Antipathy *Pascal Ory*	42
3	Anti-Americanism in the Years of Collaboration and Resistance *Robert O. Paxton*	55
4	The Cold War *Michel Winock*	67

PART II THE BEHAVIOUR OF THE INTELLIGENTSIA AND ITS INFLUENCE ON PUBLIC OPINION

5	Images of the United States in Public Opinion *Jacques Rupnik and Muriel Humbertjean*	79
6	The French Intelligentsia Rediscovers America *Diana Pinto*	97
7	Anti-Americanism and the Elite *Ezra N. Suleiman*	108
8	Sartre, Beauvoir, Aron: An Ambiguous Affair *Marie-Christine Granjon*	116

PART III ECONOMY: DREAM OF MODERNITY

9   Managerially Yours   137
   Richard Armand

10   Modernists and Protectionists: The 1970s   143
   Denis Lacorne

11   The Limits of the American Model   160
   Christian Stoffaës

PART IV THE RHETORIC AND REALITY OF ANTI-AMERICANISM IN FOREIGN POLITICS

12   French Anti-Americanism Under the Fourth Republic and the Gaullist Solution   169
   Michael M. Harrison

13   Unruly France   179
   Alfred Grosser

PART V THE US CONSTITUTION: MODEL OR MIMIC?

14   The Lawyers' Verdict   189
   Marie-France Toinet

15   The Fifth Republic and the American Model   205
   Julien Feydy

PART VI WHY ANTI-AMERICANISM IS NOT ALWAYS QUITE WHAT IT SEEMS, NOR AMERICANO-PHILES QUITE WHAT THEY SAY THEY ARE

16   United States: Model or Bête Noire?   213
   Guy Sorman

17   Does Anti-Americanism Exist?   219
   Marie-France Toinet

18   By Way of Conclusion   236
   André Kaspi

Index   244

Acknowledgements

The idea for this volume grew out of a symposium organised five years ago on French perceptions of the United States. The symposium was sponsored by the *Centre d'Etudes et de Recherches Internationales* (CERI) of the Fondation Nationale des Sciences Politiques (Paris), with the assistance of the Sterling Currier Fund of Columbia University (New York).

We wish to express our gratitude to Eric Homberger of the University of East Anglia for all his support in making this collection available to the English-speaking reader. Special thanks are due to Gerald Turner for his painstaking work on the translations.

D.L. J.R. M-F.T.

Notes on the Contributors

Richard Armand is an industrialist and a graduate of Ecole Polytechnique.

Julien Feydy is Professor of Political Science at the Université de Paris I. He specialises in constitutional issues.

Marie-Christine Granjon, docteur ès lettres et sciences humaines of the University of Paris, is a fellow at the Fondation Nationale des Sciences Politiques, Paris. She is the author of *L'Amérique de la Contestation* (1985).

Alfred Grosser is Professor of International Relations at the Institut d'Etudes Politiques, Paris. His recent books include *The Western Alliance: European-American Relations* (1982), *Affaires Extérieures: La Politique de la France 1944–1984* (1984), *L'Allemagne en Occident* (1987).

Michael M. Harrison is associate director of the Programme for Strategic and International Security Studies of the Institut Universitaire des Hautes Etudes Internationales, Geneva. He is the author of *The Reluctant Ally: France and Atlantic Security* (1981).

Muriel Humbertjean is director of sociological studies at the SOFRES (a French survey institute). She is a co-author of *Opinion Publique* (1985).

André Kaspi is Professor of History at the Université de Paris I-Sorbonne. His publications include *Les Américains* (1986), *Etats-Unis 68* (1988), *Franklin Roosevelt* (1988).

Pascal Ory is Professor of History at the Université de Paris X-Nanterre. He is the author of *Les Collaborateurs* (1983), the co-author of *Les Intellectuels en France de l'Affaire Dreyfus à nos jours* (1986) and editor of *La Nouvelle Histoire des Idées Politiques* (1987).

Robert O. Paxton is Professor of History at Columbia University. He is the author of *Vichy France* (1982), and the co-author of *Vichy France and the Jews* (1983).

Notes on the Contributors ix

Diana Pinto is a freelance writer in Paris. She has written numerous articles on European intellectuals, European history and sociology. She received a PhD from Harvard University.

Guy Sorman is the author of *La Révolution Conservatrice Américaine* (1983), *L'Etat Minimal* (1985), and *La Nouvelle Richesse des Nations* (1987).

Christian Stoffaës, formerly in the Ministry of Industry, occupies an executive position with the Electricité de France and is a professor at the Institut d'Etudes Politiques, Paris. He is a co-editor of *French Industrial Policy* (Brookings 1985), and author of *Fins de Mondes* (published in English by the University of Chicago Press).

Ezra N. Suleiman is Professor of Political Science at Princeton University. His publications include *Elites in French Society* (1978), and *Private Power and Centralization in France* (1987).

Michel Winock is Professor of History at the Institut d'Etudes Politiques, Paris. His recent books include *La Fièvre Hexagonale* (1986), and *1789 L'Année sans pareille* (1988).

Theodore Zeldin, is a Fellow of St Antony's College, Oxford. His publications include *France 1848–1945* (1981), *The French* (1983) and *Happiness* (1988).

Foreword
Theodore Zeldin

This is more than a book about France. For there are now very few people left anywhere who have not experienced, in some form, the emotions which are discussed in it. There are very few countries which have not been obliged to re-define themselves by reference to what the USA represents or is supposed to represent. But the predicament of the old world in face of the new world is ceasing to be quite what it used to be. The USA has long been seen as a vision of the future, albeit a blurred vision. The inhabitants of the old world had simply to choose between faith and doubt when confronted by it. Today, however, it is no longer enough for a person to decide whether the USA holds out a promise of liberation or a threat of stifling oppression, for it has become clear that it is not so easy to disentangle liberation and oppression.

What is new is that Europeans in particular are beginning to know the USA at first hand; more and more of them are able to study, or travel, or live there for a few months or a few years; more and more have tasted the future without relinquishing their own past. There are few who have not spent innumerable evenings relaxing in the fantasy foam-bath of American films. The USA is far less distant, in both space and time, than it has ever been; indeed, some element of its culture is to be found, however minimally, in most people. So it has become a necessity for every individual to try to understand, as this book does, how dreams and hallucinations about the USA, enthusiasms and disappointments, continue to be born and to die.

English-speaking readers may start by thinking they are being served yet more exasperating illustrations of that special combination of chauvinism and fashion-mania which is supposed to characterise the French. But they will soon realise that the perspective of the future which is opened up here is quite different, and for American readers this perspective may be alarming. So far, American attitudes have been decisive in shaping the quality of US-French relations. The basic problem has been that the French fascination with the USA has not been reciprocated. There is probably no western country, proportionately to its size, in which the French language is less spoken or less appreciated than the USA. Everything in the interactions between the two nations is overshadowed by the French sense of being undervalued and, worse, ignored. If only the Americans hated the French, and were open enemies, as the Germans once were, something could be done about it; and indeed something which might have seemed miraculous a generation ago has been done in Franco-German relations. However, this long-established deadlock may be about to be broken. In the 1990s the roles of France and the USA may well be reversed. Europe may come to replace the USA as the great adventure, and the vision of a new future. The turning point in Franco-American history may be 1992.

What is unusual about this book, to me, is the way it points to the future, suggesting that the future is far more open and uncertain than the heavy burden of past misunderstandings may lead one to suppose. The essence of a historical approach to political and social issues, such as is adopted here, is that, normally, it is based on the assumption that events are linked by a chain of cause and effect which is very hard to break, a chain once considered to be forged by the gods, who called it destiny, and nowadays produced by seemingly as omnipotent economic, social and cultural forces. But this book demonstrates how flimsy the chain is. Its conclusion is that French attitudes to the USA had more to do with the vagaries of the imagination than with actual experience of that country, or with any positive intrusion of American power into French life. It shows how trivial the reasons for sympathy and antipathy have often been, how narrow the margin is between success and failure, how readily the wind changes direction, again and again. In other words, the relations between the two countries could easily have been different. So the new question which it raises is not 'Why is it so?' but 'How could it have been otherwise?'

It may seem that that is not the business of scholars to write alternative scenarios either of the future or of the past. When tradition determined what people believed and did, scholars simply proclaimed what tradition was. But frequently, and perhaps inevitably, they invented or re-invented tradition in the process, though they did not admit it. Now that most people are increasingly interested not so much in their inheritance as in what the future can offer, writers of fiction appear to be taking over the task of nourishing the imagination, probing the hidden depths of human potential, inventing new possibilities, exploring the unforseen. The imaginative side of the scholar's role has recently been less in evidence, while the emphasis has been on collecting more and more information. There is so much information now, it is becoming very difficult to cope with, let alone master. Scholars are being forced to be more selective towards their material, on pain of becoming ever narrower specialists. And that may lead them to be bolder in what they attempt, in the questions they ask. In a world searching desperately for freedom, there is a need for a new 'free history' of its heritage, which means looking at the past not only for what happened, but also for what almost happened but did not quite, using both elements to construct pictures of reality which emphasise choice as well as inescapable constraints, becoming aware of the artistic nature of the process of understanding the past, and being willing to be a modern artist.

A book such as this one not only clarifies the myths of two countries, it also, inevitably, contributes to creating new myths. I personally believe that the transformation of US-French relations will hinge on the transformation of the myth of what it means to be a foreigner.[1] In this history and analysis of the French attitude to the USA, the reader will find ample material for constructing, for himself or herself, hypotheses about what might happen next.

Note

1. For a 'free history' of the foreigner, see Theodore Zeldin, *Happiness* (1988).

Introduction: France Bewitched by America

Denis Lacorne and Jacques Rupnik

Whether as model or *bête noire,* America has never ceased to fascinate and exasperate the French, as well as inspire all sorts of fantasies. For some, it evokes modernity and social progress, for others, imperialist violence and the summary justice of a corrupt sheriff, and for others still, the threatening uniformity of mass culture. As a kind of retribution for the American surpluses off-loaded on to a bankrupt Europe at the end of the war – and so frequently denounced by the detractors of 'Yankee capitalism' – the French have tacked their 'ideological surpluses' on to the great mythical figure of America.

According to Jean Baudrillard, 'The United States is Utopia attained': it is the 'American Dream' come true; the belief in all those values of *la vieille Europe* – 'justice, abundance, law, wealth, freedom* – has been miraculously incarnated in the New World.[1]

Nowadays, the 'American Dream' is more associated with the catch-all concept of *modernity.* In the France of the 1980s *modernity* evokes the enterprise spirit, state disengagement, Silicon Valley, genetic engineering, the conquest of space and anything else that is supposed, rightly or wrongly, to be of American origin.

The problem for a country like France is that its economic ambitions clash with its cultural identity.[2] The French seek economic power in order to maintain their position in the world. This in turn requires the integration of the French economy into world markets and a truly competitive spirit. It implies becoming business-minded, willingness to spend lengthy periods abroad, a decent command of English, and so on. But at the same time the French want to preserve a cultural heritage which is intrinsically archaic, those *vieilles valeurs* which are the very foundation of *la France éternelle* such as *l'académisme,* distrust of pragmatism, a passion for philosophical abstractions, and a taste for refined fashions and highbrow culture. The upshot is that the country's real or imagined economic power conflicts with the national identity of a people with uninhibited delusions of 'grandeur' and a desire to set themselves up as a model for the rest of the world.

Will the French ever be modern? Some have their doubts: 'We will never catch them [the Americans] up. We will never have their forthrightness. All we do is imitate and parody them, with a fifty-year lag and nothing to show for it anyway ... America is the original version of *modernity:* we're the dubbed version, or even the one with sub-titles'.[3] Others believe France does stand a chance of catching up, but they fear the negative side-effects. To them, *modernity* signifies the *'américanisation'* of the French way of life; it is the horrifying prospect of an 'American Dream' turned nightmare, which would degrade *la France éternelle* and transform it into the 'gadget civilisation' of fast-food and soap-operas ... The worst-case scenario is the 'Disneylandisation' of *la vieille Europe,*[4] paving the way for a 'cultural Waterloo'[5] brought about by the excessive importation of American TV series.

There is no easy way of summing up French perceptions of America. France is a heterogeneous country made up of countless different groups, every one of which has its 'own' image of America, which frequently changes in the light of circumstances or political events. However, it sometimes happens that this multitude of contradictory perceptions coalesces into a major trend of opinion and for a while the attitudes of the country as a whole are either exaggeratedly favourable or excessively unfavourable to American realities. But what is public opinion in fact, and to what extent can it influence or change the perceptions of groups or individuals? What is the actual influence of the media, the political establishment and the intelligentsia on the evolution of our perceptions as a community? How is it that the American factor has dominated political debate in this country, on the Right and Left alike? Is our image of America always distorted by the prism of our obsessions? Is it always determined by the vigour of domestic debate or the violence of international crises? It is questions like these that we seek to answer in our analysis of the wave of Americanomania currently seizing France. We will take a look at the major swings of opinion in French history, before considering the insistence of the political and cultural élite on preserving the 'purity' of the French language. Being largely a self-defence mechanism, this latter phenomenon has tended to escape the cyclical fluctuations of pro- and anti-American feeling. It constitutes, we argue, a 'cultural invariant'.

It is senseless to assert the existence of pro- and anti-American attitudes in France on the basis of poll findings, in the absence of any real notion of what such opinions actually signify. They can, of course, display extreme ambiguity as well as enormous variations. People can loathe Reagan while being enthusiastic about American technology and keen on jazz. Equally they can condemn the invasion of Grenada while wearing their faded jeans with pride. The range of possibilities is endless. Consider the case of Baudelaire and Sartre, for instance, both of whom were great proponents of American literature, while also being fierce critics of 'Americanism' in their day: the former denouncing the nineteenth century as 'Americanised by its zoocratic industrial philosophers', the latter diagnosing America as 'a mad dog'.

Rather than dwell on the idiosyncrasies and ambiguities of personal options, it would be more enlightening to consider those tidal waves of opinion that carry thousands of individual attitudes with them, before eventually producing 'a swing'. What better demonstration of this than the 'Reaganomania' of 1984. There was no lack of warning clues, particularly the sensational headlines of the Parisian press and the proliferation of special issues devoted to the American model: 'My model is Reagan' (interview with Jean-Marie Le Pen in *Le Figaro Magazine* of 23 June 1984); 'The new New World' (*L'Expansion*, 19 October 1984); 'Dr Reagan's miracle cures' (*Le Nouvel Observateur*, 14 September 1984); 'Reagan's incredible destiny' (*L'Express*, 2 November 1984); 'Why the French love Reagan'(*Le Monde*, 10 November 1984); 'France's declining anti-Americanism' (*Le Figaro*, 10 November 1984), and so on. Guy Sorman, France's leading exegete of American neo-conservatism, did an enormous amount to spread the gospel by publishing *La Révolution Conservatrice Américaine* followed by *La Solution Libérale*.[6]

The American model's miraculous ability to overcome the economic crisis of the 1980s is now commonly accepted. Enthusiasm reached such a peak that one even found commentators expressing astonishment that France has yet to adopt the 'Reaganomic remedy', quite ignoring the fact that in its first phase, Reaganomics caused the worst recession in the United States since the 1930s.[7] In an unprecedented move, French intellectuals eager to do their bit to assist the progress of the miracle, actually set up a 'Committee to re-elect President Reagan'.[8] The SOFRES pollsters were so impressed by the pro-Reagan tide, that they found nothing odd in asking a cross-section of French voters to indicate how they would vote if they were American electors. Not surprisingly they obtained the answer they were seeking, namely, that in France also, Reagan was more popular than Mondale.[9] There was even the Gaullist deputy who took the floor at a symposium organised by *La Fondation du futur* in the wake of Reagan's victory and expressed his joy by rephrasing one of his hero's election slogans: 'The West is a myth. Mr Reagan is a man of the West. Ergo Mr Reagan is immortal.'[10] With no less enthusiasm, Georges Suffert, author of *Les Nouveaux Cowboys* told a *Figaro* journalist: 'The 21st century has already started over there. As we cross the ocean we change millennia . . .'[11] Even the Left was not spared this wave of infatuation. 'Even Socialists think America is *chic*!', concluded an article on Reaganism in *Le Nouvel Observateur*.[12]

While most commentators are agreed that there was a swing of opinion, it is important to realise what it was a swing *away from*. Were the French as a whole Americanophobic before 1984? Such an assertion would be hard to prove, since, among other things, Americanophobia is a very imprecise concept. In reality, it is not America *per se* that has fired the French imagination and turned public opinion upside down, but the very specific policies of a particular man and his administration. No doubt one should speak of *Reaganomania* rather than *pro-Americanism*. French Reaganomania is a reaction to the anti-Americanism evident during the Carter administration and at the beginning of Reagan's first term. As Jean-Marie Domenach suggests: 'The French were scandalously "disinformed" about Reagan at the time of his election. Now they are making up for it, if not actually over-compensating'.[13]

Careful study of the Parisian press of the early 1980s confirms this impression and reveals the strength of anti-Reagan feeling. In those days, the ex-actor turned politician seemed to have stepped out of a 'props room'.[14] Everything about him confounded the expectations of French political pundits – from his lack of experience in foreign policy, to his naïve declarations of faith and his primitive anti-Sovietism. They were used to less candour, more cynicism and greater intellect. At first sight, his election confirmed the confused fears of an American-style decadence that might one day overwhelm us. That was the time when one of the future front-runners of Reaganism *à la française* denounced the 'lack of culture, public-spiritedness and civilised intimacy' in an America which 'seems to have failed as a nation...' and came to the conclusion that it was vital to 'adopt a greater degree of detachment' vis-à-vis a country that no longer had anything to offer us, not even a 'virile image of modernity'.[15]

Here and there one could come across articles extolling Reagan in 1980, but their ironical tone betrayed their authors' underlying purpose. The reason why there was affection for Reagan in those circles was that he confirmed with rare precision the most deepseated French prejudices about America. The corny side of his personality not only appealed to the French: they found it reassuring. Carter, on the other hand, was impossible to come to terms with. His behaviour gave grounds for concern and anxiety. His lack of decisiveness, the shifts and changes in his foreign policy, his sudden belated discovery of the Soviet threat and his agonising over the fate of the American hostages did not live up to the French people's image of the decisive American, let alone of the leader of a powerful imperial nation.

Reagan was someone who at last fitted the bill; in other words he matched the old stereotype of the simple-hearted, devout roughdiamond with a disarming candour: the champion of the unbridled competition, indifferent to workers' rights and civil liberties. And then all of a sudden, after recession had given way to recovery, and recovery to a 'miracle', the French recognised in these all-American shortcomings the very virtues of a Cyrano de Bergerac: 'The Gascons have found themselves a new leader again. Reagan's America – November 1980 model – naïve, impatient and hottempered, is a kind of Gascony of the world ... The Americans ... have had enough of being the global cuckolds of history which they only seemed to dominate because of their ineffectual might'.[16]

Although less marked, the shake-up of opinion on the Left was just as obvious, in spite of the die-hards of the Communist Party and the left-wing of the Socialist Party. However, the America which the left-wing government sought to emulate was quite different from the model of America promoted by the conservative opposition. Neither Reagan nor 'Reaganomics' appealed to the Left. What they found alluring and *chic*, was American technology, the enterprise spirit and the university-industry tie-up, not to mention the real or imagined adaptability of traditional American industries. That is why, during his American tour of March 1984, Mitterrand chose to make stop-overs at Silicon Valley and Pittsburgh, the symbols and variations of an industrial revolution which, the theory went, could be transferred to France. The first location reflected the desire to develop the industries of the future, the second was selected with an eye to renovating and preserving France's old iron and steel centres.

Was the American example applicable to France? 'Yes', replied François Mitterrand, 'in the sense that the American people are a tremendous reservoir of energy and initiative. For instance, the way they have managed to link enterprise and the university is a masterpiece of intelligence and practical thinking. No, in the sense that America's recovery has resulted in all sorts of casualties and is based on a number of illusions . . .'[17] The ambiguousness of that reply was a good illustration of the limits of the Left's infatuation with America, which it admired for its technology (in the same way it admired the rival model – Japan) while censuring its economic and social policies. It was over the question of Reaganite neo-conservatism that the model of America championed by the Right differed from the one accepted by the Left.

It would be a mistake to give the impression that these manifestations of pro-American feeling were a sudden phenomenon. In fact the significance of the upheaval in public opinion can only be properly assessed if it is viewed in the context of the historical developments of recent years. It then begins to look rather less dramatic or wide-ranging. For a good many reasons, analysed elsewhere in this book, the political and intellectual climate of the 1970s fostered pro-American sympathies within French society. Foreign policy, the behaviour of the leading intellectuals and the worsening image of the Soviet Union were the chief factors in creating the new climate.

The change in foreign policy was unmistakable. Former causes of contention with the United States – defence of the colonial empire, NATO, Vietnam – had all disappeared from the political agenda. French interests were no longer directly threatened as at the time of Suez and, although American imperialism had lost none of its drive or brutality, such as in Central America, there was no comparison with what had happened in Vietnam. There was no longer any conspicuous military conflict that might spark off the criticisms, fears or anti-American prejudices of the French. Paradoxically, at the very moment when whole segments of European public opinion were turning against the United States over the siting of Pershing missiles, the French refrained from any manifestation of hostility. There was no such thing as a French pacifist movement. France's strategic and military independence – that undeniable triumph of Gaullism – ruled out any debate on Euromissiles. The Pershings were needed, as François Mitterrand did not fail to remind the Bundestag, as a response to the threat from the SS20s, and as a means of cementing the strategic Euro-American connection. But it was *les autres* who would get the Pershings ... The few minor disagreements over the gas pipeline, Nicaragua or even North-South relations, did not prejudice the fundamental pro-American orientation of government policy.[18]

Conditions for a swing back in favour of the Americans date back as far as 1970, when the verbal ravings of May 1968 were a thing of the past and 'fashionable Maoism'[19] had collapsed. They were created by what has been referred to as the political silence of the intelligentsia, or rather a certain indifference to the United States on the part of the intellectuals. Paradoxically, though, this did not prevent them making trips to the United States or even spending lengthy periods at American universities. American realities were no longer a central concern of the new generation of intellectuals[20] such as Derrida, Foucault, Lacan, Lévi-Strauss or Serres, who travelled to the United States solely for the purpose of seeking disciples, widening their audience and arranging for translations of their works, although some may well have had a secret desire to commune with those on the fringe – preferably the Californian variety – whose libertarian ideology recalled, albeit in an apolitical and apocalyptic way, the great moments of May 1968. There was no longer any shame attached to visiting a country that had revealed its limitations by losing the Vietnam War and exposing itself to the ignominy of Watergate.

However, the main reason for the intellectuals' silence was their abandonment of the old prophetic modes of expression so dear to the *engagé* intelligentsia of the Sartre generation. Even Althusser was to exclude all 'socialist prophetism', from his philosophical texts, regardless of what his transitory disciples thought and however great was his concern to find an epistemological caesura between the scientific and the ideological, between the 'scientific' mature Marx and the 'humanist' young Marx who was still imbued with neo-Hegelian idealism.[21]

The success of structuralist, neo-Freudian and deconstructionist thinking turned the leading intellectuals of the 1970s away from the more down-to-earth realities of public life. With the advent of the 'primacy of the text' as categorical imperative, as well as 'symptomal reading', the pursuit of the 'floating signifier', and so on, it was out of the question for intellectuals to refer to any 'historical subject'. Shared by literary scholars, philosophers and anthropologists alike, that approach made the very possibility of behaving as an *engagé* intellectual something contemptible. The deftly cultivated esotericism of the leading intellectuals served to divorce the public at large and the mass of students from the Parisian 'centre' of intellectual life.

The brilliant students of the *grandes écoles* fell into three main groups. The most politically aware dallied with fashionable Maoism for a while before discovering the media and converting to the *nouvelle philosophie*. The less politically active and more philosophically minded joined the coteries of the new 'gurus' where they became known for their in-language and their unbelievable élitism. The pragmatists among them discovered business and managerial methods and set off for the American business schools in search of the 'new gospel' of marketing, accounting and strategic planning.[22]

Engrossed in its own factional squabbles and abstruse as ever, the intelligentsia lost its moral supremacy to the intellectual 'gurus' who were manipulated by the mass media but knew how to make use of it in their turn, and who, moreover, were ready to follow the trend. It was the gurus who were to foster a far more attractive image of America than the one purveyed by their great predecessors.[23] Edgar Morin set the ball rolling with his *Journal de Californie* 'I feel an enormous elation to find myself in California . . . it is also an intense excitement to feel myself inside the homing device of spaceship earth, to be a living witness of this crucial *hic et nunc* of the anthropological adventure . . . I am in my element here where new possible worlds are being forged, at the wellhead of mankind's tropic forces, the fermentation vat of what in my excitement I feel like giving the name of Biological Engineering or the nascent *Lebenswelt*'.[24]

Morin's example was followed several years later by the *Tel Quel* group which suddenly swung away from post-68 Maoism when it made the ecstatic discovery of an America more capable of solving economic and political problems and, moreover, richer in manifold 'aesthetic experiences . . . of a superior quality', than old Europe, which it described as 'economically' and 'intellectually' bankrupt'.[25]

Anti-American opinion among the intellectuals had not evaporated but it was being marginalised, particularly since those who continued to support it were concentrating their attacks almost exclusively on the alleged danger for French society of the insidious penetration of socio-cultural forms of the 'American way of life'. On the Left, isolated voices such as those of Régis Debray and Jean-Pierre Chevènement were denouncing *la trahison des clercs* and attacking the mediocrity of the 'pan-Atlantic discourse' and 'the alignment of French ideology on American ideology',[26] or even ' "the American Left", whose purpose continues to be the rapid Americanisation of French society and the avoidance of any revolutionary outcome of the crisis of advanced capitalism, which now encroaches on our very thinking. If there is any truly fashionable and dominant ideology these days, then this is it'. The frenzied conclusion was that the time had come to 'act against the organised *crétinisation* of our people, otherwise our children will have no other option – if they want to "change their lives" – than to pump themselves full of heroin'.[27]

On the self-styled 'new' Right, the ideologues of the GRECE (the extreme right-wing *Groupes de Recherches et Etudes pour la Civilisation Européenne*) were undertaking a systematic analysis of American 'perversions' in order to assert more effectively the correctness of their neo-Barrèsian philosophy of *enracinement* or 'rootedness' and the rather unusual political concept of a 'pagan' and neutralist Europe (that is, one without any real or potential contact with the United States). The identity of the 'New Europe' would derive from *le droit à la différence* of its component peoples, based on ancient polytheistic foundations. It was this right to be different that would be directly threatened by the 'virus of non-differentiation' that spilled over from the American racial and cultural 'melting-pot'. Hence the need to take all measures necessary to end infiltration by American ideas.[28]

When viewed in the historical context of the past 150 years, the pro-American fervour of the 1980s does not appear such an unusual phenomenon. There is a sense in which the history of Franco-American relations is one of swings of opinion *vis-à-vis* the United States. Waves of infatuation are followed by waves of disenchantment – which are sudden and exaggerated in both cases, as if opinion were only capable of finding equilibrium in motion, and even in violent fluctuations.

Are the swings of opinion not partly linked to French ambivalence with regards to a political model perceived as containing the seeds of its own destruction – the potential for a shift from democracy to tyranny? Such anxiety and ambivalence were certainly felt by de Tocqueville, who went so far as to alert his readers in the following terms: 'The political Constitution of the United States seems to me one possible form of democratic government, but I do not believe American institutions to be the only, or even the best ones that a democratic people might adopt.'[29] And why did he not consider them the best? De Tocqueville's objections were legion and the most serious of them concerned the prerequisites for democracy in a country with a long aristocratic tradition which clearly had difficulty in breaking with its monarchical past. In America, de Tocqueville asserted, the republic came into being 'without combat, opposition or ordeal, but through a tacit agreement: a sort of *consensus universalis*'.[30] It also derived from a prime cause unknown in Europe: the fact that the American people all had the same conditions, 'this generative fact from which each particular fact would seem to derive'.[31] And it was precisely this *consensus universalis* – characteristic of a nation which had been spared the disastrous effects of social revolution – which was lacking in the case of the French, who, at the time de Tocqueville was writing, were still incapable of bringing their revolution to an end and controlling the tide of their 'egalitarian passions'. Slavish imitation of the American model was therefore not appropriate since it could risk inflaming 'the passions' of the middle classes to such a degree that it would make a reality of the omnipresent threat – though still latent in the United States – of a 'tyranny of the majority.'[32]

The only model, in de Tocqueville's view, that would be appropriate to a society as unstable and inegalitarian as the France of his day, would be a mixed system capable of satisfying the political aspirations of the greatest number while preserving the civic virtues of aristocratic societies, that is, a taste for excellence, a sense of sacrifice, and a passionate attachment to freedom and the common good.[33]

And had these virtues been lost, they would have to have been re-invented on the basis of those 'artifices' which the Americans had ingeniously developed by means of citizens' associations, by multiplying the institutions and levels of political decision-making, by laying the basis of a civic religion, and by forging a pseudo-aristocracy of enlightened lawyers.[34]

The ambivalence towards the United States, an attitude so well illustrated in de Tocqueville's writings and largely shared by his contemporaries, was intensified by the outcome of the great historical upheavals of the nineteenth, and twentieth centuries. These had settled for good the question of collective representation in a manner which was sometimes favourable and on other occasions unfavourable to the American experience. Consider, for instance, the following epochs: the July Monarchy (1830-48), the Second Republic (1848-51), and the periods immediately following World Wars I and II.

According to René Rémond, the beginning of the July Monarchy coincided with a phase of 'general infatuation' of the public with the United States. The American government was the object of extraordinary admiration. Its perfection was lauded, stress being laid on the insubstantiality of its state structures and its system of checks and balances.[35] The model was the 'invisible government' so dear to Mme de Staël. But several years later, there was 'a total reversal of perceptions'. In the space of five years, what was formally a model to be imitated had become a cautionary lesson. The immoderate extension of male adult suffrage, the widespread implementation of the spoils system, riots in the cities of the North East against slavery – all such happenings served to put public opinion off a democracy which seemed to be opening the doors to the worst excesses of the 'dictatorship of the street'.[36] The backlash of public opinion was exacerbated by the question of debts inherited from the Napoleonic Wars. Their reimbursement was intended to compensate the American ship-owners for the losses occasioned by the seizure of over 500 American-flagged ships by French pirates. It took five years of hard bargaining by French and American diplomats before they agreed on the actual level and form of debt-repayment, with each side accusing the other of abuse, insulting the national honour and bad faith.[37]

By the end of the July Monarchy, the United States had become a foreign power like any other, and even a 'hostile' and 'constantly meddling'[38] force. With the Union continually expanding, and annexing, one by one, Oregon, Texas, California, and so forth, the French at that period were already expressing their anxiety about what would later be called, in Lenin's words, 'American imperialism'.[39]

The establishment of the 2nd Republic marked a new swing in public opinion which 'almost unanimously' rediscovered the virtues of the American institutional model.⁴⁰ However, that new wave of enthusiasm for America would soon be attenuated by the factional squabbles between the liberals, with their profound attachment to the virtues of the presidential system and the socialists who were scandalised by the continuation of slavery.⁴¹

The *coup d'état* of December 1851 destroyed for a long time any desire to import any elements of the American institutional model and adapt them to French conditions.⁴²

For very different reasons, French public opinion experienced an equally sudden swing at the end of the '14–'18 War. The Americans' involvement in the war, albeit belated, naturally fostered pro-American sentiments, particularly after the signing of the Brest-Litovsk Treaty. People had high hopes of the reputedly 'stalwart', 'splendid' and 'athletic' American soldier.⁴³ Limited to 70 000 men in November 1917, the American contingent would soon exceed two million soldiers by September 1918. The American war effort was therefore considerable. The Americans' popularity peaked after the successive victories of the American Expeditionary Corps at Bois Belleau (June 1918), Villers-Cotterêts (July) and Saint-Mihiel (September).⁴⁴ On his arrival in Paris after the Armistice to attend the peace conference, President Wilson was welcomed as a victor by a unanimous public opinion: 'From the extreme Left to the extreme Right – for once reconciled – came the same chorus of praise'.⁴⁵ However, in the space of a few months, Wilson's popularity took a sudden nose-dive, and by the end of that Spring it had turned into 'general hostility, and in the course of the summer, into an indifference more damaging than hate'.⁴⁶

Dissension between governments over the questions of the Sarre and the left bank of the Rhine are undoubtedly the best explanation of that extraordinary reversal of opinion. Initially the French had wanted to annex both territories. The response of the Americans and English was to invoke the nationality principle. The French press went wild and accused President Wilson of pro-German bias. There were other factors, not so deep-rooted but no less real, which account for the growing resentment among local people who felt threatened by the wealth of *les tommies* (which encouraged higher prices) and the moral depravation which reputedly prevailed around the American camps.⁴⁷

In 1919, at the time the Versailles Treaty was ratified, very few politicians or leader writers openly voiced pro-Wilson sentiments. The famed victor of 1918 and visionary of the League of Nations was now no more than a 'despicable bourgeois' whose hypocrisy and lack of realism were now denounced.

A few years later, that wave of anti-Americanism reached its climax when the Americans refused to compromise over the question of the French debt or to countenance a guarantee clause allowing the French to link repayment of the American loan to German reparations. American intransigence seemed all the more unjust at a time when Germany was the main beneficiary of American loans and investments in Europe.

To the French public 'the Americans seemed like vampires sucking the life-blood of their exhausted partners'.[48] The evocative titles of the best-sellers of those days are a telling illustration of the anti-American mood among the intellectuals: *Qui sera le maître Europe ou Amérique?* (Lucien Romier, 1927), *L'Oncle Shylock ou l'impérialisme américain à la conquête du monde* (J.-L. Chastanet, 1927), *L'abomination américaine* (Kadmi-Cohen, 1930), *Le cancer américain* (Robert Aron and Arnaud Dandieu, 1931), *L'Amérique à la conquête de l'Europe* (Charles Pomaret, 1931), *L'impérialisme économique américain* (Pierre Laurent, 1931), and so on and so forth.[49]

Though they had won the Great War, the French henceforth regarded themselves as losers in the global economic war. France had become the 'new pauper' of the community of capitalist nations. The United States and, even by that time, Japan were the *nouveaux riches*.[50]

Curiously enough, as one can judge from the dates of the books mentioned, the intellectuals had yet to grasp the importance and gravity of the crash of 1929. Thus, paradoxically, all that talk of a threat from American capitalism came at the very moment when the latter was in a state of collapse. Once the French public had become aware of the crisis, those who still believed in the virtues of the American model found themselves in an even more sticky position, and tended to abandon the New World and turn their eyes in the direction of Rome, Berlin and Moscow in search of new models capable of regenerating *la vieille Europe*.

In 1944, just as in the aftermath of the Great War, a certain ambivalence of attitude prevailed towards a 'liberator' who had entered the war late in the day and was destined thereafter to exert a decisive influence on the future of France and Europe. In the wake of the humiliation of June 1940 and the traumas of Vichy, the Liberation was to resurrect and accentuate certain features of French anti-Americanism already evident in earlier periods. In its way, Gaullism was the reincarnation of an earlier nationalism which had since taken a heavy beating. However, the international context in which it had to operate was now very different. Moreover, it had to contend at home with the considerable influence of the Communist Party on the intellectual and political life of the country. This was to give anti-Americanism a further boost in the shape of pro-Sovietism.

Gaullist nationalism at the time of Liberation was marked above all by a proud refusal to be undervalued. This gave rise to two political myths. The first was that the country had 'liberated itself', an assertion which had its roots in the very real misunderstandings between de Gaulle, Roosevelt and Eisenhower.[51] The second was the myth of Yalta: the erroneous belief that Soviets and American had shared out Europe between themselves and deliberately excluded the French on the personal initiative of the American President.[52]

These two myths were to serve as a rationale for what has been described as 'Gaullist anti-Americanism' whose target was American leadership in Western Europe: 'Saying no to the Americans was to become the underlying principle of Gaullist policies'.[53]

For the Gaullists, the upshot of that determination to assert French independence was a conscious effort to maintain an equidistance between the two superpowers, which explains the neutralist tenor of France's foreign policies from the Liberation onwards, and particularly during the 1960s. As we shall see, these attitudes towards the Big Two were to be shared by a large segment of the intellectual and political élite, and public opinion as a whole.

Some of the findings of the first post-Liberation polls are invaluable to an understanding of the complexity of public attitudes towards the United States. Polled in the heat of events in September 1944 and again in May 1945, a majority of the French considered that it was the Soviet Union which had done more than any other nation to bring about the defeat of Germany (57 per cent of replies, compared to 20 per cent for the USA and 12 per cent for Great Britain[54]). This response, which displayed an astonishingly favourable opinion of the Soviet Union in a country which had just been liberated by the joint efforts of the USA and Great Britain, should be viewed in the light of the French people's great disappointment with US policies. When asked 'Which country, over the past 12 months, do you feel has let us down most?' the

French overwhelmingly replied 'the United States' (54 per cent against 12 per cent for the USSR[55]). There are two factors, in particular, that help explain this lack of gratitude towards the American liberator and the enormous prestige enjoyed by the Soviet Union. First of all there was the German issue. When asked in June 1945 'Which countries will be in favour of treating Germany harshly enough?' the overwhelming majority (87 per cent) of the French thought it would be the Russians, while only 9 per cent expressed confidence in the Americans.[56] In other words, people feared that the Americans would again be loath to 'punish' Germany, as after World War I. In the initial period, therefore, anti-Americanism was also an expression of anti-German sentiment.

The second factor was the disappointment felt by the French over US economic aid, a disappointment all the sharper because of the enormous hopes that had been pinned on it. Indeed when they had been asked which country they thought would assist French recovery, the French had expressed greatest confidence in the United States. At the very moment when a majority of the French considered American attitudes towards France far from satisfactory, a comparable majority pinned (no doubt excessive) hopes on that very country. (This conjunction of the German and the economic factor was also to occur later, in relation to the Marshall Plan; many of the French were to consider the Germans privileged by the Americans in the matter of economic aid). In the light of this, the Soviet Union, as a world power, was seen as a counterweight to American might. It would seem that on this particular issue French public opinion coincided with the views of the intellectual and political élites. Suffice it to recall that during the years of the Fourth Republic, which was a pro-American regime according to the Gaullist and Communist opposition, neutralist theses gained wide currency via such newspapers as Hubert Beuve-Méry's *Le Monde* or journals such as the left-wing catholic *Esprit* and Sartre's *Les Temps modernes*. *Le Monde* had launched the debate in 1948 with an influential article by Etienne Gilson which posed the question: was Europe to be pro-American or neutral? The themes it introduced, such as non-alignment, disengagement from the Atlantic bloc, mistrust of Washington, and détente with Moscow, were to enjoy pride of place in *Le Monde* throughout the 1950s and form the backbone of the Gaullist foreign policies of the 1960s: 'In the final analysis, Hubert Beuve-Méry and General de

Gaulle shared many ideas, but they never shared them simultaneously'.[57] There was one idea which de Gaulle and the director of *Le Monde* did not share, however, and that was the construction of Europe. The fact is that *Le Monde* was at one and the same time anti-American and very much in favour of European construction. Hence Michael Harrison's suggestion that the 'European party' in France was itself divided between the Atlanticists and the partisans of a 'third way'. This is a pertinent remark in the sense that it helps attenuate the Gaullo-Communist stereotype which treated all partisans of European construction as Atlanticists and pro-Americans. On the other hand, it is inexact as regards the actual concept of relations between Europe and the United States held by Jean Monnet and his friends. The fact is that the real issue, then as now, was not whether one wanted an independent Europe (which was a goal which almost everyone shared), but rather a question of priorities, of what steps to take first. The contention between Monnet and de Gaulle reflected two different approaches, two distinct philosophies. 'The first – Monnet's – entailed starting the work of European construction straight away, on the understanding, of course, that once it had been established, Europe would be strong enough to assert its independence of the United States. In the light of this, to raise the problem of anti-Americanism at the outset was to put our allies – particularly the Germans – on the spot and force them to choose between France and the United States. The upshot would be to guarantee unending US domination. The second approach – de Gaulle's – maintained that France and Europe, above all the latter, asserted themselves through opposition; if European construction went ahead without establishing a clear demarcation line between itself and the United States, Europe would be condemned to being no more than an American tool. The Gaullist approach gave first priority to negative momentum and regarded reconstruction as a long-term prospect'.[58]

It is possible, of course, to show that there was greater continuity between the Fourth and Fifth Republics than people have sometimes been prepared to admit, and that the Fourth Republic also had its waves of anti-Americanism (such as the time of Suez, over decolonisation, and the like). Thus de Gaulle was only prepared to take a firm stand with the United States when he felt himself entrenched within the western world, of which America was the linchpin, when all was said and done. This is precisely what he demonstrated when it came to the major East-West crises such as Berlin or Cuba. The specific character of Gaullist mistrust of the United States derived from a particular idea of Russia and its place in Europe. In de Gaulle's eyes, 'the Russian factor', just as much as the 'Communist factor' motivated the Kremlin's actions.[59] He did not regard European frontiers as 'the artificial and provisional frontiers of Yalta, but those defined by geography text-books and atlases'.[60] This was his celebrated 'Europe from the Atlantic to the Urals'. The fact that de Gaulle perceived the Soviet Union above all as 'Russia' meant that he saw it as fundamentally European, as opposed to the United States. The latter belonged to its own 'hemisphere' and not to *l'ensemble fécond* which the General wanted to see created.[61] From such an angle the USSR was more than just a counterweight to American might. It was a 'great nation' and an integral part of the Europe then in gestation, whose nurture would demand a certain reserve *vis-à-vis* the United States.

Whereas Gaullist anti-Americanism derived from a particular concept of Russia, Communist anti-Americanism was resolutely pro-Soviet, as one may expect. From the moment the Cominform was created in September 1947, the Zhdanov Report assigned Communist parties the task of 'resisting the American plan to enslave Europe and resolutely unmasking all the henchmen of American imperialism'. One will recall the riotous demonstrations in Paris against the arrival of General *'Ridgway the Plague'*; when prominent Communist leaders managed to get themselves arrested. Ridgway was 'the man with the grenade and the packet of bandages round his neck, the man who thinks war is a team game...'[62] Equally unforgettable are French Stalinism's pro-Soviet effusions, with its odes to Stalin and even to the GPU (now KGB). However, it is occasionally forgotten that they went hand in hand with an anti-Americanism that was so out of this world that it is fun to rediscover it today.[63] It was the declared opinion of Aragon, for instance, that a Ford car was 'the epitome of that civilisation of baths and Frigidaires'. Those self-same 'Frigidaires' – which over half of the French already owned – were the target of a diatribe by Roger Vailland: 'I have never properly appreciated what purpose a Frigidaire might serve in France, where, except for two or three months a year – and not even that long some years – it is always so cold that one needs no more than a meat safe on the window-sill to keep the left-overs of the Sunday roast fresh until Monday, Tuesday or Wednesday. Those of my friends who own a Frigidaire use it mostly for making ice cubes to put in their wisky [sic] and spoil its taste. Anyway with the price of wisky what it is nowadays, their Frigidaire retains no more than a symbolic function'.[64] However, it was Coca-Cola, of course, that was the No. 1 symbol of American colonisation and was therefore not just politically dangerous but prejudicial to the nation's health: 'Soon they will be able to say "Coca-Cola over all" just like they used to say "Deutschland über alles". But what is Coca-Cola? Few French people have ever tasted it. One of the characteristics of the beverage is that it creates an addiction just like drugs. It includes sodium benzoate as a preservative ... However, the addition of sodium benzoate to drinks is banned by the French fraud department. And this is the drink that Messrs. Bidault and Schuman intend to foist on the French – along with American spies – just so as to please the OSS, the State Department and the Chase [Manhattan Bank]'.[65]

Another purpose of anti-Americanism was to get the Communist and fellow-travelling intellectuals to close ranks around the Communist Party at moments of doubt. The Rosenberg solidarity campaign often went hand in hand with endorsement or tacit acceptance of the trials in Prague and Budapest. As a one-time Communist journalist recalls: 'Fortunately for us and our consciences McCarthyism arrived just at that moment. It was absolutely marvellous. We had a good reason for rejecting the United States. There has never been anything since then to give one such a good anti-American conscience, apart from the Vietnam War'.[66]

In this way McCarthyism was able to neutralise or eclipse the realities of Stalinism in Eastern Europe and thereby lend a gloss of reasonableness to a form of anti-Americanism which rather overstepped the proper bounds of crypto-Communist activity. The latter consisted of making no distinction between the Soviet Union and the United States, and even regarding the former as the lesser evil. One still came across this attitude as late as the 1970s in the writings of authors as disparate as Alain de Benoist, Jean-Pierre Chevènement, Jean-Marie Benoist and Michel Jobert.

In a scathing attack on both imperialisms, Soviet and American, Michel Jobert, Pompidou's Minister of Foreign Affairs, went so far as to find a common denominator in the fortuitous resemblance between the words 'Cobol' and 'Kabul'. In his view, the challenge of 'Cobol' – one of the many computer languages invented in the United States – was 'more insidious and more part of our daily life than the threat from the East'. It was necessary, wrote Jobert, 'to give the Americans their due: they are more modern and more adroit than the Russians. Whereas the Kabul coup is wearing down the Soviet armed forces and souring Soviet relations with many countries, and giving the lie to its propaganda, the Cobol coup, on the contrary, is taking place unbeknown to those who are not directly affected by it'.[67]

Several years before his lightning conversion to Reaganism, Jean-Marie Benoist, a former French cultural attaché to Great Britain and professor at the *Collège de France*, had no qualms in decrying 'the twin monolithic tyrannies of uniformity ... Woodstock and the jeans uniform on the one side; the Gulags on the other',[68] before going on to draw a striking parallel between the said Gulags and the American media: 'Almost obscenely symmetrical in their hegemonic ambitions and in the mirror-image absolutism of their lust for power, the two great empires that share out the planet between themselves employ different methods reflecting the obvious radical differences between their economic and social structures. The police brutality of the "Gulag", whose operation has been laid bare by Solzhenitsyn in his explanation of how the cancer spreads throughout the social organism (a process prophesied Cassandra-fashion by Orwell in his *1984*) is the counterpart, albeit asymmetrical, of course, of the way the media and opinion polls are used as channels of propaganda by Atlantic imperialism in order to condition the people of Western Europe and the Mediterranean basin'.[69]

Texts like this are a good illustration of the frivolous facet of intellectual life in the French capital which caused Pierre Hassner to declare that 'France is the only country where it is possible to say *absolutely anything*, so long as it is said in a manner which is sufficiently systematic or romantic, apodictic or apocalyptic, best of all if one can manage to combine both, or if one has said precisely the opposite, but in the same style, just a few years or even months previously'.[70] What is most striking, though, is how such texts have dated in the few short years since their publication. This is due to one of the major phenomena of the intellectual and political life of postwar France, namely the collapse of the Soviet Union's image.

This collapse became evident in the 1970s and early 1980s. The Parisian intelligentsia had discovered a new evil, Soviet 'totalitarianism' as expressed in the works of Solzhenitsyn and the Red army's occupation of Afghanistan.[71]

The old evil – US imperialism – was superseded by a new one: Soviet imperialism. The collapse of the Soviet image hastened the electoral decline of the French Communist Party. As for the other pillar of French anti-Americanism, the Gaullist RPR party (*Rassemblement Pour la République*), it chose to be in tune with the times and dropped all negative references to the United States.

With Gorbachev's coming to power, French intellectuals modified their perceptions of the Soviet Union, without developing however, any great enthusiasm for Gorbachev's reforms. In fact, it can be argued that Gorbachev's own criticism of the Soviet system contributed further to the collapse of the Soviet 'model'. French public opinion, perhaps influenced by intellectual élites, has remained substantially less appreciative of Gorbachev's reforms than its British, German and Italian counterparts.

Is this an established or even irreversible trend? Nothing could be less certain, even if the influence of the Communist Party, now retrenched in its pro-Soviet ghetto, continues to dwindle. The fact is that one cannot rule out a resurgence of the neo-Gaullist variant of anti-Americanism. Suffice it to read Régis Debray's *Les Empires contre l'Europe*[72] to assure oneself of the fact.

A resurgence of anti-Americanism could also take place in the cultural field. This is where the French are most vulnerable and most susceptible to react with exacerbated displays of nationalism. Since the Renaissance, there has always been a French 'politics of culture' which, because it is defensive by nature, can only be defined in terms of opposition to rival cultures, of which the most recent, most dynamic and undoubtedly the most threatening is the 'American Way of Life': that all-powerful media machine with its reputation for vulgarity and commercialism which would absorb all the indigenous cultures of a colonised world into a new rootless, indiscriminating and even barbaric culture.

That culture, to which the epithets 'homogenising', 'standardising' and 'impoverishing' have been often applied, would be the product of the notorious 'melting pot' which, by mixing races and values, must inevitably generate ethical, ethnic and aesthetic confusion. For the supporters of the *nouvelle droite*, 'American civilisation' is 'monstrously non-aesthetic' because it 'has retained from its judaeo-christian origins an indifference to beauty'.[73] Being a 'mere agglomeration of men and women from all countries' the American nation is incapable of serving as a vehicle for any civilising mission. So all it has to export is its 'lack of culture'.[74] Looked at in this very singular manner, the Americans are 'condemned to cause all the cultures they touch to perish, and to uproot all traditions. By exporting their way of life, they inevitably end up killing the national soul everywhere, since they themselves are the progeny of such murder'.[75]

Pessimistic sentiments like these are shared by a large number of intellectuals who would seem to be poles apart at first sight in terms of educational background, political sympathies, social status and so on. Thus Michel Jobert considers that the French risk being dispossessed of their own language because of 'information technology which services and rules all the rest' and is backed by '*un dollar roi*'.[76]

Jean-Marie Benoist, who cannot be considered as belonging to the *nouvelle droite*, sees taking shape in American cultural imperialism a new kind of totalitarianism which will be 'more devious than [Soviet and American] economic or military imperialism'. It takes the form of 'a paranoid desire for uniformity and integration into monolithic blocs, alongside which Jacobin uniformity looks very amateurish stuff'.[77] Alain de Benoist who apparently shares the concerns of his namesake, took the anti-American tirade several stages further when he declared at a symposium organised by GRECE: 'The fact is that there exist two distinct forms of totalitarianism, very different in their effects, but equally fearsome. The Eastern variety imprisons, persecutes and mortifies the body, but at least does not destroy hope. Its Western counterpart ends up creating happy robots. It is an air-conditioned hell. It kills the soul'.[78]

Jacques Thibau, a diplomat with Gaullist leanings, shares this extreme pessimism, without, however, going so far as to lump the two 'totalitarianisms' together. 'It is not France that is colonised, but the French in their vision of their past and their future prospects. Presented in abstract and intellectual form, the cultural homogenisation resulting from the massive diffusion of American culture provokes euphoric reactions . . . it is tantamount to ethnocide, whereby the personality, existence and vigour of nations, groups and peoples are engulfed, and then replaced by universal manipulation'.[79]

Similarly violent in tone are certain Communist authors such as Anicet le Pors who, in a politico-economic text, has denounced *le parti américain* in France and its 'deliberate campaign of national depersonalisation'. Unless France pulls itself together, le Pors adds, this intensive 'brain-washing' could cause it to lose its historical memory and everything that constitutes the 'classic purity of the French personality'.[80] The author concludes by adopting the very terms of Jacques Thibau's analysis and denounces the phenomenon as 'tantamount to ethnocide'.[81]

In comparison, culture minister Jack Lang's statements in Mexico City condemning (without naming it) 'the financial and intellectual imperialism which plunders consciences ... thought patterns ... and lifestyles', seem almost moderate. In retrospect it seems odd that it should have caused such a rumpus, and led to shamefaced explanations by Lang. He even felt bound, during a subsequent trip to New York, to make honourable amends to his hosts by apologising for his 'rather shocking' language in Mexico City, and making exaggerated claims about the closeness of Franco-American cultural exchanges.[82]

Alain Finkielkraut's *La Défaite de la Pensée* of 1987 contains a violent three-pronged attack on bourgeois hedonism, the perverse effects of mass culture and the undue influence of 'King Consumer'.[83] Curiously enough this critique of 'cultural Disneylands', which is clearly influenced by Martin Heidegger, comes at the very moment when that particular philosopher is being impugned over his political 'blunder' of supporting the Nazis between 1933 and 1945.[84] Indeed Heidegger had a considerable influence on the French intelligentsia from Sartre to Derrida. The collapse of Marxism in intellectual circles made traditional attacks on consumer society suspect. A substitute had to be found.

Heidegger's teachings provided an alternative critique, which, paradoxically, placed the USA and the USSR on the same footing, regarding them both as the baleful incarnation of technological modernity. The philosopher is cited in attacks on the 'pincer-effect' whereby *la vieille Europe* is crushed between 'Russia and America'.[85] The approach is rather crude but there is no mistaking the message: the Europeans – the people in the middle – must stop aping the surrounding culture and at last develop a culture that is well and truly their own.

Although less than 2 per cent of the new words that have entered French people's everyday vocabulary are of Anglo-Saxon origin,[86] complaints about 'the flood of Americanisms' are regularly expressed by both the cultural and political élites. It is now the done thing to denounce the 'regiments of the American cultural army' which run the media,[87] and to demand exclusive use of French in international conferences so that 'the ideas of Voltaire, the prose of Chateaubriand and the poetry of Apollinaire'[88] may be disseminated more effectively. It is also perfectly acceptable to protest against 'the scheme to homogenise [the French language] by means of Angloid pidgin' [sic],[89] or even to write sarcastically about 'Anglo-American Volapuk', and dismiss it as no more than a 'universal pidgin' which is to communication 'what fast food is to gastronomy'.[90]

In the most extreme cases it is the very cultural identity of France which is allegedly jeopardised by the inordinate use of Anglo-Americanisms: 'Our people have never found themselves in such a critical situation since the Hundred Years War. For the first time in our history, our language faces the threat of extinction. America has become the last horizon for our youth . . .'[91]

Nevertheless, language has never received the attention it does nowadays from the public authorities, in a country where culture is above all a State matter. For the record, it should be recalled that de Gaulle created the *Haut Comité* (since rebaptised *Commissariat général) de la langue française* in 1966, that Pompidou encouraged the creation of the *Association de coopération culturelle et technique*, and that, in 1984, Mitterrand set up a *Comité consultatif de la langue française* under the chairmanship of the Prime Minister, as well as an *Haut Conseil de la francophonie*. One should also bear in mind that the French Army is probably the only army in the world to use conscripts for promoting the use of French abroad under the heading of 'military cooperation'. And finally the French government issues decree after decree setting up *commissions de terminologie* with the job of 'enriching' the vocabulary of a particular body of science. There is even talk of following Québec's example and making the use of French in trade and advertising compulsory by law.

In the political discourse of France, irrespective of outlook, the French language has always been more than a means of communication serving a particular culture. The language *is* the culture and any attack on it is perceived as a question of honour pertaining to the French character, the *unicité* of the State, France's civilising mission, in short, the national identity.[92]

The equation: national language=national identity is nothing new. It was expressed as early as the sixteenth century in the writings of the *Pléiade* circle, which was striving to assert the primacy of a reputedly "vulgar" language in the face of domination by the two great languages of the century: Latin – the language of the Catholic clergy and the great classical authors, and Italian – the language of culture, the arts and diplomacy. It was that period which saw the establishment of a system to defend the French language so admirably described by Joachim du Bellay in his *Deffence et illustration de la langue françoyse* (1549).[93]

It was not until it found itself in opposition to other rival tongues that French finally managed to impose itself as the national language of the intellectual élite. It was this reactional movement that gave birth to the French identity. One should not be surprised to learn that, four centuries later, a group of several hundred French intellectuals of all persuasions and professions (writers, journalists, musicians, actors and the like) have adopted the title of du Bellay's aforementioned work as the heading of a manifesto in which they declare their determination to 'preserve [their] cultural identity' through an organised campaign against 'undue penetration by Anglo-American expressions'.[94]

However deeply attached to tradition these intellectuals may be, in radically rejecting all Anglicisms they have clearly forgotten that the true '*deffence*' of the language, as conceived by du Bellay, is the ability to appropriate that '*je ne scay quoy*' which can invigorate another language and yet which falls short of verbal expression. '*Deffence*' in his sense is based on imitation, in the most primitive meaning of the word. Creative people ought to be cannibalistic about foreign words and expressions. They need to 'devour' and 'digest' them and then convert them into 'blood and nourishment ...'[95] Du Bellay's defensive strategy ruled out cultural protectionism on principle, since it was based on a receptive attitude towards the rest of the world and on a multilingual approach, in other words, on creative imitation as the only way of enriching or revitalising a language which was unsure of itself.

In the recent manifesto referred to, our latterday defenders of the French tongue attack the 'vulgarity' and 'slackness' of the language employed by the mass media. This élitist approach which harks back to the sixteenth century and which was institutionalised when Richelieu created the *Académie française*, is nowadays part and parcel of a campaign against (Americanised) 'mass culture'.

Are the learned culture of the élite and its corollary, French *bon goût*, truly preferable to the plebeian and cosmopolitan tastes of the masses who wolf down Big Macs, rave about *Dallas* and *Dynasty*, and dance to *le rock* and *le pop music*? Who is to decide, and in the name of what concept of culture, in an era when leisure, artistic products and performances are answerable to no government? The answer is definitely political. It depends on the sort of society individuals want and on their ethics of responsibility. *Jacobins*, whether of Right or Left, will always favour a centralised, coherent and rational cultural policy. *Liberals* – also regardless of political hue – will, in the name of individual liberty and freedom of conscience, reject any policing of culture. The first will be happy to give the State the job of safeguarding their cultural identity. The second will prefer the State to leave well enough alone, in favour of individual creativity and private sponsorship.

The existence of a certain American cultural imperialism is undeniable. It is assisted by factors such as the massive expansion of the American economy, the application of the science of marketing to a mass culture which is 'abundant, multifarious and easily accessible to foreigners', mass media with an 'international vocation', and a messianic spirit which equips the Americans with an 'arrogant conviction that theirs is the least bad culture around'.[96] However, one ought not to exaggerate the power of this imperialism. The American media are rich and influential but they are not all-powerful. Competition is not only possible, it exists, even from poor countries like India or Mexico. Consumers of the products of American culture, like gadget-lovers, are not passive victims forcefully injected with the American virus. The reason why they appreciate a particular film or a particular gadget is because they consider it well made, cheap and accessible, although the absence of any satisfactory alternative can also be a factor, of course. Most importantly, though, the dissemination of culture is not a one-way process: 'Too much is said about the Americanisation of the world and not enough about the cosmopolitanisation of the United States'.[97]

The easy way out for the critics of Yankee imperialism is to blame America for everything that imperils France's cultural identity, even though such dangers and the sense of decline that accompanies them often derive from a more general phenomenon, admirably described by de Tocqueville as the democratisation of western societies 'for better or worse'.[98]

French perceptions of the United States have not fundamentally changed since 1984–85. Admittedly *reaganomania* is no longer in vogue. Irangate, combined with Congress's protectionist attitudes and the twin deficits of the US budget and balance of trade, have rather detracted from the American 'model'. Nonetheless, American successes in the jobs sphere continued to be a source of admiration for the ministers of Chirac's government in 1988.[99]

In terms of foreign policy, mainstream political thinking applauds the outcome of the Reagan-Gorbachev talks and the signing of the INF treaty. But suspicion lingers about the possibility of secret collusion between the superpowers. The difference between the early and late 1980s has to do with the change in the Soviet leadership. Mr Reagan was merely a 'lame-duck President' whereas Mr Gorbachev seized the French imagination because of his reputation as a great reformer. Nevertheless, the 'model', if model there is, remains the United States.

America, as a product of the French people's collective imagination, serves as a political and social barometer which helps reveal their different moods, passions and delusions. The turmoil of pro- and anti-American attitudes, the sudden shifts in public opinion, the ambiguity of certain judgements and the existence of cultural invariants, all reflect the turbulent evolution of postwar France in which 'modernisation' has been by turns Jacobin or liberal. Could it be that these changing trends themselves are influenced by increased transatlantic communication, and is a certain stereotyped vision of the United States beginning to fade as a consequence?[100] It might be argued, of course, that stereotypes have a tendency to give way to further stereotypes and that the *americanomania* of the 1980s is just as simplistic a caricature of American realities as was the anti-Americanism of the 1950s. However, this would be to ignore the fact that French political culture is in the course of being transformed. Thus, bit by bit, the main ideological canons of the second half of the twentieth century are being shaken, particularly those that derived from the nature and heritage of the French Revolution.[101]

The bicentennial commemorations of the American Constitution and the French Revolution are perfect illustrations of the differences and similarities between the two cultures. Both countries share a common ideal, both celebrate the virtues of republican democracy, but the French, who never quite finished their Revolution, put the emphasis on their Declaration of the Rights of Man, while the Americans, whose Philadelphia Convention put an end to their revolutionary fervor, praise above all the greatness of their one and unique Constitution. The universalist pretensions of the two revolutions are what will ensure that France and the United States remain rivals, each one setting itself up as a model for the rest of the world.

Notes

1. Jean Baudrillard, *Amérique* (Grasset: Paris, 1986) pp. 152 and 153.
2. Cf. Stanley Hoffmann, 'Conclusion' in George Ross and Stanley Hoffmann (eds.), *The Mitterrand Experiment* (Oxford: Polity Press, 1987) last page of the conclusion to the French edition.
3. Baudrillard, op. cit., pp. 155 and 151, respectively.
4. Cf. *Le Messager Européen*, 1988, No. 2, p. 18; *Esprit*, June 1986, No. 115, pp. 105–13.
5. Marc Paillet, *'Le gâchis'*, *Le Monde*, 11 August 1987.
6. *La Révolution Conservatrice Américaine* (Paris: Fayard, 1983); *La Solution Libérale* (Paris: Fayard, 1984).
7. W. W. Rostow, *The Barbaric Economic Counter-Revolution* (Austin: University of Texas Press, 1983).
8. Prominent members of this committee included Michel de Rostolan, chairman of the *Cercle Renaissance*, Patrice de Plunkett, editor-in-chief of *Figaro Magazine*, Bernadette d'Angevilliers of *Radio Solidarité* and Jean-Marie Benoist, *maître-assistant* at the *Collège de France*.
9. *Le Monde*, 6 November 1984.
10. Speech by Gaullist deputy Mr François Fillon at a round table organised by the *Fondation du Futur* on the topic, 'The American elections: change or continuity?', in Paris on 8 November 1984.
11. *Le Figaro*, 3 December 1984.
12. Franz-Olivier Giesbert and Jacques Mornand, *'Pourriez-vous vivre à l'américaine'*, *Le Nouvel Observateur*, 14 September 1984, p. 46.
13. Jean-Marie Domenach, *'Dieu est moderne'*, *L'Expansion*, 19 October 1984, p. 254.
14. Jean Lefebvre, *'Chez Reagan, c'est beau comme un western'*, *Le Figaro Magazine*, 31 November 1980, p. 66.
15. Louis Pauwels, *'Lettre au futur président des Etats-Unis, quel qu'il soit'*, *Le Figaro Magazine*, 31 October 1980.
16. Jean d'Ormesson, *'Portrait de Reagan en Cyrano'*, *Le Figaro Magazine*, 15 November 1984.
17. *'Mitterrand parle'*, an interview with Jean Boissonnat, *L'expansion*, 16 November 1984.
18. Cf. Alfred Grosser, *Affaires extérieures* (Paris: Flammarion, 1984) Chapter 10, and his contribution to the present volume; Alain Duhamel, *Le Complexe d'Astérix* (Paris: Gallimard, 1985) pp. 231–2.
19. Pierre Grémion, *Paris/Prague* (Paris: Julliard, 1985) p. 301.
20. This necessarily arbitrary list of leading intellectuals ought to include in addition such distinguished historians or sociologists as François Furet, François Bourricaud and Michel Crozier who do

21. Raymond Aron, *D'une Sainte Famille à l'autre. Essais sur les marxismes imaginaires* (Paris: Gallimard, 1969) p. 89; Pierre Grémion, op. cit., pp. 183–4.
22. Michel Bauer and Elie Cohen, *Qui gouverne les groupes industriels?* (Paris: Seuil, 1981) p. 217.
23. See Diana Pinto's contribution to the present volume.
24. Edgar Morin, *Journal de Californie* (Paris: Seuil, 1970) p. 250.
25. Julia Kristeva, Marcellin Pleynet and Philippe Sollers, 'Pourquoi les Etats-Unis?', *Tel Quel* 71/73, Autumn 1977, pp. 4 and 11.
26. Régis Debray, *Modeste contribution aux discours et cérémonies officielles du dixième anniversaire* (Paris: François Maspero, 1978) p. 48.
27. Jean-Pierre Chevènement, 'Les nouveaux penseurs de la gauche américaine', *Témoignage chrétien*, 21 September 1978, pp. 6 and 7.
28. René Girard, *Le bouc émissaire* (Paris: Grasset, 1982) pp. 34–6 and more generally, Eugen Weber, 'Dextrogyrations in Paris', *Times Literary Supplement*, 10 March 1980, p. 1133, and Jacques Julliard, 'L'inégalité à la mode', *Le Nouvel Observateur*, 24 August 1984, pp. 44–6.
29. Alexis de Tocqueville, *De La Démocratie en Amérique* (Vol. I, Book II, Chap. VI), cited by Jean-Claude Lamberti, *Tocqueville et les deux démocraties*(Paris: P.U.F., 1983) p. 136.
30. Alexis de Tocqueville, *De La Démocratie en Amérique* (Paris: Garnier-Flammarion, 1981) Vol. I, Book II, Chapter X, p. 521.
31. Ibid., p. 57.
32. Ibid., Vol. I., Book II, Chap. VII, 'De l'omnipotence de la majorité aux Etats-Unis et de ses effets', pp. 343–60. See also Lamberti, op. cit., Chaps. I–III.
33. Lamberti, ibid., p. 55, 77, 192–8; Pierre Manent, *Tocqueville et la nature de la démocratie* (Paris: Julliard, 1982) pp. 41–9.
34. Tocqueville, op. cit., 'De l'usage que les Américains font de l'association dans la vie civile', Vol. II, Book II, Chap. V, pp. 137–41; 'De la constitution fédérale', Vol. I, Book I, Chap. VIII, pp. 182–250; 'De l'esprit légiste aux Etats-Unis et comment il sert de contrepoids à la démocratie', Vol. I, Book II, pp. 362–71.
35. René Rémond, *Les Etats-Unis devant l'opinion française 1815–1852* (Paris: Armand Colin, 1962) Vol. II, pp. 454–5, 543.
36. Ibid., pp. 699–701.
37. Jean-Baptiste Duroselle, *La France et les Etats-Unis des origines à nos jours* (Paris: Seuil, 1976) pp. 57–8.
38. René Rémond, op. cit., Vol. II, p. 823.
39. Ibid., pp. 817–21.
40. Ibid., p. 838.
41. Ibid., pp. 839–47.
42. See the contributions by Marie-France Toinet and Julien Feydy in the present volume.
43. André Kaspi, *Le Temps des Américains* (Paris: Publications de la Sorbonne, 1976) pp. 128–9.

44. Ibid., Ch. XIII.
45. Duroselle, op. cit., p. 115.
46. Kaspi, op. cit.
47. Duroselle, op. cit., pp. 116–26.
48. Ibid., p. 136.
49. Works cited and analysed by David Strauss in *Menace in the West, The Rise of French Anti-Americanism in Modern Times* (Greenwood Press, 1978), particularly Chap. 8, pp. 123–38.
50. Léon Archimbaud, *La conférence de Washington* (Paris: 1923), quoted in Strauss, op. cit., p. 111.
51. Suffice it to recall Roosevelt's reluctance to recognise de Gaulle as legitimate chief of the French resistance and his intention to set up in France at the Liberation 'an allied military government' just as in Italy, an ex-Axis power.
52. Charles de Gaulle, *Mémoires de guerre: le salut, 1944–1946*, (Paris: Plon, 1959) p. 102.
53. Duroselle, op. cit., p. 182.
54. IFOP polls quoted in *'Les Etats-Unis, les Américains et la France'*, *Sondages*, 1953, No. 2, p. 4 onwards.
55. Ibid.
56. Ibid.
57. Jean-Noël Jeanneney – Jacques Julliard, *Le Monde de Beuve-Méry ou le Métier d'Alceste* (Paris: Seuil, 1979) p. 92. See also the text by Michel Winock in the present volume.
58. Cf. Pierre Hassner's intervention at the foreign policy panel of the Anti-Americanism symposium. Reference also to Michael Harrison's contribution in the present volume.
59. Charles de Gaulle, *Mémoires d'espoir* (Paris: Plon, 1970) p. 225.
60. Jean Touchard, *Le Gaullisme, 1940–1969* (Paris: Seuil, 1978) p. 211.
61. Charles de Gaulle, *Mémoires de guerre*, op. cit., p. 62.
62. Paul Noirot, *Démocratie nouvelle*, June 1953.
63. See the examples of Communist anti-American silliness in Bernard Legendre's excellent collection, *Le Stalinisme français* (Paris: Seuil, 1980) and the volume edited by N. Dioujeva and François George, *Staline à Paris* (Paris: Ramsay, 1982).
64. *La Tribune des nations*, 14 March 1956, quoted in Legendre, op cit., p. 301.
65. *Action*, 15 December 1949, quoted in Legendre op. cit., p. 240.
66. Dominique Desanti's intervention at the Symposium on French perceptions of the United States sponsored by the CERI (Paris, 11–12 December 1984).
67. Michel Jobert, *Chroniques du Midi Libre*, Hachette, Paris, 1982, p. 24.
68. Jean-Marie Benoist, *Pavane pour une Europe défunte* (Paris: Hallier, 1976) pp. 143–5.
69. Ibid., pp. 87–8.
70. Pierre Hassner, *'Le totalitarisme vu de l'Ouest'*, in Guy Hermet, Pierre Hassner and Jacques Rupnik, *Totalitarismes*, (Paris: Economica, 1984) p. 19.
71. Ibid.
72. Régis Debray, *Les Empires contre l'Europe* (Paris: Gallimard, 1985).

73. Robert de Herte and Hans Jurgen Nigra, 'Il était une fois l'Amérique', *Nouvelle Ecole*, Autumn-Winter 1985, p. 46.
74. Alain de Benoist, *Vu de droite*. *Anthologie critique des idées contemporaines* (Paris: Copernic, 1979) p. 398.
75. Ibid.
76. Michel Jobert, op. cit., p. 24.
77. Jean-Marie Benoist, 'L'épuisement d'un modèle: le mythe anglo-saxon' in *Les Conditions de l'indépendance nationale dans le monde moderne* (Paris: Cujas, 1977) p. 512.
78. Quoted by Alain Rollat in 'Le GRECE prêche la "guerre culturelle" contre la civilisation "américano-occidentale"', *Le Monde*, 20 May 1981.
79. Jacques Thibau, *La France colonisée* (Paris: Flammarion, 1980) p. 267.
80. Anicet le Pors, *Marianne à l'encan* (Paris: Editions Sociales, 1980) pp. 201 and 203.
81. Ibid., p. 201.
82. Claire Devarrieux, 'Décrispation culturelle entre la France et les Etats-Unis', *Le Monde*, 20 November 1984; Raymond Sokolov, 'Changing Tunes at the French Cultural Ministry', *Wall Street Journal*, 18 January 1985.
83. Paris: Gallimard, 1987, p. 145.
84. Cf. Luc Ferry and Alain Renaut, *Heidegger et les modernes* (Paris: Grasset, 1988).
85. In a special issue of *Le Messager Européen* devoted to 'l'américanisation', the exile Czech philosopher Vaclav Belohradsky quotes approvingly the following passage from Heidegger: 'This Europe ... lies today in a great pincers, squeezed between Russia on one side and America on the other. From a metaphysical point of view, Russia and America are the same; the same dreary technological frenzy, the same unrestricted organization of the ordinary man'. (*An Introduction to Metaphysics*, Yale University Press, 1959, p. 37). Cf. Belohradsky, 'La modernité comme passion du neutre'. *Le Messager Européen*, No. 2, p. 21. Heidegger goes even further in the same text when he identifies mass culture 'the boundless etcetera of indifference and always-the-sameness' of Russian and American society with 'the onslaught of what we call the demonic (in the sense of destructive evil)'. (*Introduction to Metaphysics*, ibid., p. 46).
86. Jacques Cellard, 'Le Franglais au microscope', *Le Monde*, 16 May 1981.
87. Thibau, op. cit., pp. 93 and 100.
88. Michel Debré, quoted by Guy Scarpetta in *Eloge du cosmopolitisme* (Paris: Grasset, 1981), p. 74.
89. Jean-Marie Benoist, *Pavane pour une Europe défunte*, op. cit., p. 146.
90. Jean-Louis Cartry, 'French culture kaputt?', *Le Figaro Magazine*, 23 February 1980.
91. Jean-Pierre Chevènement, 'Pour l'indépendance nationale', *Le Monde*, 11 May 1983.
92. See the heated debate provoked in France by the publication of an article by Raymond Sokolov in the *Wall Street Journal* of 15 February 1983 entitled 'Junket of the Year; Les Intellos', on the 'decline' of French literature. Cf. '*Les intellectuels français sont-ils vraiment nuls?*',

Le Matin, 18 February 1983, pp. 1, 3–6; Philippe Sollers, 'Lettre ouverte aux intellectuels yankees', Femmes series 2, No. 2, December 1984.
93. Cf. Margaret Ferguson, 'Joachim du Bellay; The Exile's Defense of his Native Language' in Ferguson, Trials of Desire, Renaissance Defense of Poetry (New Haven: Yale University Press, 1983) pp. 18–53. See also Claude Hagège, Le Français et les siècles (Paris: Odile Jacob, 1987).
94. 'Manifeste contre l'invasion des ondes et pour la diversification des échanges audiovisuels', Le Monde, 24 January 1985.
95. Joachim Du Bellay, Deffence et illustration de la langue françoyse (Paris: Librairie Marcel Didier, 1948) pp. 42–3.
96. Claude-Jean Bertrand, 'L'impérialisme culturel américain: un mythe?', Esprit, May 1985, pp. 68, 69, 70, respectively.
97. Ibid., p. 74.
98. Cf. Pierre Manent, 'Democracy in America after 150 Years...', Wall Street Journal, 29 January 1985.
99. Such as the admiration expressed by the minister for social affairs and employment, Philippe Seguin, at a symposium held at the OECD headquarters in January 1988. Cf. Le Monde, 23 January 1988. The Communist L'Humanité of the same day bore the headline 'M. Seguin fasciné par le modèle Reagan' and called for action to combat a policy which 'increased unemployment and poverty'. The Communists' presidential candidate also denounced M. Seguin's 'jobs fast food' (sic).
100. The French have never gone in very much for world travel, let alone living abroad. There has been no French emigration to the United States to compare with that from other European countries, hence nothing to 'bridge' the old and new worlds. Until very recently, the main effect that tourism has had on the USA's image is through the presence of American visitors in France. The fact that French tourism is on the increase and travel to the USA is also à la mode shows that there is much less fear of American might, and suggests that people are wanting to know what US society is really like. The image of America as a mighty and arrogant world power is being replaced by that of an open society – a society 'sans Etat'. Alongside the Washington-based reporters whose coverage is confined almost entirely to goings-on on Capitol Hill, there is an influx of French journalists more au fait with developments in American society, particularly the trends in culture (and counter-culture). Where Le Monde under Beuve-Méry and Fauvet displayed a degree of anti-Americanism over foreign politics, Libération now promotes a more pluralist and non-stereotyped image of today's America that does more for the reputation of the United States than half a dozen born-again Reaganite leader-writers.
101. For instance, François Furet, Penser la Révolution française (Paris: Gallimard, 1978); Jacques Solé, La Révolution en Question (Paris: Seuil, 1988).

Part I

The Origins of Anti-Americanism: History and hysteria

1
The Pathology of Anti-Americanism
Theodore Zeldin

I should like to consider this subject as a medical case history. To hate a whole nation, to love a whole nation, is a clear symptom of hysteria. The pathology of the phenomenon can perhaps be usefully clarified by examining it from four clinical standpoints.

(1) PREDISPOSITION

The French are not the only people who have shown dislike for the Americans. So the question should be, not just when did they show their dislike, and when did they attenuate it, but is there anything special about their dislike compared to that exhibited by other countries? If all the world suffers from influenza at the same time, that is a different problem to one particular individual catching cold frequently, irrespective of the weather. Is there a greater French disposition to hate foreigners in general? Unfortunately, no comparative studies of this kind of animosity have been undertaken; each nation is too absorbed by the details of its own relationships. The more I study France, the more I am convinced that the study of national history is unsatisfactory; the nation is not a self-sufficient entity except in a narrow political sense; the most important cultural and economic frontiers are not the national ones; the problems of nations need to be seen in a global context, as instances among many more or less similar ones. To judge the significance of a nation's attitude to foreigners we need an Index of Xenophobia, a thermometer of susceptibility, to measure the degree of fever produced by contact with foreigners in different countries. The French assume too readily that they are particularly sensitive. I do not think they are. To illustrate this, let me compare the history of the attitude of Britain to the USA.

Britain has had many more reasons for taking an interest in a former colony, linked to it by ties of blood and language, and which long continued to be an important trading partner. But what has characterised the relations of the two countries over the last century has been, above all, ignorance. In 1898–1932, for example, only between 8 and 16 per cent of foreign news in English newspapers was about the USA, and this is a statistic of the serious newspapers; one third of this news, moreover, was concerned with crime and sex. So Britain's knowledge of the USA was not dissimilar then to the information that the Russians have about the USA today – much of it was derogatory. The greatest British expert on the USA was Viscount Bryce, whose *American Commonwealth* (1888) held almost the same status as Tocqueville's *De La Démocratie en Amérique*; everybody who cared about America, we are told, read it; but in the first 25 years after its publication, only 9000 copies were sold. Compare that with the 17 reprints of Tocqueville's book in France 1835–88, and eight reprints of the British translation. (To compare Bryce and Tocqueville is not to compare equals, but after Bryce's book was published, Tocqueville ceased to be reprinted until interest was revived after 1945).

The USA was held in suspicion by the British both as a source of threatening innovations and as a backward province lacking in refinement. In 1900 a resolution was introduced into the House of Commons denouncing the demoralisation caused by American theatrical plays being put on the London stage. At that time, British teachers were already complaining about the invasion of Americanisms into the English language; by 1940 they had counted about 1000 which they judged reprehensible. The extent of their animosity can be seen from their objections not only to US spelling but even to the smell of US glue, which, they said, made American books doubly repulsive. Resentment against America's economic advance was equally strong. In 1902 a campaign was started to protest against the invasion of American cigarettes. In 1909 the first American department store was opened in London, Selfridges, but it was careful to promise that it would not be too American in character, that if it showed American *zip*, it would also have English *poise*. By 1940, 40 per cent of US factories situated in Europe were in Britain, and they aroused as much disapproval as admiration. For British prejudices about the Americans were certainly ambivalent. On the one hand the Americans were supposed to be good businessmen and hard workers, and to have a high standard of living, but on the other hand they were regarded as not truly democratic, their political spoils system in particular was despised. Lord Bryce could find few achievements that were distinctively American, though he conceded that the Americans were more thorough in working out ideas borrowed from Europe (the same complacent comment was later applied to the Japanese). In 1936–37, English schoolboys aged 13 to 16, asked what they thought of the US, defined it as the place where one could get rich quickly, and which produced good sportsmen, but they considered Americans boastful, and incapable of speaking good English; America was not more democratic; American manufactured products did not have the quality of British goods; the boys were divided on the question of whether they were more interested in the US than in Europe, and on whether Britain could learn more from Europe than the US. The ambivalence was accentuated by the war of 1914–18, when the British suddenly became aware that the Americans were not Britons in exile, nor even predominantly of British stock. But the hostility to America was probably restrained by the many British writers who not only found a good market for their books in the US, but often obtained their first successes there. H. G. Wells learnt his socialism from Henry George, not from Europe. We still need to calculate precisely whether there was more anti–Americanism among British or French intellectuals.

To compare British and French attitudes to the US may be a little unfair, because of the former's greater ties with US. So a necessary supplement is to compare the attitude of the two countries to Japan, which they confronted at about the same time, on roughly the same terms; that reveals their attitudes to foreigners in the purest form. Both simplified, stereotyped, caricatured, Japanese civilisation, finding what they wanted to find, despite genuine curiosity on the part of a few talented individuals. On the British side, Gilbert and Sullivan's *Mikado* summed up the unwillingness to treat foreigners as anything but laughable. On the French side, the import of Japanese art styles and the export of Impressionism showed that there were always some French people who prized the universal element in culture.

(2) POSOLOGY

But how does France distribute its affections or animosities between the nations? To judge the strength of its feelings towards the USA, one must place them in the context of all the feelings that it has at the same time for other foreign countries. The thread that runs through French history is hate for one's immediate neighbour, and preference for more distant strangers. This is the natural reaction of the provincial who quarrels with the next village, often feels an inferiority complex about his origins, and envies or admires the residents of the capital city. The principle is easily extended on an international scale; in every century the French have discovered a new set of foreigners to admire: Greeks, Romans, Italians, the English (for their political constitution), the Germans (for their science), the Americans (for their prosperity), the Poles (for their heroic resistance), the Japanese (for their cooking as well as their art). But their admiration has never resulted in a committed marriage, only in flirtation, or in a fashion that has always been élitist. The polls about French sympathy for foreign countries are seldom precise enough to show exactly what is admired: sometimes it is no more than a liking for jazz or a brand of cigarettes.

In 1598 Sir Robert Dallington made this comment on the French: 'When ye see all other Nations painted in the proper habit of their country, the Frenchman is always pictured with a pair of sheers in his hand, to signify that he hath no peculiar habit of his own, nor contenteth himself long with the habit of any other, but according to his capricious humour, deviseth daily new fashions ... [They are] the most fickle kind of men, sudden to begin & more sudden to end'. This stereotypical view of the French not only obfuscates the great variety of reactions of different segments of the population towards the strange and the new. It also glosses over the superficiality of much of the interest in foreign ideas and the misinterpretation which is a constant feature of it. The search for foreign models often says more about the discomfort of an individual in his own skin than about his tastes. My own view of national culture (including both French and British culture) is that it cannot be compared to a tree with roots firmly planted in its natural soil; in modern times at least a better analogy is the import-export firm.

(3) EPIDEMIOLOGY

Who is susceptible to catching Americanophilism? It is important to answer not just in terms of classes, generations, or economic pressures, but also of individuals, because the precise nuance of the attachment is what matters most. Suppose one drew a map of nineteenth- or twentieth-century Europe, with a red dot indicating every person with some feeling of attraction for the USA. It is very likely that France would be revealed as the most affected. Enthusiasm for America spread in France despite the governing classes' efforts to vaccinate themselves against it. They valued classical education which gave them a peculiar, esteemed way of speaking and writing; the prestige of state employment kept their eyes firmly directed at Paris as their Mecca; the limited ambitions of their family firms encouraged them to isolate themselves as far as possible from foreign competition; they clung to their provincial roots even when they apparently abandoned them. But good taste could also be boring. The traditional avenues of social promotion were like motorways covered with the debris of car crashes: so many people failed to achieve their aims, or to obtain full satisfaction from their conventional success, that bad taste had its attractions too. Pro-Americanism could be a sign both of superior, snobbish taste – or of contempt for the canons of taste. French popular culture was receptive to many features associated with the US. Those who attended not the lycées, which taught respect for philosophy and the classics, but private vocational classes like the Cours Pigier, those who were working their way up the ladder in commerce, those who read Jules Verne and Benjamin Franklin, were readily infected by enthusiasm for the so-called land of opportunity. Benjamin Franklin's *Way to Wealth* sold 70 editions in English (on both sides of the Atlantic) but 56 editions in French translation, and only 11 editions in German. It would be interesting to discover the precise figures of these sales. They may mean that France was the European country most interested by the American myth. Perhaps that is because it did not have enough suitable heroes of its own. Ivon Gattaz, the former leader of the Employers' Organisation, was inspired in his youth by the example of American millionaires. The British had far more millionaires than the French; they had less inducement to seek other heroes abroad; even British aristocrats were far richer than French millionaires. However, one must distinguish between true and false pro-

Americanism. Much use has always been made of foreign examples simply as ammunition to fight purely domestic battles.

Which sex is most susceptible to being pro-American? It is surprising that no session was devoted to women in the conference out of which this book arose, because perhaps the most fundamental obstacle to fraternity across the Atlantic has been disagreement about women, and also about food. In Britain as well as in France, throughout the nineteenth century, the mysteriousness of the American woman, her disregard for European conventions, her apparent rejection of male domination, made her appear a dangerous threat, a threat much more profound than economic competition. In the 1970s it might have appeared that France and Britain were differently receptive to the writings of American feminists; in the 1980s the relations have altered; this is a subject in international relations that still awaits more detailed investigation.

(4) IMMUNOLOGY

Fashions of enthusiasm for different foreign countries raise the question of how individuals grow to be resistant, or immune, to their own national traditions and myths, or alternatively to foreign influence. I believe that individuals are developing more and more immunity, as insects have done to pesticides. The conclusion of my own work is that the individual of today (not only in France but throughout the western world) is basically different from the one Tocqueville wrote about. Tocqueville expected people to become more and more conformist. But neither democracy, nor education, nor the media have had the effect he predicted. As the range of choices available to the modern individual has increased, so he (and she) has been forced to make a unique selection; he has found that it is not so easy to conform, even if he knew what to conform to; he has misinterpreted the messages of his teachers and the television as often as he has understood them. He is a member of a large range of minorities. So there are now 55 million minorities in France. The breaking up of monolithic opinions is occurring in all western countries. Each individual has his own way of being pro- or anti-American; each is struck by a slightly different ratatouille of qualities that he attributes to the USA; each often alters his views over the course of his lifetime. I certainly have never returned from my visits to the USA with quite the same reaction, since it is so vast and rich a country, that not to alter one's view of it is equivalent to refusing to alter one's view of the world in general, as one experiences it more fully. The history of Franco-American relations is thus an opportunity for analysing the intimate history of individuals, as well as a way of confronting one's European heritage.

George Bernard Shaw said half a century ago that one must distinguish between civilised America and barbarian America. No, that is only a beginning, an elementary statement, for to hate or love half a nation is still too simple; still too hysterical. To judge America, is to judge oneself. So what we should seek to discover about French judgements of the USA is not so much what proportion were for or against, as what proportion understood the significance of what they were saying when they expressed their approval or disapproval.

2
From Baudelaire to Duhamel: An Unlikely Antipathy
Pascal Ory

I shall make no bones about it: I have come to the conclusion that the term 'anti-Americanism' is not a very apt one and that the concept it denotes is not particularly operative. In its very construction, it is a loaded expression. It suggests more or less implicitly a parallel with the great 'negative faiths' such as anti-freemasonry or anti-semitism – ideologies whose terms of reference changed considerably during the period in question.

However, the moment one starts investigating the principles of anti-Americanism in France, or its most evident occurrences – whether among academics, ordinary people, performers or politicians – it becomes glaringly obvious that systematic criticism of the United States here never acquired the reductionist and unifying character of the negative ideologies, and therefore never developed into an autonomous tendency. Whatever importance it might have assumed in the output of various personalities – albeit only ever a passing phase – it never became an obsessive theme in the way that the 'Jewish menace' did in the case of Edouard Drumont, or Freemasonry in the case of Bernard Fay – the latter, incidentally, a dyed-in-the-wool Americanophile of the inter-war period.[1] To my knowledge – during this period at least – hostility towards the United States was never 'organised' in the sense of motivating the formation of a specific group or association, or the creation of a journal. In a nutshell, what makes research in this area difficult is the instrumental, or even secondary nature of Americanophobia in the Third Republic.

It was not until other avenues of research led me to examine the very origin of the noun *'américanisation'* and the verb *'américaniser'* that I was to discover the role played by writers such as Baudelaire or the Goncourt brothers in first airing this phenomenon.[2]

A cursory scan of French literature dealing principally with the United States reveals another obvious factor which makes the phenomenon a very relative one: extreme positions of total rejection or unbounded approval are very much in the minority. In fact it is quite likely that approval – illustrated by such names as Tardieu, Siegfried and Maurois[3] – greatly outweighed antipathy. The most common attitude among the French falls somewhere between these two poles, and it is not unusual to find that critical passages from the pen of an admirer like André Siegfried sound, when taken out of context, not unlike similar passages from the works of a basically hostile writer such as Georges Duhamel.

Finally, one inevitably comes across comments which are impossible to locate on an attraction/repulsion axis. It either depends on the context, or it is irrelevant. This particularly applies to Americans portrayed in French fiction during the 1870–1914 period. How is one to assess such conventional figures as 'the emancipated young woman' and the 'hard-pressed and a trifle eccentric business-man'? Where are we to place the 'innocents' of Eugène Labiche's best-selling *Trente millions de Gladiator* (1875) relative to Victorien Sardou's satire *L'Oncle Sam* of 1873 or to Jules Verne's portrayal of national characters, which was actually extremely pro-Anglo-Saxon? The most popular literary genres, such as adventure stories, children's fiction and comic- strips tended to manipulate stereotyped American characters and situations in a mish-mash which is virtually indistinguishable from European self-satisfaction and a traditional fascination with exotic goings on.[4]

What is most important at this point, therefore, is the content of the argument. One should not be surprised that the mythological stock in trade changes so little or so slowly in the course of time: that is an inherent characteristic of mythological stocks in trade. What is more surprising is to find that both admirers and detractors tend to employ the same images – 'merely' lending them a different complexion.

Are we, however, to rule out any period influence? Certainly not if we accept the view that this was a crucial epoch which saw not only the permanent establishment of republican rule in France, but also the first extended experience of democracy that the country had known since the fleeting or ambiguous syntheses of the first two Republics or the so-called 'liberal' Empire. In that particular historical climate, certain classic forms of rejection would seem to have crystallised fairly rapidly, albeit tempered by the state of economic, political and cultural relations between the two societies at the particular period under consideration. And over this lengthy period of three quarters of a century, what seems to me the essential factor is that France never ceased behaving as a top-ranking power even when made to endure humiliation, threats or isolation. This conviction, which, it must be said, was justified in terms of events and material circumstances, hardly waned except on two occasions: the national crises which mark the beginning and end of the period, namely the early 1870s and the late 1930s. And by chance, these just happened to coincide with analogous periods of crisis and decline in the United States. Throughout the inter-war years – a period marked by US diplomatic retreat on the European continent and the Great Depression, which no longer deceives historians about the extent of American power – this psychological situation did much to compensate for certain misgivings which were voiced by a handful of French intellectuals, in stark contrast with mainstream opinion.

Of course, there is no denying that the new century brought with it a change of tone. Right up to the beginning of World War I, the terms of the debate about the United States seemed less heated and there was much less urgency to the discussion of its negative or positive attributes. Even though increasing contacts had led to a gradual *rapprochement* between the two countries, the United States was physically remote and – importantly – there was little French emigration to America at a period when emigration from the other European countries was reaching its peak. America scarcely intervened in political disputes between the European powers which were the central concern of those country's rulers and the supreme perspective of national mythologies. Last but not least, the USA's economic dynamism affected the man in the street far less than in Great Britain, for example, where *'Made in USA'* served as a counterweight to *'Made in Germany'*.[5]

And as for cultural relations, all opinion polls, such as on the occasion of the various Universal Exhibitions, served to confirm the French citizens' imperturbable sense of superiority. Even such a denouncer – or maybe it should be 'announcer' – of the 'American Peril' as the engineer Paul Sée authored a study whose conclusion was that one of France's best trump cards was still 'its leading rank in the field of luxury industries, arts and literature'.[6] Moreover, this is the field where changes were slowest in coming, and even as late as 1939, the commissioner of the French Pavilion at the New York World Fair could be heard to exclaim *à propos* the theme of 'The World of Tomorrow': 'When America asks this question we can only smile and answer quite calmly: the world of tomorrow, like the world of yesterday and the world of today will be of French inspiration'.[7]

But the new century arrived just at the moment when the United States was emerging as a great power, first economically, then politically and finally – between the wars – culturally. At this point, almost everyone's attitudes to America lost their exotic or fairy-tale colouration, and the French started to take America seriously. A concrete manifestation of this change was the publication, within three years of each other, of two symmetrical and contemporaneous works of reference about America: André Siegfried's *Les Etats-unis d'aujourd'hui* (1927) and Georges Duhamel's *Scènes de la vie future* (1930).[8]

This new climate brought about the fusion of two critical standpoints which were interlinked but so far had expressed themselves in quite separate ways. On the one hand, there was fear and rejection of foreign *domination* and on the other, the fear and rejection of *modernité* which America most clearly epitomised, hence the adjective in the title of Duhamel's book, the entire argument of which hinged on this idea. It was the key to his passionate rejection of that model of civilisation and provided the *leitmotif* of all the author's essays.

The most strictly material criticism was to be found in the works of the economists such as Paul Sée, whom we have already mentioned, or Professor Octave Noël of L'Ecole des hautes études commerciales who, three years previously, had denounced the USA's growing hegemony in a book entitled *Le péril américain*.[9] However, apart from the fact that it was never any more than a counterpart of the much more frequent denunciations of the English or German 'perils', the most interesting feature of such criticism is the *profession de foi* which often accompanied it, together with an exposition of the spiritual values which were allegedly at stake.

Thus Noël's well-documented study opens with a definition of good and bad chauvinism, contrasting the former ('this essentially European concept . . . born out of an excess of patriotic sentiment')

– clearly regarded as something noble and positive – with American jingoism which '*in reality* (sic) is no more than a manifestation of a ferocious egoism dictated by the appetites or aspirations of a people whose excessive intellectual and physical efforts have been directed over the past century towards the endless increase of wealth and material goods, and the achievement of comfort'.[10]

Nevertheless, where the peril was perceived as mainly quantitative, the solutions proposed tended to be of a material kind, such as the exploitation of France's chief advantages, including its agricultural potential and, above all, its colonial reserves.

The tone shifts rapidly to one of alarm or even pessimism as soon as the discussion takes a cultural or predominantly cultural turn. In this connection, it is no doubt necessary to recall the little-known circumstances in which the expression *américanisation* – used with negative *culturaliste* overtones – first made its appearance in France. 'The poor man is so Americanized by the zoocratic industrial philosophers that he has lost all notion of the difference between the phenomena of the physical and moral worlds, and those of the natural and supernatural.'[11] The 'man' Baudelaire is referring to here is modern humanity, which in his view was already on the downhill slope of technical materialism. Two years later (1875), in the preface to his translation of Edgar Alan Poe's *More Tales of the Grotesque and Arabesque* he was to condemn an epoch in which 'Americanomania has virtually become a socially acceptable fad'. Most important is the context of the first quotation; it is a reference to the first Universal Exhibition in Paris, that triumphal assertion of a technical and industrialist blueprint – somewhat tinged with Saint-Simonism – for the human society of the future.

It therefore comes as no surprise to discover that the noun derived from Baudelaire's verb appeared in the Goncourt brothers' *Journal* of 16 January 1867 *à propos* the second Exhibition: 'The Universal Exhibition, the latest blow in what amounts to the Americanisation of France – Industry outdoing Art, steam threshing machines in place of paintings ... – in a word, the Material Federation'. At precisely the same period (the first part of the *Grand Dictionnaire universel du XIX siècle* appearing in 1863 and the complete volume in 1866), Pierre Larousse defined of the new word *américanisme*: 'unbounden and exclusive admiration of the government, laws and customs of the Americans, and chiefly of the inhabitants of the United States'.

I would surmise that because they adopted a negative stance towards democratic institutions, those first manifestations of Americophobia were bound to decline after the final establishment of the Republic and the gradual implementation of liberal democracy *'à la française'*. This imposed on partisans and adversaries alike a political agenda light-years away from political debate in the United States. By contrast, when the pace of industrialisation – a process inaugurated during Louis Philippe's reign – accelerated during the years of the Second Empire, we encounter a new set of arguments, chiefly cultural, which were a synthesis of old attitudes and a new reality.

These attitudes were already evident in the first accounts by French travellers to America at the time of Independence, such as the Marquis de Chastellux. De Tocqueville's subtle analysis was subsequently to lend it a force of conviction that stood the test of time. The United States was regarded as the probable, or – more and more frequently – the inevitable future, if not of Europe, then certainly of France. What was essential about the new reality was the growing importance of technology, particularly in the form of mechanisation, standardisation and speed. It was not just a material 'reality', but also a cultural one, of course, since our aim here is to try and capture (approximately as always) the epoch in which this phenomenon and its images were gaining currency. The important thing is that these characteristics represented the same basic conviction, at least as far as those who rejected them were concerned, that is, the triumph of the quantitative over the qualitative. In strictly cultural terms it amounted to the supremacy of 'mass culture' over 'high culture'. In that respect, anti-American xenophobia would seem to have borrowed most of the stereotypes of the 'second wave' of Anglophobia whose targets were the City's domination and Manchester's 'tentacles'. But it was actually more radical, because once the monarchical and aristocratic filters had gone there was no common past left.

This would seem to be the point of synthesis for the attitudes we are studying and the period in question. For in the sense that democracy introduces the law of 'the many', universal suffrage – whose establishment was not entirely unconnected with the aggravation of 'artistic' individualism of which Baudelaire and the Goncourt brothers were among the best examples – introduces the law of the multitude. Nonetheless it was not until rulers, mediators, artists, and so on, became aware of the spread of industrialisation that the United States became established as the byword of modernity.

From the end of the nineteenth century onwards, examples abound of America being used in this sort of abstract way. When Barrès describes his friend the Marquis de Morès, he makes him 'both a positive Americanist and the last living reader of the courtly romances'.[12] A generation later, Montherlant uses similar, albeit more ironic, terms to describe his Baron de Coëtquidan[13] who fancies himself as a 'modern (that is, "Americanised") man'. In their boldly drawn predictions of tomorrow's world, Anatole France, in *L'île des pingouins* of 1908, and Jean-Richard Bloch, in his *Destin du siècle* of 1931, both describe the future in much the same way. What is astonishing, though, is that these two men of the Left – in fact of the extreme Left at their time of writing – put entirely opposite complexions on their respective prophecies. Anatole France, as one may expect, reproaches that future for destroying 'all remaining pockets of freedom, spontaneity, consideration, moderation, humanity and tradition', while Bloch is already an enthusiastic witness at 'The Birth of a (*technological*) Culture' which he portrays in the most positive light.

And even when a Barrèsian writer like Paul Adam at the beginning of the century (*Le Trust*[14]) or young spiritualistic intellectuals of the inter-war years such as Robert Aron or Arnaud Dandieu (*Le Cancer américain*), seem to have their gazes fixed on America, their eyes are focussed chiefly on 'the way that industry and banking dominated the entire life of the period'.[15] This was the aspect they chronicled or warned against.

The recurrent theme of womanhood as part of the overall image of the United States throughout the period in question also needs to be seen in the same light. The idea of the 'emancipated woman' crops up repeatedly from the Second Empire onwards, at least in American stereotypes,[16] but the disfavour which generally attached to it says much about the gap between the two cultures. And one cannot help being struck by the staying power of this attitude which started out as amused or scandalised surprise and ended up as pitying condescension. Incidentally, when in 1938 the Marxist poet François Drujon, wrote in *L'Amérique et l'avenir*[17] of the choice between *'femmes poupées'* and *'femmes fatales'* he was not far in spirit from the description of 'nylon-stockinged slaves' which Catholic writer Jean Canu coined for American womanhood in his *Villes et paysages d'Amérique*.[18] Yet again, however, both these works are friendly to the United States, broadly speaking. Moreover, as André Malmaison was to point out a few months later in *Terre d'Amérique*: 'Is not much of present-day dissoluteness in the civilised world due to the misuse of women's capacities and qualities?'[19]

Looked at from this angle, there is nothing at all original about Duhamel's *Scènes de la vie future*. What makes it important in terms of the discussion of anti-Americanism is the success which the book enjoyed. In *Le livre de l'amertume*, a journal penned jointly by Blanche and Georges Duhamel during the years in question, we read that the book had already run to 150 editions by August 1930, having first appeared the previous April.[20] As for its critical acclaim, this can easily be judged not only by the large number of reviews but also the inevitable reference to it for years afterwards in the accounts of travellers to America and observers of that country. However, such references mostly turned to Duhamel's disadvantage as he tended to serve as a foil to modernist attitudes.

It matters little, therefore, that Duhamel derived his knowledge of the United States (except for what he learnt from some preliminary reading) from a six-week stay in the USA in Autumn 1928, crammed with university lectures and organised trips, or that his animosity was undoubtedly motivated entirely by personal circumstances. The enormous response to the book is not entirely unrelated to its date of publication – which coincided with the first shock-wave of the Wall Street crash – but it has far more to do with its lively tone and the simplicity of its anecdotes, which was striking, coming from the pen of a writer considered to be a model of bourgeois moderation. The main reason for its impact, however, was the fact that it was a highly 'authorised' re-exposition of the classic case against America, that is, materialism versus idealism, the machine versus humanity, utilitarianism versus disinterestedness, vulgarity versus refinement, industry versus art . . .

One might be tempted from this to believe that Duhamel is voicing the views of a dyed-in-the-wool Americanophobic 'silent majority', but there are no real grounds for doing so. In fact there is good reason to assume that what affected Duhamel's readers of those days more – whether positively or not matters little – was a steady diet of pejorative accounts of phenomena which were actually already familiar, and till then had been favourably accepted by the public, for instance, the cinema, jazz, advertising, and so on. There was nothing more popular in the France of 1930 than American cinema, nothing more common in dance music than the syncopated rhythms of the sort of jazz that was as adulterated and 'whitened' in the Champs-Elysées as it was in Broadway. Through Duhamel's eyes, the first of these becomes the notorious 'entertainment for helots, a pastime for the illiterate', the second 'the triumph of barbaric silliness' and the third 'seems to have been dreamt up to arouse the reflexes of a sedentary mollusc'. Everything else gets similar treatment. As for his violent portrayal of the Chicago slaughter-houses, it is important chiefly as a counterbalance to such starry-eyed accounts as that of Edouard Herriot[21] published at about the same time. In contrast to the latter's model of rationality Duhamel saw a 'Realm of Death'.

On the other hand, what is striking for the present-day reader is just how far-reaching Duhamel's critique was. America for him was no individualistic paradise offering unbounden opportunities but instead a levelling, conformist and exclusively materialist society peopled by 'miserable care-worn creatures stupefied by drudgery', all reduced to the 'same level of uniformity'. Boredom and anxiety held sway, both of them combatted and nourished at one and the same time by collective illusions; it was rule by the State, that tendentious God-substitute. In short, Duhamel, that paragon of intellectual liberalism, taxes the United States with precisely the same shortcomings that anti-Communists attributed then (and still do now) to Soviet-style Communism, in other words, the spirit of the bee-hive or the ant-hill.

The Duhamelian – one might almost say Orwellian – interpretation;[22] is all the more striking in that it came at a time regarded by historians as the apogee of authentic (economic) liberalism, and in the wake of the author's analogous picture of the Soviet Union, *Voyage à Moscou* published in 1928, which was equally guarded but far less aggressive.

Without doubt, the fact that the USA/USSR parallel was becoming an explicit component of an increasing number of books about America of the inter-war period is a further explanation. For whereas, of course, the Sovietophile is by no means *ipso facto* an anti-American, the Americanophobe, whether liberal or conservative, eventually concludes that there is a greater threat from the West than the East, and regards America as the more negative example.

From all I have said so far, it is obvious that the anti-Americanism of the period cannot be situated with any sort of accuracy on a Right-Left axis. Its cultural expression undoubtedly bore all the hallmarks of the Right, in the shape of misoneism and a pessimistic attitude to progress. It was no coincidence that Octave Noël wrote in *Le Correspondant* – a die-hard Catholic journal – that the extreme Right applauded Duhamel, or that various press campaigns of the period against American cinema or jazz based themselves on his book. Nor can it be denied that the anarchist Left applauded Duhamel's 1930 onslaught on America and that traces of it can be detected in the account of Bardamu's American sojourn published two years later.[23] If one shares my view of Céline as a right-wing anarchist, one has here a splendid example of political extremes converging.

But could there be anyone more moderate than the moderate Duhamel? It would therefore be going too far to classify all anti-Americans as extremists, or, by the same token, all pro-Americans as moderates. For conservative writers such as Siegfried or Maurois, it is possible to find counterparts on the Left such as Georges Boris. This is not possible, however, in the case of an Anglo-Saxon-style liberal like Emile Boutmy, who had serious reservations about the evolution of the American political system.[24] In *New York* and *Champions du monde*[25] (two books that appeared in the same year as *Scènes de la vie future*), a writer as representative of his epoch as Paul Morand – who has been rather too glibly dismissed as 'cosmopolitan' by critics past and present – certainly displayed an insatiable curiosity, but his overall assessment was unfavourable.[26] At this point it is scarcely relevant any longer to propose a separate history of Americanophobia. From now on we need research into a phenomenon which is much more extensive and so far uncharted: French xenophobia.

Until World War II, when the US burst on the scene as a political power, what I would describe as the 'second wave' of political Americanophobia was scarcely ever more than marginal. Since it was essentially a condemnation of that country as a prototype of capitalist and racist social injustice – and a puritanical society to boot – it was a phenomenon of the Far Left. Even in exceptional circumstances, such as the Sacco and Vanzetti affair between 1921 and 1927, the violence of Anarchist, Communist and Socialist organisations was so much part and parcel of the Left's close combat with the Right in France that a specifically 'American' component scarcely emerged. The ringing calls from Paul Vaillant-Couturier in *L'Humanité* of 24 August 1927 – the morning after the execution of the two anarchists – to 'boycott Yankee capitalism' and exact 'collective reprisals' against 'the Yankee idlers living in France', led in fact, to violent confrontations with the French police force and a working-class raid on 'Montmartre, capital of the fun-loving dollar'. These should be viewed more in terms of proletarian 'emotions' than as anything to do with a particular country. Moreover, it is a well-known fact that F. D. Roosevelt's social experiments, which were virtually contemporary with the anti-fascist coalition, evoked a very positive overall response among various currents of the French Left, including the Communist Party. The New Deal was seen as the first step towards the socialisation of the country and great support was voiced for the – albeit modest – diplomatic initiatives of the Democratic administration. On 9 October 1937 *L'Humanité* was even to carry the headline '*Bravo Roosevelt!*' when FDR's administration came out publicly in support of the Chinese, then victims of Japanese aggression. It was within the ranks of the old-time orthodox liberal Right that the US economy was to encounter the greatest hostility from 1933 onwards.

I would pause here on the distinction between cultural and political anti-Americanism. So long as US hegemony is not perceived as an immediate issue by French public opinion, attitudes to the United States are not split in terms of the two main political ideologies. Rather they serve to crystallise, reveal and epitomise two cultural ideologies. I refer to two implicitly antagonistic arguments, and if I may be permitted to crown this value judgement, two fantasies – two visions of Paradise. On the one hand there is an aristocratic *lost paradise* of the 'lord of the manor' or artistic variety (if not actually a bit of each), while on the other is the plebeian 'singing tomorrows' of the liberal or democratic variety (or a bit of both).

One may, of course, qualify the first fantasy as 'right-wing' and the second as 'left-wing', in which case Americanophobia is automatically a right-wing phenomenon. However, as we have demonstrated, it is time we stopped seeking systematic expressions in partisan terms.

This is undoubtedly the most fascinating aspect of anti-Americanism, although the theme's extreme volatility makes it a rather controversial area of study. In fact it is a specific case where ideological families cannot be categorised in party political terms. A case worth keeping an eye on.

Notes

1. Cf. Bernard Fay, about whom it is seldom remembered that he was a translator of Gertrude Stein; see, for instance, his *Civilisation américaine* (Paris: Le Sagittaire, 1939). For an example of a synthesis of anti-semitism and anti-Americanism, see Roger Lambelin, *Le Règne d'Israël chez les Anglo-Saxons* (Paris: Grasset, 1921).
2. Reference to a work to be published by Editions du Seuil under the title *L'Américanisation culturelle de la France, mythes et réalités*.
3. André Tardieu, *Notes sur les Etats-Unis* ... (Paris: Calmann-Lévy, 1908); André Siegfried, *Les Etats-Unis d'aujourd'hui* (Paris: Armand Colin, 1927; André Maurois, *Chantiers américains* (Paris: Gallimard, 1933); *Etats-Unis 39* (Paris: Editions de France, 1939).
4. Cf. two works from the same period which are still widely read: *Bécassine voyage*, by de Caumery and J. P. Pinchon (Paris: Gautier-Languereau, 1921) and *Tintin en Amérique*, by Hergé (Brussels: Editions du Petit Vingtième, 1932).
5. Cf. the campaign by a journalist called Williams on the latter issue in 1890. Economic operations by American firms in Great Britain were taking shape at the time.
6. Article published in the *Bulletin de la Société industrielle du nord de la France* in 1902, republished in booklet form a year later.
7. Marcel Olivier, in *Plaisir de France*, No. 58, July 1939, p. 5. Cf. my article: 'Plus dure sera la chute: les pavillons français aux Expositions internationales de 1939', *Relations internationales*, No. 33, Spring 1983, pp. 81–90.
8. Although it came out after the Wall Street Crash, Duhamel's book deals with the United States of 1928.
9. Article published in *Le Correspondant*, of January-June 1899, subsequently re-issued as a booklet.
10. Cf. the text quoted by Marie-France Toinet in her contribution to the present volume.
11. This text, subsequently republished by *Les Curiosités esthétiques*, first appeared in 1855 in one of the articles of art criticism that Baudelaire contributed to the journal *Le Pays*.
12. *Scènes et doctrines du nationalisme*, Vol. II, p. 62. Hence it is an article formerly published in the press.
13. *Les célibataires*, p. 770 in the 'La Pléiade' edition, (Paris: Gallimard, 1959).
14. Paris: Fayard, 1910.
15. Paris: Rieder, 1931.
16. Cf. the thesis by Simon Jeune, *De F. T. Graindorge à A. O. Barnabooth. Les types américains dans le roman et le théâtre français (1861–1917)* (Paris: Didier, 1963).
17. Paris: Corrêa, 1938, p. 132.
18. J. de Gigord, Paris/Liège, p. 27.
19. Paris: Fayard, 1939, p. 318.
20. Paris: Mercure de France, 1984.
21. *Impressions d'Amérique* (Lyon: M. Audin, 1923).

22. It was an attitude also shared by Drujon, although he took it from a quite different angle. For him, 'standardised shops and standardised food ... are not to be found in the Soviet Union but the USA. The standardised life-style is a by-product of advanced capitalism not of socialism' (*L'Amérique et l'avenir*, op. cit., p. 159.)
23. Louis-Ferdinande Céline, *Voyage au bout de la nuit* (Paris: Denoël, 1932).
24. See the point made by Marie-France Toinet.
25. *New York*: Flammarion, 1930; *Champions du Monde*, Grasset, 1930.
26. For example, 'I wrote a few years ago: "France has no option but to turn American or turn Bolshevist". Nowadays I believe that we must do everything in our power to avoid both these precipices' (*New York*, op. cit., p. 263.)

3

Anti-Americanism in the Years of Collaboration and Resistance

Robert O. Paxton

French attitudes towards the United States during 1940–44 were as deeply divided as French attitudes about anything else in those years of conflict, and they evolved rapidly with the roller-coaster of the war. The Vichy regime began with the relative warmth of Roosevelt's 'Vichy Gamble',[1] but it became the first French regime to take active steps against the penetration of American culture, and in November 1942 in North Africa it became the first French government to exchange hostile fire with Americans since the 'undeclared naval war' of 1799–1800. The Resistance based its whole gamble on American military success, but relations came to be poisoned at the top by Roosevelt's refusal to recognise the Free French as the government of France until the summer of 1944.

Both Vichy and Free France needed American assistance, and both resisted American influence. Vichy leaders preferred America generous but distant. They hoped for both moral and material support, but considered the United States incapable of constructive military impact upon Europe, inappropriate as a constitutional model for Europe, and harmful culturally to Europe. Resistance made sense only on two contrary assumptions: an eventual American participation in the defeat of Hitler, and the continued relevance for France of the democratic model. But the embrace of Free France's giant ally could seem stifling.

VICHY: THE LIMITS OF AMERICAN USEFULNESS

It was American neutrality that made the American tie valuable to

Vichy leaders at the beginning. They yearned for an early end to the war; there is no contemporary evidence for any 'double game' whereby the armistice covered preparation for a return to the war on the British side. The United States offered two potential benefits: diplomatic recognition and supplies.

Mindful of the cloud upon its legitimacy, Vichy treated the arrival of a prestigious American Ambassador in January 1941, Roosevelt's personal friend Admiral William D. Leahy, as a major event. American diplomatic recognition swelled the number of states (already considerable) that accepted Marshal Pétain's regime as legitimate.[2] It also strengthened links with other major neutrals, a group whose influence Vichy hoped to enhance.

Economic aid was the other main advantage sought from the United States. The Murphy-Weygand agreement of 26 February 1941, which provided food and fuel to North Africa under the supervision of American consuls to prevent these shipments from reaching Axis-occupied areas, consolidated the era of public warmth opened by Admiral Leahy's arrival.[3]

It is during this brief honeymoon, during the first five months of 1941, that one finds articles quite favourable to the United States in the Vichy-controlled press. One writer praised the US Military Academy at West Point, where 'even' Jews and Blacks were admitted, and whose instruction in general culture and close relations between officers and men ought to be emulated by Saint-Cyr.[4] American aid, wrote *Le Temps*, proved that the United States kept alive the best in the European spiritual tradition.[5] This cordial tone soon vanished as American support for Britain became more and more open.

Beyond that, there was little sign that Vichy wanted or expected a close relationship. Vichy's choice of ambassador to Washington, Gaston Henri-Haye, the right-wing Senator and mayor of Versailles, sent a clear message that traditional ideological affinities and personal friendships would play little role in the relationship.[6] Marshal Pétain himself seems to have begun with only positive feelings for the United States, which he expressed in largely personal terms: comradeship with General Pershing, and warm memories of his official role in 1931 during the 150th anniversary of the French-American victory over the British at Yorktown. It is hard to find significant differences between the American policies of his first two ministries. Laval was too busy in the autumn of 1940 opening up German contacts to spend much time on the less demanding American link. Admiral Darlan, more opportunist, went further than Laval in seeking a bargain with Germany in 1941, only to turn back, after Laval supplanted him as head of government in April 1942, to discreet contacts with American officials. In both cases, they sought correct relations and certain material benefits from the United States, along with a continuation of American neutrality.

Both Laval and Darlan lectured Americans on the 'realities' of the world situation as they saw it, and urged the United States to stay out of the war.[7] Their American strategy rested upon finding and exploiting differences between the Americans and the British. It was American hostility to the British blockade that made the Murphy-Weygand supply agreements possible. At each French clash with the British, from Mers-el-Kébir in July 1940 to Syria in July 1941, Vichy leaders looked hopefully, but fruitlessly, for a separate United States response.[8] When the United States entered the war alongside Britain on 7 December 1941 it was a black day at Vichy.[9]

Vichy leaders sometimes tried to use the American tie to persuade the Germans not to impose new obligations on them which would compromise those relations.[10] That tactic's effectiveness depended upon some German interest in retaining good Franco-American relations; such interest diminished sharply during 1941 as the Germans sought more and more French contribution to the lengthening war effort. It vanished completely when America entered the war, though even then the Germans did not insist upon rupture of Franco-American relations. When Darlan attempted to use the argument of American displeasure to block the return of Laval in April 1942, he provoked the very result he had hoped to avoid.

What the Vichy leaders most emphatically did not want from the United States was armed liberation. Vichy's foreign policy assumptions – that the war was over, and that prolonging it could only bring ruin and revolution – were based in part on a conviction of American military incapacity. That conviction was partly empirical, partly ideological. Its empirical root was the three years it had taken in World War I for the United States to become willing and able to project armed forces onto the European continent. Even then, American troops had had to be equipped with striking power – all their heavy artillery, for example – by the French.

Ideological reasons led Vichy leaders on to doubt that the United

States could ever make war effectively against Nazi Germany. Vichy inherited from the civil-military controversies of the Third Republic – the battles over the length of military service, in particular – the conservative view that only hierarchical, deferential, agrarian societies possessed military capacity. The United States, rootless and pleasure-seeking, could only produce 'soldats d'opérette', Darlan told Italian Foreign Minister Ciano in December 1941.[11]

Only internal revival, according to the Vichy diagnosis, could bring France authentic salvation. 'Le renouveau français', Marshal Pétain told his fellow Cabinet members at Cange on 13 June 1940, 'il faut l'attendre bien plus de l'âme de notre pays, que nous préserverons en restant sur place, que d'une reconquête de notre territoire par des canons alliés'.[12] Restoring 'l'âme de notre pays' meant accentuating those qualities that set France apart from the United States – or at least from the stereotype of the United States widespread among conservatives in the 1930: a mass society without roots or deep spiritual values, held together only by material interest. Only reversing the tide of 'américanisation' could make France strong again and the French people soldierly. This diagnosis of recovery is linked to the Vichy leaders' diagnosis of the fall of France in 1940. Thus, both the external project of Vichy – neutrality – and its internal project – revival from within – implied the rejection of a stereotyped version of 'American' qualities.

VICHY: AMERICAN THREATS

Of the three arguments available in the twentieth century to tie moderate and conservative French opinion to the United States, two were inoperative during the Vichy years. The 'fellow democracy' argument vanished with the discredit of the Third Republic. The 'bulwark against Communism' argument hardly worked when the United States was, in effect, allied with Stalin after December 1941. That left only the rather threadbare 'traditional ally' argument, emptied of any content except momentarily converging interest. Hence the Vichy leaders drew freely upon two currents of non-Socialist anti-Americanism widespread in the 1930s: the anti-modernist critique of French conservatives, and the more radical corporatist, personalist critique of the younger 'non-conformistes'.[13]

One Vichy strategy of internal revival was anti-modernist and corporatist. France would become strong again by becoming more organic,[14] more hierarchical, and more committed to patriotic and religious values. Although the United States was rarely named in the literature of the Chantiers de la jeunesse, the Ecole d'Uriage, or the Légion des combattants, its stereotyped image was clearly the negative example – individualistic, egalitarian to excess, materialistic – whose opposite Vichy traditionalists and personalists wished to create in France.

Traditionalists and corporatists saw youth as their most vulnerable point. Perpetual adolescents in their tastes and amusements, American 'grands enfants' seemed to possess fatal powers of attraction over adolescents elsewhere. Vichy inherited from such Third Republic quarrels as the struggle over 'l'école unique' the conviction that the high cultures of Europe were besieged bastions, defending themselves against the facile amusements of America and American-influenced adolescents.

Vichy was the first French government to fight actively against American cultural infiltration. This effort was only part of a broader campaign to moralise French youth, to replace Third Republican frivolity with an austerity more befitting a time of national sorrow,[15] and to refortify the 'barrières' demarcating the educated élite.[16] Vichy's campaign against jazz is well-known.[17] The Ministry of Education subsidised a film demonstrating the corrupting effects of American films on French youth.[18] Defiant French youth responded by calling themselves 'les swing'.[19]

The second Vichy strategy of internal revival was authoritarian modernisation. Darlan's equipe of young technocrats saw economic rivalry rather than cultural decadence as the American threat. François Lehideux, for example, Minister of Industrial Production, urged in a speech at the Ecole Libre des Sciences Politiques in February 1941 that Europe be organised 'en face des américains'.[20] As head of the Comité d'organisation de l'industrie automobile, Lehideux had already been discussing with Col. Thönnissen of the German automobile industry the possibility of combining French, German and Italian production to achieve 'world supremacy'.[21]

Darlan, unlike Laval, saw a grand vision of France as the maritime and colonial arm of the 'new Europe' occupying the space opened up by British decline. The term 'Eurafrique' enjoyed great vogue in 1941: Africa as the hinterland of Europe, managed for Europe by France. Without Africa, 'la France tombera en tutelle de l'Amérique ou de l'Asie'.[22] The trouble with this ambition, of course, was that the United States rather than the 'New Europe' was stepping into Britain's imperial shoes. It is not surprising that colonial officials expressed the most acrimonious bitterness against the United States.[23]

Whether viewed as a cultural contaminant or as an economic rival, the United States did not offer a model to Vichy leaders in their search for a strategy of internal revival. Neither side in the 'fureur destructive' of this insane war, wrote Thierry Maulnier in May 1941, offers 'l'image harmonieuse et complète d'un ordre vraiment acceptable'.[24]

VICHY: VARIATIONS IN SPACE AND TIME

The official Vichy position discussed so far was not necessarily shared by everyone, not even by those in public service. Nor was it constant over time.

At the beginning, there was room in the Vichy coalition for some who wanted closer co-operation with the United States. They were gradually forced out during 1941, under the combined pressure of several developments: the growing involvement of the United States in the British war effort, increased German demands for French assistance in its war effort, and Admiral Darlan's efforts to exploit them to obtain a more favourable Franco-German settlement. A notable example was General Paul Doyen, who resigned his position as head of the French Delegation to the Armistice Commission at Wiesbaden in July 1941. The long statement he prepared for Marshal Pétain urged that the French government remain close to the United States which would be the 'grand arbitre' of the future.[25] Similarly, General Weygand, who had opposed Darlan's proposed concessions to the Germans in North Africa in the summer of 1941, was dismissed as the delegate of the Vichy government in North Africa in November 1941.

As best as we can judge from imperfect evidence, a majority of the French public thought of the Americans as potential liberators. The best test case we have is public response to American entry into the war in December 1941. While a few prefects (Vienne, Haute Savoie) reported mixed reactions and gloom about the lengthening war, the vast majority reported hope in an Anglo-Saxon victory.[26] Although the personal popularity of Marshal

Pétain remained high, particularly in the unoccupied zone, a majority of the French people did not accept, or no longer accepted by December 1941, his doubts about an eventual American liberation army.

At the other extreme of the Vichy coalition, others wanted to break definitively with the democracies. They offered a third strategy for internal revival: the creation of a 'muscular' regime openly aligned with the Axis. Jacques Benoist-Méchin, for example, based his rejection of the United States on both reason and sentiment. He reasoned that American economic interests clashed more fundamentally with France's eventual maritime and colonial destiny than did those of continental Germany. His sentiment was that Anglo-Saxon victory would mean the 'lente décomposition de notre civilisation'. In 1941 Benoist-Méchin advocated reliance upon Japan rather than the United States to uphold French sovereignty in Indo-China, believing that by playing off Japanese against German ambitions in the area he could assure French independence. He also advocated Japanese assistance to keep the British out of Madagascar.[27]

The Paris collaborators, unlike Vichy, attacked the United States from the beginning, without waiting for American entry into the war. Their rejection of American society and culture was anti-capitalist and racist rather than conservative. Before American entry into the war, they denounced the United States as a Jewish-dominated plutocracy and the home of 'le jazz judéo-nègre-américain'. Later attacks focused upon US military aid to Bolshevism, that other well-known Jewish conspiracy. Their assumption that Americans would make poor soldiers, incapable of intervening in Europe, was based, like Hitler's, upon theories of racial and cultural 'mongrelisation'.[28]

French opinions of the United States naturally varied with time. We have already pointed to American entry into the war in December 1941 as the crucial turning point from the Vichy perspective. The next major watershed was the transformation of the United States from a distant belligerent to an invader of French soil, first in North Africa, and, more ominously still, in the metropole.

Allied invasion could follow any of several scenarios, all of them bad from the Vichy perspective. Those with a low opinion of American military capacity feared a weak landing force whose success would depend upon internal French assistance. Whether such a commando raid succeeded or failed, it would unleash 'insurrectionary war' in France and open the door to Bolshevism.[29] Not much better was the scenario of a powerful landing, for another long war of attrition like that of 1914–18 would then ensue on French soil. Generals Weygand and Noguès no less than the political leaders warned Americans clearly and plainly that they would defend North Africa and the metropole against 'quiconque', as they indeed did in November 1942.[30]

The Allied aerial bombardments that began with the RAF raid on Boulogne-Billancourt in March 1942 and gained intensity as D-Day approached inevitably produced some ill feeling. Most of the French population was remarkably patient with the death and destruction caused by high-altitude bombing, accepting them as necessary for liberation and placing the fundamental blame on the Germans.[31] Even some observers unsympathetic to Vichy, however, believed that British pilots were braver and more accurate than the high-flying Americans.[32] The quite natural dread that even ardently anti-German French people must have felt for the approaching agonies of armed liberation have vanished from memory, for the campaign was quite unlike 1914–18 in its rapidity.

ANTI-AMERICANISM IN THE RESISTANCE

The leap of faith required in dissenting from the Vichy view in 1940 included faith in the United States' eventual military weight in Europe and in the virtue of the democratic model.

After the United States entered the war in December 1941, the entire spectrum of resistance opinion, from Communist to conservative, accepted a close Franco-American relationship as indispensable for both liberation and for postwar reconstruction. For some, this was a practical necessity; for others it was the expression of a 'commune patrie' of political liberty.[33]

Since the Resistance was, by definition, 'une défense de la vie française',[34] Resistance planning for postwar reconstruction drew reluctantly on American examples. Even in the political realm, where interest in American examples was highest (stronger executive, supreme court), most Resistance planners rejected the presidential system 'contre lequel toute notre tradition historique s'insurge'.[35] In the economic realm, the supposed American economic system of unbridled *laissez-faire* was universally rejected for

France. Even conservatives advocated Colbertian resistance to American projects for a postwar world economic system based on free trade.

As Henri Michel showed, the distant Soviet Union generated far fewer criticisms within the Resistance than did the nearby Americans, at least after the Russians entered the war.[36] The early Resistance felt betrayed by Roosevelt's 'Vichy Gamble'. Then the long delay in the promised Anglo-Saxon landing disappointed; the Communist Resistance press pointed with particular pride to the Russian war effort, but it was by no means alone. Allied bombing created serious strains.[37] The greatest thorn in the relationship, of course, was Roosevelt's refusal to recognise de Gaulle's movement as the government of France until June 1944. The underlying problem, of course, was the disparity of power within this alliance. The Resistance reacted 'avec une sensibilité aiguë contre ce qu'elle considère comme tout acte arbitraire qui ne se justifie que par sa faiblesse et la force des autres'.[38] 'Nous accueillerons le général Eisenhower avec des fleurs et des drapeaux, mais nous nous considérons comme des alliés et non comme des vassaux.'[39]

A LONGER-TERM PERSPECTIVE

The years of collaboration and resistance do not appear to have added any new element to the existing lexicon of anti-American feeling. The familiar terms that one still encounters today are already there. The Americans were 'des grands enfants'; they were naive, materialist, rootless, 'des primaires', as Darlan told Charles Rist in October 1941.[40]

Circumstances had changed, however. Once the home of the 'noble savage', the United States had then been rediscovered by nineteenth-century Frenchmen as the prefiguration of the future – an often dismaying future.[41] A further transformation in 1917 had revealed a United States capable of decisive impact upon the old world. During the period of collaboration and resistance arose a new spectre: American 'tutelle', which Vichy and Free France – kin in more than one way – both resisted.

Notes

1. William L. Langer, *Our Vichy Gamble* (New York: 1947).
2. More than 40 states, from the Soviet Union to the Vatican, recog-

3. Negotiated outside embassy channels, to bypass Ambassador Henri-Haye, according to J.-B. Duroselle, *L'abîme* (Paris: 1982) p. 297.
4. Victor Dillard, 'Cadets américains', *Revue des deux mondes*, 1 avril 1941.
5. *Le Temps*, 5 avril 1941.
6. Pétain had first chosen an ambassador with strong personal ties to the American leadership, Paul Reynaud. We do not know why the less congenial Gaston Henri-Haye replaced him after Reynaud was injured in an automobile accident. On occasion there were efforts to replace Henri-Haye by someone on better terms with American leaders. See Charles Rist, *Une saison gâtée* (Paris: 1983) pp. 183ff., for a plan to send Rist to Washington in October 1941. Darlan was cool to the idea, and one perceives that by then any change in the status quo threatened to provoke unwanted German responses.
7. Laval, for example, in a declaration to United Press correspondent Ralph Heinzen, published in the *New York Times* in May 1941. See numerous conversations between Darlan and American diplomats in *Foreign Relations of the United States*.
8. Darlan thought in July 1941 that the US would stay out of the war and usurp British world markets [German Foreign Office Archives, Series T-120, reel 587, frames 243612-20]; he told Charles Rist in October 1941 that the US was building a large fleet in order to 'se débarrasser des anglais' and to make Britain a platform for overseeing Europe.
9. Vladimir d'Ormesson, 'La grande pitié du monde', *Le Figaro*, 9 December 1941.
10. For example, in the negotiations concerning the disarmament or removal of French naval units at Alexandria when the North African battle drew close to Egypt in summer 1941.
11. Quoted in Duroselle, *L'abîme*, p. 300.
12. Général Emile Laure, *Pétain* (Paris: 1941) p. 433.
13. J.-L. Loubet del Bayle, *Les non-conformistes des années trente* (Paris: 1969).
14. Marshal Pétain liked to say that France had almost died of individualism. Cf. *La Revue Universelle*, 1 janvier 1941.
15. 'Le plaisir abaisse', Marshal Pétain told French youth on 29 December 1940. Gérard Miller, *Les pousse-au-jouir du maréchal Pétain* (Paris: 1975) p. 192. The old roué spoke from rich experience in the matter.
16. Edmond Goblot, *La barrière et le niveau* (Paris: 1925). Vichy reimposed fees for secondary education and increased the study of Latin.
17. W. D. Halls, *The Youth of Vichy France* (Oxford: 1981) pp. 177–8.
18. *Ibid.*, p. 171. The Third Republic had imposed a quota on foreign films in 1928, but it was less stringent than the British quota. After 1940 American films were forbidden in the Occupied Zone at once, and in the Unoccupied Zone after 15 October 1942; new American films were already rare in Vichy France, however, because of currency controls.

19. Gérard Walter, *La vie à Paris sour l'occupation* (Paris: 1960) pp. 170–2.
20. F. Lehideux, 'La lutte contre le chômage', Ecole Libre des Sciences Politiques, *Conférences d'information*, no. 1, 7 février 1941.
21. German Foreign Ministry archives, series T–120, reel 5584H, frames E401074 *et seq.*: Auswärtiges Amt, Richtlinien Pol. II, Bundle 5/1, 'Kartei Frankreich M-Z'.
22. *La revue universelle*, 25 juillet 1941. The concept also appears in some Resistance planning. Cf. Marie Granet, *Défense de la France* (Paris: 1960) p. 278.
23. Admiral Bléhaut, Minister of Colonies, told a German naval officer in May 1944 that while he hated England he despised [méprisait] the United States, and considered Americans 'au même niveau que les nègres'. Ministère public c/ Bléhaut, fascicule 2, p. 31.
24. *La Revue Universelle*, 10 mai 1941.
25. *Délégation française auprès de la commission allemande d'armistice*, vol. IV, pp. 644 *et seq.* This letter was widely distributed as a resistance tract, but J.-B. Duroselle believes that few at Vichy paid attention to it. *L'Abîme*, pp. 289, 297.
26. Archives nationales, Paris: F 1C III 1135 *et seq.*
27. Memoirs of Jacques Benoist-Méchin, *A l'épreuve du temps*, 3 vols. (Paris: forthcoming).
28. Pascal Ory, *Les collaborateurs* (Paris: 1976) p. 151, says that the Paris collaborators treated Americans as 'grands enfants' more to be scorned than feared. Michèle Cotta, *La collaboration* (Paris: 1964) pp. 197–203, prints some particularly virulent citations about 'Jew-York' and American depravity and corruption. Hitler frequently told his generals that he did not expect an American landing in Europe before 1945. Cf. the Halder diaries.
29. Robert Havard de la Montagne, 'Second front', *La Revue universelle*, août 1942, p. 190.
30. I have examined these issues more fully in *Parades and Politics at Vichy* (Princeton: 1966)
31. Prefects' reports suggest mixed feelings: approval in the abstract, resentment in the immediate vicinity of the raids. Rist, *Une Saison gâtée* reports no ill feeling even among the victims against Allied pilots fallen in their midst.
32. This is an insistent theme in personal recollections. I find an early example in André Gide, *Journal*, 16 March 1943.
33. *Bir Hakeim*, 6 October 1943, quoted in Henri Michel, *Les Courants de pensée de la résistance* (Paris: 1962) p. 250.
34. *Les Cahiers: Etudes pour une révolution française*, 1er fascicule, juin 1942, p. 52.
35. *Les Cahiers politiques*, no. 3, Août 1943, p. 5. Even Michel Debré thought the presidential system would cause 'nos enfants à être gouvernés par un général à la manière des pronunciamentos'.
36. Michel, p. 251.
37. *Ibid.*, pp. 240–4.
38. Jacques Vintras, 'La France, allié souverain', *L'Aurore*, no. 12, juin 1944.

39. Pierre Breteuil in *L'Avenir*, no. 13, 1er mai 1944.
40. Rist, *Une saison gâtée*, p. 202.
41. François Furet, *Penser la Révolution française* (Paris: 1978) traces this rediscovery to Tocqueville.

4
The Cold War
Michel Winock

At the time of the 'Cold War', in the climate of all-out ideological warfare, the phenomenon of anti-Americanism grew beyond all measure, far outstripping all other periods. However, there was nothing very new about it even in terms of the anti-American diatribes of the time which tended to form part of a continuing pattern.

The East-West conflict naturally mobilised Communist and progressive activists on the political front alongside other left-wing intellectuals, but the arguments used in that particular battle were taken from an arsenal of grievances previously amassed against what supposedly constituted the very basis of American civilisation, in other words, an 'anti-culture' which was intrinsically anti-French and anti-humanistic.

Before pursuing this point further, it is worth recalling the importance of the Communist/Socialist rift of 1947. The Communists' anti-Americanism was confirmed at their Congress in Strasbourg at the end of June 1947. The Cold War had just begun. Only one month earlier the Communist ministers had been excluded from the Ramadier government. In a torrential address to Congress, Maurice Thorez was to denounce 'American expansionism' assisted by a plethora of quotations from Lenin: 'The omnipotence of monopoly finance capital, the search for market outlets, the export of capital, the development of militarism – these are the characteristics of imperialism as Lenin defined them'. That set the ball rolling: henceforth all interpretations of international politics would be based on the Leninist theory of imperialism.

Two camps confronted each other: two worlds, two universes. On one side 'an aggressive and decadent world, riddled with contradictions'; on the other, the block of true democracies under the leadership of the USSR, the 'bastion of world peace'.[1] The one bloc desired peace, the other was preparing for war.

This stark and categorical opposition between two blocs, two systems, was to become a *leitmotiv* for Communist journalists and intellectuals, and for a large proportion of their fellow travellers. It was one of the latter, Claude Aveline, who provided a clear illustration of this in *Lettres Françaises*:

> On the one hand, Capitalism: a capitalist-based system, society and civilisation. On the other, Socialism: a socialist-based system and society. More and more, this alternative is taking the concrete form of two blocs whose mutual hostility is becoming increasingly overt as time goes by. Understanding between them is out of the question, and even the diplomats of either side scarcely conceal the fact. One of these blocs must go. The world must choose ... In this battle between the blocs *"engagé"* writers – who are my concern and among whom I count myself – have deliberately opted for Socialism. We believe it to be an inevitability, and as such we welcome it. We no longer believe that the capitalist system has further scope for improvement. We do not believe that, by some miracle, capitalist society will become more humane and just. We believe that capitalist-based civilisation is bankrupt. And since its predicament is the result of fraud, there is no way of saving it, except superficially, by means of ever more cynical or treacherous deceptions. In the end it will go, taking with it the authors of its ruin, because it has already cost too much and continues to cost its victims dearly.[2]

During the Cold War years, the Communist Party's permanent watchword was the 'fight for peace'. By definition this implied solidarity with the USSR and an anti-American stance. The justification for the latter was very simple. Defence of the Soviet Union in all fields, particularly the defence of its foreign policies, had become the touchstone of 'proletarian internationalism'. It had become imperative for the western European Communist parties to make use of all the 'formal freedoms' of the liberal democracies to wage a campaign against everything that threatened the USSR's interests which were synonymous with world peace. The USA and NATO were the prime targets. Thus the national and regional Communist press orchestrated protests against the presence of US troops in France, following the creation of NATO. To quote from a study on the US military presence in the town of Châteauroux between 1951 and 1967: 'By 1952, *La Marseillaise* [a Southern

Communist daily journal] had launched a violent anti-American campaign, ramming home the same handful of points day in day out'; specifically, the American was 'an amoral individual'; 'the [American] occupation jeopardises living conditions'; it was 'a danger for the town', a 'danger to traffic', and so on.[3] From that time onwards, the walls of French cities were covered with painted slogans *US go home!* France did not want to be occupied again.

Actually, this latter idea had been mooted in the Communist press even before NATO was set up. A 1948 article entitled '*France, pays occupé*' took up the matter of the invasion of French cinemas by American films in the wake of the Blum-Byrnes agreements of 1945–46.

> In the same way that the French paid tribute to Leni Riefenstahl during the Occupation, so now, in a display of the same kind of intuition and servility, *Le film français* devotes an entire issue to adulation of 20th Century Fox's "illustrious" Director General, Joseph M. Schenk ... It is always from the West that darkness invades the world. But there are no stars in this particular night, which has all the oppressiveness of the Middle Ages but unrelieved by faith or hope in an afterlife. It is a darkness without any ray of light: a night of inquisition, degeneration, obscurantism, of ultimate and final degradation. It is self-perpetuating darkness. That is the darkness now beginning to invade us. But it is an act of desperation, a vain endeavour to protect the last remaining lairs of a lost past from the victorious onslaught of the Light. The time to stand firm and resist is now.[4]

In contrast to their Communist counterparts, neutralist intellectuals, writing in such publications as *Le Monde*, *L'Observateur* (later *France Observateur*), *Esprit* and *Les Temps Modernes*, adopted a rather more subtle attitude to the United States though their judgement was generally severe. At the risk of oversimplification, we can cite two quotations from *Les Mandarins* by Simone de Beauvoir which give an idea of the state of mind of those particular intellectuals in the period between 1947 and 1956. Henri, one of the novel's main characters, declares: 'I'm well aware that things aren't entirely perfect in the Soviet Union. I'd be more amazed if the opposite were true. But when all is said and done, they are the ones who are on the right track'. And this is echoed in a statement by the heroine, Anne: 'What America means these days is the atom bomb, sabre-rattling, and nascent fascism . . .'[5]

1950s America laid itself open to the strongest criticism. The McCarthyite madness and the witch-hunts that it give rise to; Foster Dulles' 'big-stick' diplomacy – these were all things that fostered the picture of a warmongering United States, blinded by anti-Communism and dragged into imperialism by its corporations. At the time of the Rosenberg trial, Jean-Paul Sartre put it quite categorically: 'Don't be surprised if from one end of Europe to the other we are shouting: Watch out, America is a mad dog! Let's cut every tie that binds us to her lest she bite us and we go mad too'.[6]

However, as we said earlier, the language of anti-Americanism is not solely political. Anti-Sovietism, whose language was equally unbridled at that period of the Cold War, was confined to the political and ideological spheres. The targets of criticism in the Soviet Union were the system's Marxist-Leninist foundations, the new Stalinist autocracy, the reign of terror, and so on. Russian culture was not called into question. Only the state superstructure was challenged, and this could be put down to a historical accident. In contrast, for the anti-Americans it was the very essence of the United States, its very culture and history which indicted it.

At the time of his clash with Hubert Beuve-Méry within the editorial board of *Le Monde*, René Courtin ascribed ethical motives to the Director's neutralist attitudes: 'He's no Stalinist and hasn't the slightest sympathy for the Russian régime. However, he has an even stronger hatred for American civilisation. Russia is odious but not totally despicable. She is poor and has an understanding for selfless effort and anonymous, communal labour. She will therefore "stand the test" '.[7]

It was a coming together of two different strands of anti-Americanism: the political and the cultural. The French intellectuals of the 1950s – whether Communist, progressive or neutralist – were not merely hostile to the State Department and the fascistic overtones of McCarthyite America. Basically they rejected a cultural model identified in their minds with *'la culture de masse'*. Despite his trumpeted attachment to *'le peuple'*, the intellectual was a scholar, a repository of high culture – the sort that still holds sway in France – for instance, the influence of the Left Bank writers, the prestige of the *Ecole normale supérieure, l'agrégation*, the importance of *engagé* literature, the political clout of intellectual opinion, and so on. Such French realities were totally foreign to the United States, which did not offer its writers or professors any sort of comparable status. Most disturbingly, ever since World War I, the United States had been developing the characteristics of modern mass culture, in which advertising and the majority of radio (and subsequently television) broadcasts, not to mention strip-cartoons and Hollywood cinema, offered a forceful challenge to 'intellectual power'.

In this way, leaving aside purely transitory characteristics, anti-American criticism had increasingly established itself as a form of 'resistance' to the 'big-business colonisation' of the French way of life. Communists and fellow-travellers were even better placed to use the weapon of cultural criticism in their political campaigns at a time when the products and by-products of American mass culture were beginning to spread, particularly in the wake of the Marshall Plan. The Blum-Byrnes agreements of 28 May 1946 wiped out France's debts to the United States. In return, the Americans managed to make considerable inroads into France's protected markets. As a result, there was a massive invasion of American films. The rest is history: the insipid *Readers' Digest*, Coca Cola, comics, blue jeans, and so on. Not only did devotees of Soviet socialism have plenty of sticks with which to beat Yankee imperialism, they also had no lack of allies on all sides. France was being colonised: Marx and Racine, unite and fight!

'Your myths are already flooding France', wrote Vladimir Pozner to *'an American friend'*, 'I come across these old acquaintances on our screens, in book-shop windows, on newspaper stands and even in official speeches. I can recognise the second-hand gear which no one has even bothered to disguise in any way: the films, the best-sellers, the magazines, the digests, comic strips, coloured pin-ups. Long live great American democracy! Long live the American Technicolor paradise! Have you read *Amber*? Have you seen *Gilda*? Did you know the French edition of *Readers' Digest* runs to a million copies? Buy one today while you've the chance! "My dear, yesterday I drank a bottle of *the best* Coca-Cola – it was really something, I can tell you"!'[8]

The anti-American criticism of the 1930s, typified by Georges Duhamel's best-selling *Scènes de la vie future* had already targeted mass-production and mass-consumption as the machinery of the new civilisation of 'l'homme standard'.[9] In the land of Henry Ford and Taylorism, of assembly lines and the Chicago slaughter-houses, everything – work and leisure alike – was organised on an inhuman, mass scale. Thus in 1948, 20 years after Duhamel's distressing trip to the homeland of Rockefeller, Armand Salacrou, one of the former's colleagues, was to bring back from a recent American trip a report which bore witness to a continuing transpolitical aversion:

> On your very first day in New York just go into the first bar you come to: the way the barmen serve you will be just like Chaplin's workmen screwing on bolts in *Modern Times* ... With every passing day you sink deeper and deeper into organised solitude, and you become aware of those beings who are overcome by the impossibility of extricating themselves from it. I happened to attend the one thousand eight hundredth performance of '*Oklahoma*' ... During the interval, I suggested to my companion that we make a trip to the bar. (I had in mind the charming bustle in the bar at the Saint-Georges or at the little café of the *Théâtre Montparnasse* where the *patron* tells jokes ...) My friend and I arrived at the end of a queue ... The queue advanced one by one until at last I found myself in front of a tap of iced water and above it an automatic dispenser of cardboard 'glasses'. You pull off your cup, drink up quickly and then throw away the soggy utensil – which is already disintegrating in your hand – into a new and improved waste-basket, and the next person in the queue is already removing the cardboard cup which was also waiting its turn in its automatic dispenser. I will never ever forget that encounter with a slow queue of silent men, and a queue of cardboard cups both waiting for a tap of cold water ...[10]

It is an important and highly symbolic scene which reveals the profound contrast between a civilisation of human beings and one of androids, between the civilisation of the *bistro* (red wine and conviviality) and the bar civilisation (drinking-water, paper-cups and anonymity). At the time of prohibition, Duhamel had depicted the Americans' dreary, clandestine alcoholism. In the wake of World War II, Salacrou only sees water-drinkers. But it matters little, the same solitude haunts this antiseptic, conformist robotised people ruled by the dollar.

The spread of mass production and consumption went hand in hand with a dwindling of cultural models. Another article in *Les lettres françaises* provided facts and figures to show that in 1948 the number of book-titles published in France was higher than in the United States:

> It goes to show that the United States is a standardised and rationalised country, admirably launched on the path of automation, which sees no need to worry the public with too many book titles ... After all, one bible, one arithmetic book, one engineering handbook, a digest of commercial legislation, five children's flying stories, ten spicy novels for ladies, and twenty books of anti-soviet propaganda for reservists should appease all desire for reading matter, shouldn't they? ... The other thing it goes to show is that we here are sick to death of having Yankee superiority shoved down our throats ... A state the size of Europe that isn't capable of putting out even half the book-titles we publish in our country the size of a (holey and well-darned) pocket-handkerchief squeezed between the English Channel and the Mediterranean! Is that the ideal, the model, the leader they want us to look up to? *Allons donc!*[11]

In the same journal, Henri Malherbe, winner of the 1917 *Prix Goncourt*, passed the following judgement on the American novel: 'Mass produced goods manufactured by shrewd industrialists, mechanically luxurious like the cars made over there'.[12]

Mass produced goods, mass produced culture, mass produced feelings. In every field the aim was to produce the same thing. Even human beings seemed to come out of the same mould: the prototype pin-up ended up becoming a model for a new type of womanhood against which the Communist press felt compelled to take up cudgels: 'A contest which we are entitled to comment on: Pin-up Girls versus "Filles de France" [the Communist girls' movement, trans.]'. In these terms, the Communist youth newspaper, *L'Avant-Garde*, warned its female readership against the 'glorification of the pin-up' – 'the pin-up, that is, woman American-style, a painted doll whose sole aim in life is to fall in love, marry a rich man and have a good time with the least effort'.[13]

The point is that while Communist literature made use of such comments, cameos and ready-made judgements, with all their exaggerations and grains of truth, to further the cause, it did not invent them: they existed already and went on thriving in the hands of writers of every hue, including those under the least suspicion of connivance with the Soviet camp. Out of a thousand possible examples I will choose the case of François Mauriac. Unlike Georges Bernanos, Mauriac was no spokesman of *l'Ancienne France*. Nor, for that matter, was he a raving misoneist or a political opponent of the United States. In fact he was very representative of received ideas about America within the literary establishment. The following quotation is from 1959, though his judgement would scarcely seem to have altered over the years:

> In the final analysis, my sympathies are for the leader of a great country for which I certainly have a lot of admiration. However in many aspects of its genius it is a country which is more alien to me than any other. I have never visited it . . . What would be the point? America has done much more than visit us, it has transformed us. The rhythm of our lives has been attuned to its own. Its music accompanies our days on millions of records. Thousands of films in every Parisian and provincial cinema impose on us its way of thinking in every area of life: a particular female stereotype – the interchangeable star which any Brigitte or Pascale from the slums can become. But over and above the cult of technology and the idolatry surrounding it, of all the things invented by men and to which men submit, it is the mania for speed, this 'sturdy' that affects all the sheep of the West, the trepidation that none of us can escape – immoderation in everything, which is least in tune with our *génie*.[14]

That sums up the disquiet felt by the French élite of all political hues: *le génie français*, quintessential France, the culture and civilisation of an old country which has influenced the entire globe were threatened with adulteration, nay disintegration and obliteration by an invasion ('l'occupation') of American standards. The criticism voiced by that élite – leaving aside the political variety – was directed as much against material as against spiritual products, as much against manners as mentalities.

The question is whether such anti-Americanism was not an attitude confined to the élite – and the literary élite at that. If we take an average of the opinion polls conducted in France between 1952 and 1957, we indeed find that the image of the United States was unequivocally positive, even among Communist voters.[15] The American Way of Life may have horrified the bourgeois intellectuals but it fascinated a society which aspired after higher living standards and was just tasting the first fruits of economic growth.

Michel Winock 75

Leaving aside political considerations, the aversions or hostility of the intellectual élite towards the American model had two main causes. Firstly, there was the advent of a mass culture which jeopardised the status of the intellectuals in French society. Secondly, there was a well-established anti-modernist, anti-industrial and anti-technological streak in the intellectual élite, encapsulated in such works as Georges Bernanos' *La France contre les robots*.

In all such cases, America assumed an allegorical function. Those who visited America did so clearly in order to confirm their prejudices. The majority, like François Mauriac, preferred not to go there on the grounds that French culture had already been transformed and virtually adulterated as a result of American influence. At all events, America was treated not so much as living reality as a counter-myth. The survival of French civilisation (and for many, Civilisation *per se*) required the blanket rejection of the United States as the embodiment of anti-culture and anti-humanism.

Notes

1. Jean Baby, 'L'impérialisme américain et la France', *Cahiers du communisme*, January 1948.
2. Claude Aveline, 'L'engagement et le choix', *Les lettres françaises*, 29 April 1948.
3. As cited in François Jarraud, *Les Américains à Châteauroux 1951–1967*, from the author, Les Cassons-Arthon, 36330 Le Poinçonnet, 1981.
4. Pierre Daix, 'France, pays occupé', *Les Lettres françaises*, 28 October 1948.
5. Simone de Beauvoir, *Les Mandarins*, pp. 254 and 515.
6. Quoted by Raymond Aron, *L'opium des intellectuels*, (Paris: Gallimard, 1968) p. 310.
7. Quoted by Jean-Noël Jeanneney and Jacques Julliard, *Le Monde de Beuve-Méry ou le Métier d'Alceste* (Paris: Seuil, 1979) p. 104.
8. Vladimir Pozner, 'Lettre à un ami américain', *Les lettres françaises*, 25 November 1948.
9. See L'homme standard', *Esprit*, No. 271, March 1959. In it Sidney Lens writes: 'A standard man is being created in the United States, immunised against radicalism in spite of his social needs, and with a horizon limited to reality near at hand ... Hundreds of thousands of young people become delinquents rather than socialists. They are the ones that Robert Linder has called "rebels without a cause"'.
10. Armand Salacrou, 'Le pays de la solitude', *Les Lettres françaises*, 25 November 1948.

11. Pierre Abraham, 'Littérature américaine', *Les Lettres françaises*, 14 April 1949.
12. Henri Malherbe, 'Les Français n'achètent plus les romans américains', *Les Lettres françaises*, 24 March 1949.
13. *L'Avant-garde*, 25 February–2nd March 1948.
14. François Mauriac, *L'Express*, 29 August 1959, and *Nouveau Bloc–notes 1958–1960*, p. 238.
15. Cf. Jean-Baptiste Duroselle, *La France et les Etats-Unis des origines à nos jours*, 'Points Histoire' (Paris: Le Seuil, 1976) p. 195.

Part II

The Behaviour of the Intelligentsia and its Influence on Public Opinion

5
Images of the United States in Public Opinion
Jacques Rupnik and Muriel Humbertjean

After having been the most markedly anti-American country in western Europe for much of the postwar period, is France on its way to becoming the most pro-American? According to the polls taken on the eve of the US elections of November 1984, 44 per cent of the French were self-confessed pro-Americans as against only 15 per cent who declared themselves anti-American.[1] Moreover, the French would seem to prefer a Reagan-style America, that is, one that is strong, prosperous and confident in its might, to the America of his predecessor which, rightly or wrongly, they identified with dwindling American power.

Before seeking to explain this *volte face*, there are two points we ought to make. First, France's history is quite different from that of any other European country, and second, there is a certain correlation between French attitudes towards the United States and French attitudes towards the Soviet Union.

Out of all the European countries, France displayed the least sympathy for the United States in the immediate postwar years. Whereas in Great Britain, Germany and Italy the percentage of favourable opinions outnumbered negative ones by some 50 points, in France positive and negative were almost equally balanced (+4 per cent in 1955, −3 per cent in November 1957).

Conversely, favourable opinions are showing a marked increase in France at the present time, just as we are witnessing an upsurge of anti-Americanism (or at least a decline in pro-Americanism) in certain other European countries such as Great Britain and West Germany (44 per cent favourable opinions against 15 per cent in France, compared with 39 per cent/19 per cent in West Germany and 39 per cent/20 per cent in Great Britain), not to mention the strength of anti-American feeling in southern Europe, particularly in Greece and Spain.[2]

Another factor is that attitudes towards the United States are also linked to attitudes towards the Soviet Union. This correlation emerges clearly if we draw a curve representing the difference between favourable and unfavourable opinions towards the superpowers over the past 30 or 40 years.[3] Naturally the correlation is more or less pronounced depending on the period. One may observe a certain symmetry in attitudes towards the Soviet Union in the long term, and a negative correlation at certain periods, such as in the 1980s. In retrospect, the last decade was a transitional period during which the respective images of the superpowers have altered within French public opinion. Having been the odd-man-out in its part of the world during the Cold War of the 1950s, because of its anti-American stance and its slightly indulgent attitude towards the Soviet Union, France is again out of step as a result of its pro-American volte face and an anti-Sovietism as pronounced as it is new.

To make sense of the particular French shifts in attitudes towards the United States, one should bear in mind that they can be traced back to the immediate postwar period.

Two striking facts emerged from our examination of French perceptions of the United States over the past 30 years. Leaving aside 'seasonal variations', the gap in the evolution of general attitudes towards the superpowers remained fairly constant over the long term.[4] From the mid-1950s to the mid-1960s there was a progressive improvement in the images of both superpowers; over the subsequent decade these images remained fairly steady. By the second half of the 1970s (and more precisely from 1976 to 1981), those images declined (slightly in the case of the United States, more radically as far as the Soviet Union was concerned). Finally, since 1981 there has been a spectacular reversal in perceptions: a collapse of the Soviet popularity rating alongside an equally spectacular overhaul of the USA's image.

One explanation for these overall trends in French public opinion might be that they reflect a concern to preserve national independence by calling a plague on the houses of both superpowers. But the notion of balance or even equidistance in relations with the USSR-USA 'couple' should not blind us to certain short-term variations in the images of the two countries at the time of major international crises.

The Soviet intervention in Hungary certainly led to a sharp drop in pro-USSR opinions, but its effects were only short-term and

Sputnik soon eclipsed the memory of the tanks in Budapest. But it was above all the Suez Crisis (generating strong anti-American feelings) which helped offset the disastrous effects of Budapest: by 1957 the image of the United States had rapidly deteriorated to the point where negative opinions of America outweighed favourable opinions for the first and only time ever. The invasion of Czechoslovakia in 1968 was seen merely as *'un accident de parcours'* by French public opinion, wherein it shared the position of France's political establishment. On the other hand, Vietnam would seem to have tarnished the United States' image at the end of the 1960s. If détente had done much to improve the image of the USSR in the eyes of public opinion, the 'new Cold War' of the early 1980s did just as much to speed the deterioration of French attitudes towards the Soviet Union which was now clearly paying the combined price of the 'Solzhenitsyn effect' and the 'Kabul factor'. In contrast, attitudes towards the United States started to improve in 1982.

This brief summary of the main trends of French opinion towards the USSR and the United States gives rise to two possible comments. First, it demonstrates a bipolarity of perceptions: attitudes towards one superpower affect attitudes towards the other. Thirty years ago the French were not only the most anti-American people in Europe, they were also the most pro-Soviet. Today's anti-Sovietism is accompanied by a refurbishment of the USA's image which would seem to be unique in Europe.

This bipolarity in French perceptions of the international situation can be traced back to an endeavour to maintain balance and equidistance in France's relations with the superpowers, in order to guarantee national independence. In this specific case, French public opinion would seem to have been at one with that of the country's intellectual and political élite (and not only with the Gaullists and Communists). Suffice it to recall the wide coverage given to ideas of neutralism in the 1950s, both in the press (for example, *Le Monde* under Hubert Beuve-Méry) and in such journals as *Les Temps Modernes* or *Esprit*.[5] During the 1960s a consensus was to be forged around General de Gaulle's policy towards the United States.[6] The 1970s saw the emergence of a revised and amended version of what can only be called an attitude of 'pseudo-equidistance' among such diverse authors as Gaullist Foreign Minister Michel Jobert and the leader of the Socialist Party's left wing, Jean-Pierre Chevènement.

French attitudes towards the United States and the Soviet Union have been influenced by people's perceptions of the relative might of the two superpowers. Herein lies the idea of balance whereby it is legitimate to assert independence, to call for an end to the blocs and to criticise the United States so long as it is perceived to be militarily and economically stronger than the Soviet Union. The decline in American power at a time of rising Soviet influence helps explain the recent shift in favour of the United States.

However, attitudes towards the superpowers also reflect a self-image. The balanced attitude towards each of the *'deux Grands'*, albeit tainted with anti-Americanism and an indulgence towards the USSR, is characteristic above all of the Gaullist years – a period when the French entertained illusions of *grandeur* and a belief in France's great power status. For instance, in 1964 42 per cent of the French assigned France the role of 'leading world power'.[7] By the end of 1971, this percentage had fallen to 36 per cent. On that occasion, the French placed their country at No. 3 in the world power stakes (with the Gaullists and Communists placing France higher on the international scale than the centrists, and much higher than the Socialists).

Another detail to emerge from the 1971 poll was that 66 per cent of the French thought that France would improve its standing over the next ten years, or at least maintain it. The percentage was even higher among the mass public, in contrast with a more pessimistic attitude on the part of the élite. In that same period, 46 per cent of the French considered France's role to be at its greatest when General de Gaulle was in power (1958–69), compared with 22 per cent who favoured the reign of Napoleon Bonaparte, and 14 per cent who favoured the period of the French Revolution.[8]

By 1984 only 23 per cent of those polled still considered France to be a world power (54 per cent believed it to be a middle-ranking power).[9] Likewise, the majority no longer believed that France would have 'greater world importance' in 20 years' time, whereas they had no doubts about the USSR (+19), the USA (+24) and China (+42).

This trend might be explained by the following hypothesis: so long as France perceived itself as a world power, it did not have to think about forging an alliance with one or other of the superpowers – hence the notion of balance and even equidistance in its relations with the USSR and USA. Now that a more 'realistic' notion of French power has started to prevail, it is easier to regard France as part of the western 'camp' in the face of mounting Soviet might. This also explains the waning of the Gaullist concept – long shared by Communist voters – of independence from the United States or of an entirely separate stance. The attitudes towards the USSR and the USA at the time of the Liberation was marked by an inferiority complex.[10] Sixties' anti-Americanism had more to do with a certain idea of *'grandeur'*. The recent decline in anti-American feeling goes hand in hand with a more realistic image of France's position in the world.

Pierre Hassner has suggested three levels for analysing international relations: first, the interaction of States (strategic interaction); second, the degree of economic interdependence; and third, the interpenetration of societies.[11] This distinction is particularly relevant to the matter under consideration here. If one excludes opinion indices which *overall* are favourable or unfavourable to the United States, one can see that French opinion is capable of being very negative on the matter of interaction between States while accepting the interdependence of social and cultural models.

It is this lack of connection between different levels of perception of the United States that explains to a certain extent the mixture of aversion and fascination which is so typical of French attitudes towards that country. In this respect they differ fundamentally from attitudes towards the Soviet Union. The change in the latter's image has, on the contrary, to do with the extent to which the international power aspect accords with the model of society.

At the time of Liberation, the Soviet Union was not just perceived as the power which had done more than any other to bring about the defeat of the Nazis. It was also seen as a society whose image attracted not just the Parisian intellectuals, but the Left in general, particularly the working class. This is what emerges from an IFOP poll of 1947.[12] To the question 'which country is the best place to live in?', 43 per cent of the French chose their own (while being astonishingly pessimistic about its situation[13]), followed immediately by the USA and the USSR whose scores were respectively the lowest and highest compared with the rest of Europe. Whilst the Cold War had the effect of confining positive attitudes towards the Soviet Union to Communist voters, the Khrushchev era and the period of détente extending towards the mid-1970s saw a marked improvement in the Soviet Union's image. In our view, the recent pro-American swing can only be properly explained in terms of the earlier collapses of the Soviet image in French opinion.

In 1974 the French had a very favourable attitude towards the

TABLE 5.1 *Regarding countries like the Soviet Union and people's democracies, would you say that in each of the following fields the socialist system was more of a success or more of a failure?*

	Previous ORTF/SOFRES poll Sept. 1972			Previous Figaro/SOFRES poll Nov. 1980			December 1982		
	Success	Failure (in %)	Don't know	Success	Failure (in %)	Don't know	Success	Failure (in %)	Don't know
Economic development	39	29	32	26	46	28	15	61	26
Workers' participation in management	33	26	41	25	42	33	18	49	33
Reducing social inequalities	34	31	35	28	43	29	22	52	26
Health care for all	—	—	—	47	16	37	36	25	39
Equal educational opportunity	—	—	—	40	25	35	27	34	39
Respect for individual and political liberty	14	58	28	8	70	22	9	73	18
Raising living standards	43	30	27	20	53	27	14	65	21

Poll conducted 2–9 December 1982 for a group of provincial newspapers.

Soviet record. In five areas out of seven, a greater proportion thought the USSR was more of a success than a failure. In 1980 the ratio was reversed, and in 1982 only in respect to public health did people still entertain any illusions.[14]

Whereas in 1974, perceptions of the Soviet system were split along Left/Right lines (although favourable opinions were in the majority in *all* political categories), by 1980 things had changed. Only the Communists continued to regard the Soviet achievement as positive 'in general terms' (though not in respect to civil liberties).[15]

There are two further explanations that might be suggested. The first is what has been termed 'the Solzhenitsyn effect' and the tardy discovery by the intellectuals and the public at large of 'the Gulag' – an expression that has since become synonymous with the Communist system. The second factor is the 'Kabul factor' and more generally speaking, the reaction to 'Soviet imperialism'. In 1975, at the time of the Helsinki Agreements, 58 per cent of the French considered the USSR to have a 'sincere attachment' to peace (while only 43 per cent thought the same of the United

States). By 1977 (the year of Soviet incursions in Africa), only 28 per cent supported this view, and the figure was to fall to 24 per cent following the invasion of Afghanistan.[16]

In other words, the 'Solzhenitsyn effect' combined with the 'Kabul factor'. The collapse of the USSR as a model society was also to mean the end of the USSR as an international power counterbalancing 'imperial' America to the great benefit of world peace. With it went the 'Gaullo-Communist' consensus about the Soviet Union which had been the chief pillar of anti-Americanism.

Whereas in the case of the Soviet Union the respective images of a model society and a world power have proved to be inextricably linked, in the case of French perceptions of the United States the two aspects would seem to have remained quite distinct. The rejection of what was often perceived as 'imperialism' in terms of foreign policy is not incompatible with a certain receptiveness towards various trans-Atlantic social and cultural phenomena. The link between these two levels concerns economics: the problem of dependence and the question of the socio-economic model.

Whether considering the issues of defence or economic relations, one can see major fluctuations in the image people have of American policies. In the matter of defence, the French oscillate between two poles of perception: fear of American adventurism on the one hand and the desire for a firm and determined ally, on the other. When it comes to economics, they hesitate between a condemnation of reckless imperialism and a fascination with the 'powerhouse' of the developed world. To a great extent, these swings seem linked to the image of the US President.

By adopting a policy and rhetoric of national independence, the French have long been able to maintain an ostentatious distance from the Atlantic alliance and American foreign policy. It has been a psychological distance which is not totally devoid of a certain condescension towards France's less fortunate European neighbours who are obliged to huddle beneath the American nuclear umbrella.

A poll conducted in Autumn 1984 for the *New York Times* in a number of European countries provides striking evidence of this. Asked to indicate whether in their view Ronald Reagan's foreign policy had increased the danger of war in Europe, half of the English and 38 per cent of the Germans answered in the affirmative. Only a quarter of the French gave this reply. It was not that the French now regarded the American President as an apostle of peace; it was just that there was a greater proportion of them who considered that American policy had nothing to do with it: 38 per cent believed that Reagan's foreign policy had not affected the risk of war in Europe, as against 22 per cent of the English and only 13 per cent of the Germans. It is a psychological gulf that used to take the form of a criticism of US adventurism, though now it is giving way to a reaffirmation of Atlantic solidarity.

Confidence in the USA's capacity to act wisely over international issues can be plotted on a curve on which the blips coincide with international crises. Whereas in 1961 34 per cent of French people doubted the 'wisdom' of the Americans, the proportion of sceptics rose to 55 per cent in 1962 at the time of the Cuban missile crisis, representing a jump of 21 per cent in one year. The gap was not closed until after 1963, falling to 39 per cent in 1965 and 36 per cent in 1968, before making another leap as a consequence of the Vietnam war: 49 per cent in 1970 and 55 per cent in 1972 (IFOP). At that time the United States was seen as one of the countries which posed the greatest threat to world peace – after China, but a long way ahead of the Soviet Union: 39 per cent of the French thought the United States to be a threat to peace, while only 25 per cent thought the same of the Soviet Union (SOFRES).

In 1978 the USA's image had again become far more pacific, with America being cited at fifth place in the warmongers' table with 16 per cent of the votes, way behind the USSR with 40 per cent and even Cuba (24 per cent). Carter's personal image no doubt played a considerable role in restoring confidence in American foreign policy. The discredit in which the Carter administration is currently held has caused us to forget the earlier 1977 enthusiasm for a 'moral' President. When asked to draw an Identikit portrait of Carter by indicating the most appropriate epithets to describe him, the French were not stinting in their praise. Personable, honest, courageous, sincere, vigorous, dynamic, were among the first adjectives mentioned. In contrast only 4 per cent of the French considered Carter 'weak' or 'mediocre' (Louis Harris France).

The influence of the US President's personal image has been most obvious since the beginning of the Reagan era. Two polls, the first carried out in mid-term (in 1982) and the second just prior to Ronald Reagan's re-election in October 1984, are extremely eloquent in this respect.

Judgements of Reagan right up to the mid-point of his first term in office were extremely severe, with 53 per cent of the French

TABLE 5.2 *Confidence in the US President in the event of world crisis.**

	November 1977 Carter		November 1982 Reagan	
Complete confidence	6	} 46	4	} 31
Moderate confidence	40		27	
Little confidence	17	} 25	28	} 55
No confidence	8		27	
Don't know		29		14
		100%		100%

* This table and the ones that follow were drawn on the basis of SOFRES polls.

declaring that they had no liking for Reagan, as against 33 per cent who found him likeable. Not a single social group showed him leniency. In fact the US President found favour only with the Gaullists.

As we can see, the picture is one not just of antipathy but of actual mistrust. The gap between Carter and Reagan was enormous. In 1977 46 per cent of the French were ready to trust Carter in the event of a world crisis, whereas in 1982, only 31 per cent of them expressed their confidence in Reagan. Such suspicion of the new US President was accompanied by a significant revival of concern about American adventurism, as shown by two indicators in particular. First, French people's confidence in America's ability to act prudently in world affairs sank to quite a low level in 1982, with 40 per cent of those polled expressing their confidence, as against 47 per cent expressing the opposite (a similar level of no-confidence was registered at the beginning of the Vietnam War). Second, the USA once more acquired a pronounced 'warmongering' image, with 16 per cent of the French citing the United States as one of the greatest threats to peace in a 1978 poll; this proportion had topped 23 per cent by 1983.

Between 1982 and 1984 the US President's image underwent a complete overhaul and French public opinion did a somersault. This is the only conclusion that can be drawn from a poll in *Le Monde* on the eve of the US elections of 1984. The US President had been viewed initially by the majority of the French as an uncouth cowboy and cynical jingoist. This image gradually waned and French opinion increasingly acquired an attachment to the impression of success, strength and tenacity created by Ronald Reagan.[17] The image of America's world policies was considerably

TABLE 5.3 *Do you consider US policy positive or negative as regards its attitude towards:*

	the Soviet Union			Central America		
	+	−	Don't know	+	−	Don't know
	%	%	%	%	%	%
All	34	31	45	13	46	41
Party preference:						
Communist (PCF):	15	52	33	10	55	35
Socialist (PS):	27	41	32	7	58	35
Gaullist (UDF):	42	25	33	15	39	46
Republican (RPR):	55	20	25	22	39	39

rectified, even if it did not yet achieve the levels it had under the 'peace-loving' Carter. Favourable opinions which had swooped from 46 per cent to 30 per cent between 1977 and 1982 rose to 40 per cent. Conversely, negative opinions, which had previously soared from 24 per cent to 51 per cent, now fell to 38 per cent. Favourable and negative opinions about US opinion are now running virtually neck and neck.

This was no clean bill of health, however, and views continued to be qualified. Thus, French opinion remained split on the question of the United States' attitude towards the Soviet Union (for: 34 per cent; against: 31 per cent) and expressed a clear disapproval of American policies on Central America. On the latter point, critical attitudes were in the majority among all voters.

It can be seen that in France, Atlantic solidarity coexists with a supreme wariness about American policies. The failure of the peace movement to get off the ground in France is a prime indicator of this fact and is vividly illustrated by the way French opinion has swung between Atlantic solidarity and the temptations of neutrality.

Thus, between 1980 and 1984 one may observe a considerable swing in favour of the Atlantic alliance, from 21 per cent to 37 per cent, a proportion that has since remained steady. The proportion in favour of the neutralist option fell from 36 per cent to 21 per cent. (See Table 5.4.)

This phenomenon cannot be ascribed solely to President Mitterrand's pro-Atlantic alliance. There were in fact three other factors involved. First of all there was the mounting Soviet threat and the *fear of Soviet might*. In 1977 40 per cent of the French placed the Soviet Union among those countries representing the greatest

TABLE 5.4 *Which of the following options would best assure French security in your opinion?*

	SOFRES Feb. 1980	SOFRES Nov. 1980	SOFRES Sept. 1983	Sept. 1984
To be part of a military alliance of W. European countries plus the USA	21%	35%	36%	37%
To be part of a military alliance of W. European countries but independent of the United States	28%	22%	22%	25%
To be part of an alliance with the USSR	1%	4%	1%	3%
Not to be part of any alliance; to adopt a stance of absolute neutrality	36%	24%	27%	21%
No opinion	14%	15%	14%	14%
	100%	100%	100%	100%

threat to world peace, a proportion that rose to 47 per cent in 1981 and 57 per cent in 1983 (SOFRES). Secondly there was concern over the relative weakening of NATO in military terms, with as many as 38 per cent of the French expressing lack of confidence in NATO's capacity to defend western Europe against possible attack, compared with 39 per cent voicing confidence. The third factor concerned confidence in America's *determination* to support France in case of danger. Polled by SOFRES in 1976, 62 per cent of the French believed that France and Europe could rely on the military protection of the Americans in the event of a general conflict, against 24 per cent who thought the opposite. Confidence continued to grow, particularly after 1982, and reached the record of 79 per cent in 1984.

As one can see, the French have experienced an odd change of heart regarding America as an ally. It is akin to the evolution of attitudes towards the country's independent nuclear capability known as the *force de frappe*. Each of them is expected to supply a sort of quasi-magic protection, without too many questions asked about the facility's actual technical and military credibility.

Having become the best students of the Atlantic class, the French have made no bones about lambasting their European allies for their lack of consistency, with 52 per cent having no confidence in the other European allies' support for the United States in its relations with the Soviet Union.

This underlying trend was confirmed in a SOFRES poll con-

TABLE 5.5 *If the security of France were to be seriously imperilled by a Soviet military attack on western Europe do you believe that the United States would come to our assistance?*

	1982	1983	1984
Yes	64%	72%	79%
No	17%	14%	9%
Don't know	19%	14%	12%
	100%	100%	100%

ducted in June 1987 (Table 5.6), although two comments suggest themselves. During Reagan's second term in office there was a relative decline in his popularity as a 'lame duck' President. In contrast, the 'Gorbachev effect' improved the image of the Soviet Union, though Gorbachev's personal image was strikingly better than that of the Soviet Union *per se*. Despite the decline in Reaganomania, the image of the United States has not suffered, whereas the attraction of Gorbachev has only served to slow down the continuing collapse in the Soviet image.

We noted earlier that increasing French fears about US military adventurism have gone hand in hand with a growing assertion of Atlantic solidarity. In similar fashion, French support for US economic policy has grown in pace with increasing monetary

TABLE 5.6 SOFRES POLL *June 1987*

Attitudes towards the USA

Favourable	58%	+50% differential
Hostile	8%	
Neither	30%	

Attitudes towards the USSR

Favourable	22%	−11% differential
Hostile	33%	
Neither	38%	
Don't know	7%	

Image of Reagan

Positive	47%	+29% differential
Negative	18%	
Neither	2%	
Don't know	7%	

Image of Gorbachev

Positive	31%	+9% differential
Negative	22%	

disorder and the giddy flight of the dollar.

The crisis seriously tarnished the image of American economic policies: in 1977 39 per cent of the French disapproved of the USA's attitude to world economic problems, with only 18 per cent in favour (50 per cent 'Don't knows'). In 1982 – half-way through Ronald Reagan's first term in office – the French considered the country's economic relations with the United States to be extremely unsatisfactory, with US economic policies coming in for far sharper criticism than those connected with the military alliance.

Still harsher were opinions on the economic crisis, with two thirds of the French (62 per cent) considering (in 1982) that the United States was allowing the crisis to continue without making any real effort to halt it. (Managerial personnel were the most critical of all at 66 per cent). While criticism of American economic policy was strongest among left-wing voters (Communist 76 per cent; Socialist: 72 per cent) it was also the majority opinion on the Right (UDF: 53 per cent–27 per cent; RPR: 52 per cent–29 per cent).

A recent poll explicitly linking the 'ultra-liberal ideas being developed in the United States' and the policies that ought to be pursued in France, showed clearly that a majority of the French are also 'in favour of much less State intervention, even at the cost of a reduced welfare role'. While there is a clear rejection of state intervention (47 per cent, as against 27 per cent), one should not jump to the conclusion that the French have been converted to 'Reaganism'. In the same poll, 41 per cent (as against 28 per cent) were against Mr Reagan's economic and social strategy being followed in France. The accompanying article in *Le Monde* rightly concluded that it was a matter of 'le libéralisme, oui; le *"reaganisme"* non'. But it is equally undeniable that the 'neo-liberal' language of that year had taken Reagan's 'conservative revolution' as an implicit and often explicit model of how to overcome the crisis. Does this mean that public opinion would be loath to follow the 'neo-liberals' beyond a threshold marked by the social cost of a

TABLE 5.7 *Your assessment of Franco-American relations in the following area*

	Mostly satisfactory	Mostly unsatisfactory	Don't know
Economic matters	17%	56%	26%
The military alliance	31%	30%	39%
Cultural exchanges	42%	25%	33%

hypothetical importation of 'Reaganism'?

The fact remains that the most 'Americanophile' of the French are those who most favour a 'liberal solution' to the crisis. It reflects the Left/Right split of domestic politics, with RPR voters regarding themselves as the most 'liberal' (and half of the RPR's supporters in favour of Reaganite policies for France), while Socialist and – above all – Communist voters are much more reticent.

Now that the American reality has begun to be regarded as a model for 'overcoming the crisis', it has been transformed into an item of political and ideological debate in France, though perceived essentially in terms of domestic concerns. Generally speaking, it certainly looks as if the attraction of a strong and prosperous America was linked to disaffection with the Socialist government in France. This hypothesis is indirectly confirmed by the fact that in those European countries pursuing policies similar to the Americans' (for example, Thatcherite Britain or Chancellor Kohl's Germany) Reaganism is much less popular, to say the very least. A further factor, of course, was the deployment of US nuclear missiles in those countries. This has not been an issue in France which, yet again in the European context, turns out to have been the exception that proved the rule as far as attitudes towards America are concerned.

This discussion of the image of American military and economic power brings us back to our original hypothesis that the various components of French perceptions of the United States are in some sense decoupled. It would be almost impossible, of course, to devise an unequivocal explanatory model valid for all situations, since the overriding image of American policies manages to reconcile confidence and suspicion, aversion and fascination. Aversion for what was perceived as 'adventurism' in foreign policy is compatible with attraction for a trans-Atlantic social model, or for American social phenomena or cultural modes. The link between these two levels – state power on the one hand and overtures towards a social and cultural model, on the other – is the economic factor. On the one hand, there is the issue of independence symbolised in the public mind by the dollar, and on the other the American socio-economic model which exerts a force of attraction through its astonishing capacity for growth, innovation and adaptation.

The attractiveness of American society and culture is particularly marked at the present time, as people wonder how to 'overcome the crisis'. But it is nothing new *per se*. In 1962 an IFOP poll asked French people to express their opinions on the USA's strengths and weaknesses. According to the replies, the former lay not in American military might (which was ranked fifth place) but above all in the country's economic wealth, as well as in the youthfulness and dynamism of the American population. Conversely, America's weaknesses were attributed to that society's vulnerability to crises, as well as to the 'puerile and arrogant character' of the American people.

Incidentally, that particular image of the Americans has always remained fairly constant and remained unaffected by any vicissitudes in the relations between the two states. According to a SOFRES poll in October 1984, the three adjectives which, in the view of those questioned, best fitted the Americans were 'dynamic', 'hard-working' and 'open-minded'. On the negative side, the epithets most favoured were 'authoritarian' and 'arrogant'.

It is worth comparing these descriptions with the image of the United States which emerged from the large-scale poll carried out by IFOP in 1953. In answer to the question 'What are the first things that spring to mind when you think about the United States?', the most common replies were: 'power', 'wealth', 'youth' and 'dynamism'.[18] As one might expect, the question of 'power' provoked certain reservations as regards the military dimension and all those factors that come under the heading of 'imperialism'. One senses that by then the Americans' high standard of living was an attraction and also that America was now identified with *modernité*. However many faults were attributed to the American economic system (capitalism, commercialism, the All-mighty Dollar, and so on), it was nonetheless a system that knew how to apply scientific progress not only to industrial efficiency but also to lifestyle.[19]

What, since the 1960s, has applied to the social model's attraction, would seem to be even more pronounced in the cultural sphere. In 1953 39 per cent of the French considered the Americans uneducated, but the same proportion declared themselves ready to use their managerial methods. This dichotomy between cultural and political aspects seems to be confirmed by the fact that there has continued to be a great receptiveness towards American culture even at periods when the political and military images were deteriorating. A survey conducted in October 1984 indicated that a relative majority of those polled had no qualms about American cultural influence with respect to cinema, language, music, dress, advertising, and the like. The largest contingent to think this way are the under-34 age-group, followed by managerial personnel and professional people. Television is the exception that proves the rule, with a majority of the French believing American influence to be excessive. Admittedly, French television had never broadcast so many American B-serials as after Jack Lang took over the French cultural ministry on a platform of resistance to what he termed 'cultural imperialism'.

What is really interesting about these trends in French opinion is that they were always totally out of step with the cultural anti-Americanism of a majority of the French intellectual élite. Commenting on a 1953 opinion poll which indicated that the French were not particularly enamoured of such symbols of American mass 'culture' as jazz or Coca-Cola, whereas they were extremely partial to American household appliances,[20] Theodore Zeldin wrote: 'In the fifties, the autonomous values of that intellectual world – the heirs of the clergy, ceased to exert uncontested power. The Americans knew how to live more comfortably and comfort was not necessarily incompatible with culture.'[21]

The attitude of the French, and particularly the young, has evolved since the 1960s in a direction generally more favourable to American 'mass culture'.[22] As far as the intellectual élite is concerned (particularly those with a literary education), political anti-Americanism for a long time went hand in hand with a virulent anti-Americanism of a cultural variety. This latter attitude was based on a clear-cut opposition between American mass culture (or anti-culture), that is, the *American way of life*, and true (or 'high') culture of which the well-read among the French were the repositories. The trouble is that the French 'masses' have never seen things that way and have not made the same distinction between various cultural levels, nor do they seem overly concerned about the effects of the inroads of American 'mass culture', so long denounced by the intellectuals as a particularly harmful phenomenon and even a threat to the national identity.

This split between the masses and the intellectual élite that goes back to the 1950s is crucial to an understanding of the specific features of French anti-Americanism as well as of the recent volte face in public opinion. In fact, in the sense that the socio-cultural model has not been rejected, there has been nothing to prevent anti-Americanism from being rolled back (or even a transition to

'Americanophilia'), as soon as the anti-American basis of French foreign policy (in terms of 'equidistance' and 'balance') is no longer appropriate in the face of growing Soviet power.

Notes

1. SOFRES poll for *Le Monde*, 16 November 1984.
2. Greece is the country that has experienced the most spectacular anti-American swing. In 1957 favourable opinions had a 75-point lead over negative attitudes. In 1982 the latter led by 38 points. A special section in *Liberation* for 5 July 1985 provides information on the wave of anti-Americanism in Spain (cf. also K. Adler and D. Wertman in *Public Opinion*, August–September 1981, pp. 8–13).
3. Cf. figures from *IFOP/Faits et opinions*.
4. A curve can be drawn for the relationship between the percentages of favourable and negative opinions. Since 1978 it has been difficult to compare the figure with the previous period in view of the elimination of the 'don't know' category (which has served to boost pro-US opinions).
5. For the relationship between anti-Americanism and neutralist thinking see Raymond Aron, *Mémoires* (Paris: Julliard, 1981) p. 277.
6. Cf. Alfred Grosser, *Les occidentaux* (Paris: Fayard, 1981) p. 277.
7. Poll cited by Jean Charlot in *'Les élites et les masses devant l'indépendance nationale d'après les enquêtes d'opinion'*, in a report of a symposium held at the Institut Charles de Gaulle published as *Les Conditions de l'indépendance nationale dans le monde moderne* (Paris: Cujas, 1977) p. 45.
8. Ibid.
9. Gallup poll for *L'Express*, 27 January 1984.
10. Cf. the polls carried out in the immediate postwar period by IFOP under the direction of Jean Stoetzel, reproduced in the study 'Les Etats-Unis, les Américains et la France' in *Sondages*, 1953, No. 2.
11. Pierre Hasner, 'Dominant States and Vulnerable Societies: the East-West Case', *in* Leo Lindberg (ed.), *Stress and Contradictions in Modern Capitalism* (Lexington, Mass.: 1975) p. 409.
12. IFOP poll quoted by Hadley Cantril and William Buchanan, *How Nations See Each Other* (Urbana: University of Illinois Press, 1953) p. 72.
13. In response to the question 'Which countries are worst off?', the French placed their own country in second place after Greece, but ahead of Spain, Germany, Italy, Great Britain, Indochina and Palestine: in that order! Cf. Cantril and Buchanan ibid., p. 28, where the authors speak in terms of 'pathological tension' in France in relation to the conflict between self-image and the situation.
14. SOFRES, *Opinion publique 1984* (Paris: Gallimard, 1984).
15. Olivier Duhamel, Jean-Luc Parodi, 'La dégradation de l'image de l'Union soviétique' in *Pouvoirs*, 1982, No. 21, p. 173.
16. Ibid.

17. This is confirmed by the B.V.A./Europe 1 poll carried out on 20 April 1985 on the eve of the Bonn summit, in which 57 per cent of the French (compared to 48 per cent of them in 1984) were in favour of President Reagan (with only 27 per cent hostile reactions). For the sake of comparison, 38 per cent were in favour of Mrs Thatcher against 48 per cent unfavourable opinions.
18. *Sondages*, 1953, No. 2, p. 9.
19. At the beginning of the 1960s, a net majority of the French were convinced that the USSR was leading the United States in scientific research. (It was the period of Soviet successes in space and an American presidential campaign in which Kennedy spoke of a 'missile gap' – which was mythical anyway). But in the same poll the Americans came out well ahead as regards academic freedom, the range of discoveries, and medical research, and above all with respect to the capacity to make scientific discoveries available and useful in society. Cf. Leo P. Crespi, 'The image of US versus Soviet Science in Western European Public Opinion' in R. L. Merritt and D. L. Puchala (eds), *Western European Perspectives on International Affairs* (New York: Praeger, 1968) pp. 54–77.
20. 'Ce que les Français pensent des Américains' in *Réalités*, 1953, No. 91, pp. 18–22.
21. Theodore Zeldin, *Histoire des passions françaises* (Paris: Encre, 1978) II, p. 157.
22. This is what emerges from all the most recent polls. To the question 'If you had to leave France, in which country would you like to go and live?', 43 per cent of young people from 18 to 24 choose the United States, whereas the average for the population as a whole was only 29 per cent (cf. the SOFRES poll conducted in October 1984 for *Le Pèlerin*).

6
The French Intelligentsia Rediscovers America
Diana Pinto

It is easy enough to recognise the anti-Americanism of the French intelligentsia in the early postwar years; but its contemporary pro-Americanism is more difficult to assess. Perhaps the trans-Atlantic change of heart should be seen as both a consequence and a symbol of the diminished role of the intellectual in French society. But how did French intellectuals change their view of America? The notion of a 'pilgrimage' or 'journey' does not seem convincing, implying as it does a straight transition from dimness to enlightenment. Perhaps their idea of America was just a residue of the attitude towards France's own more central culture and to the ideals of the revolutionary Left. It took a profound change, under internal and external influences, before the American complex could be understood in all its political, social and cultural diversity.

If we are to use a metaphor, it is better to think not of a pilgrimage but of a voyage at sea. The passengers set out with confidence in their guiding star, sure of their destination and well aware of the perils they face. But in mid-voyage the compass fails, the star is dimmed, the land they were heading for looks suddenly forbidding, while the sea they had feared so much grows calm.

And these were the three key elements in the political worldview of the French intelligentsia in the postwar period: the gleaming star of French culture; the promised land of Revolution incarnate in the Soviet Union; the threatening sea of American power and influence. Today's pro-Americanism, a complex phenomenon with many roots, reflects the shattering of that worldview, and forms a temporary refuge from the collapse of previous beliefs and objectives. One of the ironies of history is that the French intelligentsia's receptiveness to America has led it to political silence, and to a more and more modest role as a militant force. The overt pro-Americanism to be found in cultural journals and in fashionable writings and ideas is the work of a new intelligentsia, mainly media-based. This group, which varies between the pragmatic and the ideological, has emerged to fill the gap left by 'the silence of the intellectuals' (to use Max Gallo's term). The motives for this pro-Americanism may turn out to be rather more short-term (not to say opportunist) than they seem at present; perhaps it is the 'golden' silence of the leading intellectuals that form the most positive and fruitful link between the two cultures.

In the self-confident years following the War, all was crystal clear. France radiated its own culture – a culture of unquestioned and universal value, whose intellectuals were like so many beacons. The Soviet Union, the home of Socialism and victim of Nazism, remained – despite its misdemeanours – the land of the future, a monolithic shelter from capitalist storms, and lodestar of all genuine and revolutionary progressive activity. America was a turbulent sea, forever threatening, and liable to flood the surrounding countries in Western Europe or Latin America. To intellectuals who were simultaneously élitist and revolutionary, and deeply hostile to what they regarded as an almost boundlessly energetic and unprincipled materialism, America seemed culturally and economically totally rootless, and yet extremely menacing. The only good Americans were those summoned before the House Committee on Un-American Activities, Black writers or jazz musicians, sensitive Southern Whites (opposed to the materialist Yankee culture), or political activists and trade-unionists who behaved like their French counterparts. Anti-Americanism ruled the day.

In the 1960s and until the beginning of the 1970s this picture changed solely in matters of detail, which only later were to emerge as important. Now the star of French culture glowed with the new 'isms' of the social sciences and their pretensions to a cold and clinical style of thought, whether it was that of Lévi-Strauss, Barthes, Lacan, Althusser, Foucault, or even Bourdieu. Their literary and cinematic counterparts were the *nouveau roman* and the *nouvelle vague*. French culture, which had once borne a positive message of 'civilisation', gave itself over in the 1960s to ultra-refined 'rereadings' attacking the great traditions, while creativity gave way to the stripping-down exercise of *'déconstruction'* which, however brilliant, was doomed inevitably to a dead-end.

A 1960s intellectual aspired to be 'clinical', rather than politically *engagé*. He did not so much abandon his role as change its content. Now it was the Third World, first Cuba, and then China, rather than the Soviet Union, of which France's intellectuals dreamed. The promised land remained *progressiste* and *révolutionnaire*.

As for the American sea, it became more stormy and menacing; with the war in Vietnam, it invaded the very territory of the earthly paradise. France's intellectuals strove to keep their ship steady, more than ever determined to surmount the storm and to struggle against the raging elements of capitalism and imperialism. They drew comfort from new trans-Atlantic voices which emerged to challenge the American 'system' and its consensus: there was the discovery of poverty in America, and the struggles of the Blacks for civil equality; there was the challenge of the radicals; the hippies with their 'counter-culture'; and the students protesting against American involvement in South-East Asia. They were like so many new actors, whom the French insisted on viewing through European eyes (as if they were extensions of what was happening in Paris, Berlin or Rome) and they had to be interpreted in Marxist and revolutionary terms. A deeply negative view of the 'real' America persisted.

Before the United States could be recognised as a complex reality, calling for a direct and open-minded approach on the part of French intellectuals, the ship they sailed in had to lose her bearings. It was from the 1970s that, with the disgracefully delayed discovery of the *Gulag*, the promised land at last came to be seen as an imprisoned country frozen in its totalitarian mould, not only in the Soviet Union but also in China, Cuba and Vietnam. The consequences of this revelation were inevitably profound for an intelligentsia which had always regarded the Soviet Union not only as *la mère du socialisme*, but above all as the child of the French Revolution and hence the best proof of the universal political and social influence of the French Left.

The French intelligentsia now discovered that both its theories and its causes were palpably false, and felt guilty at praising a totalitarian system which long after the intellectuals of other countries had undergone a change of heart they had continued to insist was progressive. The result was a major rethink of the national past. They railed against their former idols, even seeking out early signs of the *Gulag* mentality in their own previously venerated Revolution, and identifying anti-semitism at the very heart of French ideology. French culture had already been pared down philosophically and artistically, as well as in literary terms; it was now to be subjected to a political and historical scouring. Indeed all certainties were at an end. It was the beginning of a long, slow reappraisal, which is still going on, by an intelligentsia in search of a new identity, this time a cultural identity, and one involving genuine allegiance to democratic and libertarian values.

America came to be seen in all its 'splendour' when French intellectuals – like sailors blown off course, no longer trusting in the star, and their backs turned on the promised land – began to look at the sea beneath, and ask whether it was not perhaps a creative force rather than the element that barred them from Utopia.

Recognition of the United States as a dynamic and creative system came slowly during the 1970s, encouraged by American military defeat in Vietnam, which at least made the giant seem more human and comprehensible. Several factors were crucial in this conceptual shift – and above all a recognition that American radicals and opposition movements were the genuine American article and not mere copies of the European Left. They were full members of a movement, a long-run change which affected a whole society, and not merely its fringes.

Such books as Edgar Morin's *Journal de Californie* set the tone for a new look at America, where racial and social struggles as well as the activities of the radical opposition seemed so well accommodated by a supple and pragmatic political system in a way that the theorists of capitalism and imperialism had never dreamed of. Watergate showed the French public, if not the Paris political class, that one of the established powers of the American 'consensus', namely the press, could take the all-powerful President of the United States to the very edge of impeachment, using fully legal means and with no compromise to freedom. It was beginning to seem appropriate to read, not *The Nation* or the *Monthly Review* perhaps, but certainly the *Washington Post*, if one wanted to understand and judge America properly. Hostile certainties were beginning to collapse.

Real contact with the United States came via the American universities, not those of the agitated 1960s, but of the serious intellectual activities of the 1970s. Deprived of its previous intellectual myths, the French intelligentsia now found in the American universities a reverence for learning hitherto inconceivable on the part of the materialist 'barbarians'. At precisely the time when French intellectuals were losing faith in their own position as guiding lights of political commitment, they found the idea of the learned man in a Republic of Letters, miraculously intact in America. For the first time American voices began to play a significant part in French intellectual debate (for example, Robert Paxton's researches in the controversy over Vichy), and French scholars discovered an intellectual flexibility and open-mindedness behind American thought and activity. In place of monolithic oversimplification – the keystone of all closed explanatory systems, such as Marxism – there was an open style of thinking, kept suitably modest by the influence of logical positivism, and above all grounded in intellectual and political pluralism. Thus there developed, little by little, an idea of the intellectual as competent in certain areas but in others no longer entitled to pontificate *ex cathedra* – least of all on behalf of an *engagement* bordering on the messianic.

France's intellectuals abandoned Sartre for Tocqueville and Popper, preferring the sober mediocrity of democracy to the evils of a *nomenklatura*, however forward-looking it might appear. The best evidence for the newly acquired humility of the intellectuals of France, and their new-found attachment to that democratic camp which they had so long scorned was the triumphal acclaim which greeted Raymond Aron's *Mémoires* (1983). However, this *leçon américaine* owed less to a noisy pro-Americanism than to 'the silence of the intellectuals'. Engrossed in their own work, they were now mistrustful of all political commitments beyond basic adherence to the most elementary (and at the same time most complex) commitment of all – the issue of human rights. They had become reluctant to take up public positions at the exact moment when *leur gauche* was assuming power.

The rediscovery of America by the French intelligentsia occurred through a sort of implicit understanding – a realisation that the historical and philosophical values of democracy were in all cases similar, and that France now had to regain the place it had once held in the eighteenth century ('the age of democratic revolutions'); it could no longer be the leading inspiration of twentieth-century totalitarianism. Through long study of the origins of totalitarianism, and mature reflection on the role of liberalism and the market economy in developing a stable basis for democracy, the French intelligentsia, as it were to its soul, became aware of the real values of America and no longer merely of its *marxisant* marginalia.

This conversion to western liberal democracy does not mean that we should speak of the contemporary French intelligentsia as being 'Americanophile'. In fact, their rather isolated and specialist studies have turned increasingly on questions of cultural rather than political identity – questions which have tended to push them towards a European field of enquiry, in pursuit of a scholarly community of historical and literary values of a type not to be shared with their American counterparts.

Is there a contradiction between the geography of culture and the geography of basic values? When French intellectuals were indulging in anti-Americanism, they hero-worshipped the American novelists, whom they thought to be the underdogs of the system. Now that France, because of a common commitment to democracy, had become open to America as a general system, French intellectuals began to pay homage to all those voices coming out of Central Europe, be it Milan Kundera, Czeslaw Milosz, Thomas Bernhardt, Peter Handke or, further removed in time, Hugo von Hofmannsthal or Joseph Roth. The demise of Marxist ideology, now finally understood, has left a frightening gap; and it is precisely here that cultural research is attempting to reknit the two halves of Europe's identity. In the 'era of Silicon Valley', the imagination of French scholars turns to the Capuchin crypt or the convolutions of the Prague spirit.

The striking, even clamorous pro-Americanism that we see around us now does not result from the conversion of the old intelligentsia to democratic values, pluralism, and an openness to evidence – though these are indeed symbolised by the United States – but has its origins in other cultural, economic and political spheres. It is the product of the media-based intelligentsia that took over from the old intelligentsia (which was increasingly committed to 'anti-exhibitionist' silence). The new 'Americanophiles' are to be found among the intellectual gurus of changing fashions, among practical intellectuals drawn to inter-cultural do-it-yourself, and among the new intellectual ideologues. These three types of 'media' intellectual have derived philosophical underpinning from the complete reversal of the views of the leading intellectuals of France with regard to the Soviet Union and the United States; but they have geared their pro-Americanism to rather more contingent issues. They echo the new hopes and dreams of a society weary of the constraints of traditional political life and culture, and eager for new experiences.

It is the intellectual gurus who have sung the praises of the new individualism. Former radical critics of 'the System', even Marxists, were won over all the more easily to pro-Americanism since they had never been very firmly attached to the orthodoxies of the Left. Ensconced in the cultural sections of *Le Nouvel Observateur* or *Libération*, or gravitating towards the magazine *Autrement*, they travelled in France exactly the same road as American radicals of the Jane Fonda type, transforming the values of rebellion into support for the spirit of initiative, of the individual, the sportsman, the traveller. Their America is an imperfect mixture of French fantasies, glimpses of the real world of American fashion, a good deal of Paris snobbery, and a new cosmopolitanism turning on 'status' and 'status objects' rather than on ideas. (See the issues of *Autrement* devoted to California or New York). This pro-Americanism reflects the thirst for distance, for novelty, and for new leaders of fashion eager to break out of a France which suddenly seems provincial. Imitating all aspects of America, these intellectual gurus have reversed the traditional contempt of the French for things foreign, and made a religion of everything that emanates from the United States. Thus, American films are all the rage again, and regarded as better than those made in France even when they are worthless as works of art. (We are a long way from the time when the French intelligentsia would identify the '*sens culturel*' of great films which had been misunderstood in Hollywood).

American music is much favoured, of course, and American books seem more exciting than French publications. As for fashion, the 'preppy' style has been all the rage; the only thing missing is the ivy on the walls of French universities. America sets the tone for a life with all the rhythm of a marathon race. The slogan precisely sums up the vision, at once élitist and fashionable, which the gurus have given us of a country which no one dreams of studying in depth in other respects. These cultural pictures of America are closer to advertising than to American reality; they are aimed at a public given over to entertainment and escapism, and show very clearly how poverty-stricken French dreams have become. The wearied intellectual gurus are avid for what has been called 'the Humour Society' ('*la société humoristique*'). In the light of glasnost, will their pro-Americanism be a passing fashion?

The pragmatic intellectuals sing the praises of a France receptive to technological innovation and able to rise to *le défi mondial*. They fret over the backwardness of French life, with its various political and social bottlenecks, and look to America for the secrets of success, for the tricks they can borrow to fashion a future for France. It is in precisely such circles, whether close to the government or not, that the 'Silicon Valley' model is so popular, symbolising as it does all that has been missing in France – flexible structures, the spirit of initiative, risk-capital, intimate links between research and production, and so on. Such pragmatic intellectuals as Alain Minc and Michel Albert are more interested in American reality than the intellectual gurus, technological modernity being to them an economic and social fact rather than advertising puff – and therefore all the more difficult to transplant.

But the pro-Americanism of these pragmatists should not be exaggerated. In order to renovate France, they are ready to take whatever ideas they find most appealing. When America languished in moral and economic crisis under President Carter, the pragmatists sang the praises of Japan – at the same time (and rather ironically) preserving the legend of the Italian economic miracle, a model chaotic but effective, with all that that implied for civil society in the absence of state intervention. To place their current attitudes to America in perspective we should remember that in the 1930s (when France was undergoing a crisis of economic confidence better concealed than today's) the pragmatists, certain of the failure of American capitalism, had turned enthusiastically towards the economic achievements of the Soviet Union, and proclaimed the virtues of *Gosplan*. Now that the American economy is slumping again after its recent revival, and that the industries of Silicon Valley, thrown into crisis by 'the law of inevitable concentration', have become simply part of an uninspiring industrial machine, and with worries over the American deficit if not unemployment, these intellectual pragmatists may easily abandon their American enthusiasm for more promising vistas.

The America of the intellectual ideologues is essentially the political and economic incarnation of the liberalism they want to see in their own country. Not until the Socialists came to power in France, and the American nation took a conservative President to its bosom, could this sort of *intellectuel américanophile* gain access to the French media. Giscard's France and Carter's America could not have created the climate in which such things were possible.

Today's intellectual ideologue approaches the United States with exactly the same reflexes, concerns, and concepts as the postwar intelligentsia, though he may see the United States as the incarnation of Absolute Good, where before it was in its way, an Empire of Evil. In both cases the intellectual procedure is the same: the complex and contradictory reality that is America, with its mixture of good and bad qualities, has been set aside, and its place taken by a stylised image without any finer shades. The America of these new French ideologues was only a mirror-image of their pet political projects, whether these involve reducing the role of the State, setting market forces free, or simply extolling the virtues of liberalism or 'business'. They saw Reagan as the perfect anti-Mitterrand. Rapturously praising each of his economic and social decisions as though in the name of some health-giving law of the market-place, the intellectual ideologues indirectly criticised the French Socialist regime, encouraged and sustained by the current pro-Americanism of the French people (though that is not in the least political).

For quite some time it seemed as if the advance of these liberal attitudes ran parallel to the rethinking undertaken by the *deuxième gauche*, since this too stressed the need to change relations between the State and civil society. But with the growing politicisation of French political life, in which the truce or state of grace between the parties was soon forgotten, the breach between Right and Left has deepened. The *deuxième gauche*, vastly taken by many aspects of the pro-American views held by the gurus and the pragmatists, nevertheless reserved judgement during the general panegyric for President Reagan, preferring to return to the fold (that is to say, to the Left) under the slogan of *la République*.

At the same time the pro-American ideologues hardened their position and became militant supporters of Reagan and his conservative revolution. The euphoria of their prospectus, following Reagan's electoral majorities, showed that this kind of ideological pro-Americanism (*Figaro Magazine* is a perfect example) possesses certain characteristics which other versions do not. One might even say that in spite of their devotion to American society and its economic liberties, these intellectuals have remained in a sense the most 'French' of all, making judgements about American society *en bloc* just at the point when the traditional intelligentsia had learned to avoid wholesale generalisations, to take or leave as seemed appropriate, and above all to judge events as they unfolded.

If anti-Americanism does re-emerge in France, it will be in reaction against this ideological pro-Americanism. Indeed yesterday's pro-American opposition, now that it has regained power, has often adopted new anti-American strains and protectionism in an attempt to distance itself from the *modèle américain* in a somersault back to nationalism, or a desire to regain the middle ground of politics. Conversely, a new cultural anti-Americanism may emerge in reaction to American saturation of the visual imagination.

Will we ever return to the anti-American triumphalism of the postwar period? This seems unlikely: both America and France have changed too much. The response to the anti-American outbursts of Jack Lang (erstwhile minister of culture), when Socialism was in the ascendant, is the best proof of that. That crusade against American *impérialisme culturel* failed in face of the silence of the intellectuals and the ironic lack of interest of a public much keener on anti-Socialism than on anti-Americanism.

In Sartre's day, America was a global giant capable of imposing a *Pax Americana* on a world in ruins, where it was the only economic power. Radical French intellectuals, anxious about their national cultural heritage, were devoted to the revolutionary ideas incarnate in a Soviet Union enfeebled by the War. It was easy in such circumstances to be anti-American.

That stance affirmed the historical and spiritual values of a France closed in upon itself. Forty years on, American power has been relatively reduced on a world stage which has many other players and where the Soviet Union is a strong and threatening and now mesmerizing power. France, more or less enthusiastically, has now joined in the international economic 'game': the new generation is sold on the ideas of openness, travel and adventure, ideas historically absent in a nation from which there had been few emigrants. In such circumstances America was bound to seem a beacon of modernity. However, it is the new and glittering identity which France has unexpectedly acquired through economic growth which has made the virulent anti-Americanism of the postwar period out-of-date.

The crisis of the intellectuals is both symptom and symbol of the modernisation of France. It marks the end of a process which has taken them all the way from a committed anti-Americanism to an unusual silence which promises a great deal. Whether the *intellectuels médiatiques* – gurus, pragmatists or ideologues – praise America today or curse it tomorrow, the fact is that the structure of anti-Americanism as it was in the postwar period has simply collapsed. There are not a few observers who regard the journey in which the spirit of the traveller has so profoundly changed as yet another modern version of the road to Damascus.

7
Anti-Americanism and the Elite
Ezra N. Suleiman

There is little doubt that the image of the United States in France has substantially changed over the last few years. When we recall the fervent anti-Americanism of Left in the 1950s and of the Right in the 1960s we can't help but be struck by the transformation of attitudes and sensibilities that have opened the door to American mass and high culture. The transformation of attitudes has even resulted in general support for American foreign policies.

Survey data show that while France manifested the strongest hostility towards the United States in the postwar period, it is now probably the least hostile of the European countries. A recent survey showed that only 15 per cent of those questioned in France considered themselves 'anti-American', whereas the figure was higher in both Germany and Britain.[1] Although the appetite for American mass culture continues to grow, France has been remarkably receptive to American art, music and literature. It is no longer just Faulkner and Hemingway who represent American literature. The translation of works by Grace Paley, Toni Morrison, Stanley Elkin and many others suggests that, in this area at least, the French are far less provincial than the Americans.

What accounts for the change in attitudes towards the United States? What groups in the society have been most and what least affected by this change? Finally, does the mass appeal of the United in France have any effect on political and economic relations between the two countries?

AMERICAN ANTI-AMERICANISM

The root cause of anti-Americanism in France has generally been attributed to the intellectuals. Similarly, today pro-Americanism in France is also credited to a change of heart among the intellectuals. That intellectuals shape the cultural attitudes of a society is perhaps more true of France than elsewhere largely because of the pre-eminent role that they have long assumed in the society. Unlike in the United States, the intellectual in France is not expected to be restrained in his opinions and pronouncements by a lack of specialisation. He is expected to play a role in several institutions simultaneously.[2] His access to the media allows him a degree of influence that probably has no equivalent in the United States.

But French intellectuals have generally been in a contradictory situation because they have not had the 'free floating' role that social theorists have considered to be the hallmark of the intellectual function. What Karl Mannheim referred to as the 'unattached' intellectual has by and large been an aberration in France. Intellectuals in France have generally belonged to or become spokesmen for political movements or parties, preferring often to remain loyal to the ideological causes to which they attached themselves, while sacrificing the freedom that normally accompanies the intellectual function. It was precisely this penchant to become 'attached' that led Benda in the 1920s to denounce *La trahison des clercs*. What the intellectuals betrayed was their calling.

The French intellectuals' view of and attitude towards the United States was not directly linked to the country itself. It resulted rather from a *representation* of the country. It was, in short, a by-product of the intellectuals' other attachments. When the Soviet Union represented the ultimate 'good' society, it was natural that America should be viewed as its antithesis.

Now, as the intellectuals' attachments to certain political parties, movements and platforms changed so did their view of America. Neither American capitalism nor foreign policy have undergone a major change since the end of World War II. Yet we have witnessed a remarkable shift in the attachments and attitudes of French intellectuals. Michel Winock points to some of the factors that explain the French intellectuals' rejection of old beliefs.[3]

There is, however, another factor that needs to be taken into account in the French intellectuals' attitudes towards the United States; namely, that the French intellectuals have often taken their cues from their American counterparts. French intellectuals have not had a monopoly on anti-Americanism. During the inter-war period, the American intellectuals' opposition to fascism led many to take a pro-Soviet position.[4] Throughout the postwar period, from the Cold War and the McCarthyite witch-hunt to the war in Vietnam, American intellectuals were in the forefront of the opposition to their government's policies.

If, then, the ideological travels of many American intellectuals have ended at the conservative station, this has coincided with the distance travelled by their French counterparts. The ideological distance travelled by a Podhoretz or a Kristol is no different from that travelled by an Annie Kriegel or a Le Roy Ladurie. The recently acquired patriotism, nationalism and aggressive anti-Sovietism of many American intellectuals has had its impact in and beyond the United States. The pro-Americanism of French intellectuals today is therefore not without its debts to the American intellectuals who have rediscovered the moral virtues and superiority of their own country.

The pro-Americanism of American intellectuals was ripe for export. Just as a conservative tide was swept into power in the United States, the Socialist threat returned to France. Socialism has governed France since 1981, and for much of the time it had the assistance of the Communist Party in this task, the very party that so many of France's intellectuals had turned their backs on. The French intellectuals were therefore ready to embrace an America that had at its helm a conservative, anti-Communist, anti-Soviet, anti-statist government. Moreover, this was a government that affirmed its commitment to the defence of Europe and its willingness to counter Soviet threats. The French intellectuals turned away from their 'leftist' government and looked for inspiration again to the American intellectuals and to America.

CONSISTENCY OF THE 'CLASSE DIRIGEANTE'

The French intellectuals have manifested an inconsistent attitude towards the United States. Their view of America has been determined either *a priori* by the ideological stances of the political movements to which they belonged, or by the attitudes of American intellectuals towards their own society. While one normally thinks of intellectuals as being the most likely to hold steadfastly to a position, and those that belong to governing élites as being most likely to shift positions on account of their ingrained pragmatism, this is clearly not always the case. Indeed, it may be a paradox, but it is nonetheless correct to suggest that the governing élites in France have had a far more uniform and consistent attitude towards the United States than has the French intellectual élite. Their views have been more steady and less wavering than those of the intellectuals.

This is not to say that the governing élites always displayed the same sentiments or that their views were not sometimes tinged with hostility. It does mean, however, that they never had much doubt as to where they stood in the bipolar conflict. Nor was there ever much doubt that they shared many of the values of American society. To the extent that they displayed a hostility towards the United States, this was what might be called a *conjoncturel* hostility, as opposed to the ideological hostility of the intellectuals who questioned the fundamentals of American society and American foreign policies. Among the members of the *classe dirigeante* – in the administration, in business, in the liberal professions – the ideological content of their erstwhile anti-Americanism was minimal.

The *conjecturel* anti-Americanism of the de Gaulle era was another matter. De Gaulle after all was attempting to effect a transformation of French foreign policy. He was seeking to manoeuvre his country into a position where it could have, or seem to have, a degree of independence from its chief ally. This was true not just in the foreign policy realm. It was equally the case in the economic sphere. Who was the main rival? Who was setting up most of the obstacles to the competitiveness of French firms?

The de Gaulle era, which saw a serious discord between France and the United States, was the period of the *défi américain* and the questioning of the American hegemony. De Gaulle's actions also helped strengthen the Left's anti-Americanism by raising the spectre of economic imperialism and military hegemony. They also created a new hostility towards the United States among those who were not counted previously, or even then, ideologically hostile to the United States.

De Gaulle thus created some kind of an anti-American consensus in which conjunctural disagreements with the United States could be confused with a more fundamental (ideological) hostility to all that this country represented. It was a brilliant tactic also because de Gaulle's target was a safe one – a sure friend and ally who would not renounce its commitment to the West even if it was questionable whether it would risk a nuclear attack on itself for the sake of defending its allies.

The *défi américain* clearly did not endear America to the French business community. But the hostility was bound to be mixed with admiration: American productive capacity, technical competence, training of managers, aggressive marketing, all these were admired by French business. That French business should have felt a fear of being taken over just as it was getting 'off the ground' is understandable. And yet, as a 1970s study showed, French members of the élite were not unfavourable – certainly not more so than other European élites – to American multinationals.[5] The French business and administrative élites have more knowledge of and contact with technology and its potential transferability, with business techniques, with market changes and adaptations. Consequently, they are generally in contact with that part of America that matters most to them. Anti-Americanism and pro-Americanism have often co-existed within French society, and even within specific groups, because American society presents itself in so many different guises, each of which has some significance.

The *classe dirigeante*, even when it was critical of specific American foreign policies, was able to overlook what it considered the misguided nature of such policies because a central feature of American foreign policy was a commitment to European defence. According to one study of élite opinion carried out in the mid-1960s, 'most respondents think that the only serious conflict between France and the U.S. lies in the realm of defense, that is, the *force de frappe* and NATO policy. A number of respondents (14%) mentions trade policies, "economic penetration" or "American investments"'.[6] This same survey also showed, however, that despite the differences between the two countries, and these differences were at their height during the period in which the survey was carried out, '87% of our respondents mention the United States as a country with which France has had and will have common interests over a long period of time'.[7]

The conjunctural differences between France and the United States led to mutual resentments. But they did not lead to mutual rejection. At no point did the French governing élite cease to view the United States as an ally. Political realities dominated the perceptions of the French élite. The survey of élite opinion carried out at the height of the Franco-American differences observed that

'Whatever the nature of the American system, it is argued by many that France needs the U.S. until a united Europe is established. The basic realities are such that France "cannot do without the U.S." for the time being. Both in diplomacy and in defense, and perhaps even in order to build Europe, France needs American support: French independence must be qualified by the realities of American power and the need for American support'.[8]

The political and administrative élites have generally tended to look on the US as an ally, even if they have sometimes questioned the depths of America's commitment to Europe. The US has, after all, not seemed to welcome with alacrity signs of a movement towards a more unified Europe![9] The scepticism of the 1960s remains, even if it is masked today by the apparent pro-Americanism in France.

AMERICAN 'FLEXIBILITY' AND FRENCH 'RIGIDITY'

The French governing élite distinguishes between the differences over policies and the 'realities' of American and French society. The French business élite has been hostile to specific American foreign economic policies, but American technology and dynamic capitalism represent something of a model. This does not mean that the French élite has been ready to imitate American practices. Critical as it is of the rigidity of French institutions, and admiring as it has been of American mobility, flexibility and innovation where, as the French business élite sees it, no texts or organisational structures are sacred, no fervent attempt has been made to import American practices. Admiring the use that American institutions make of talent is one thing; doing away with French élitism and replacing it by 'promotion based on merit' is another.

The capacity for innovation, mobility and professionalism within American society has long been admired by the French governing élite. In many years of interviewing the administrative, political, business élites, and the liberal professions in France, I found that the comparisons between French rigidities and immobilism, on the one hand, and the American capacity for adaptation and change on the other were always spontaneously made. The governing élite in France always has the feeling that it operates within narrow institutional constraints where its margin of manoeuvre is extremely limited. It sees itself hemmed in by both the self-protective capacities of individual groups bent on preserving their privileges and the omnipresence and omnipotence of the State. It is precisely this view that explains the remarkable success of François de Closets' *Toujours Plus*! There is an evident contradiction in this perspective: if the State is so powerful, why has it not been able to resist the lobbying of individual groups in their quest to preserve their privileges?

The view of America as a society in which talent and professionalism predominate in all institutions is widely shared in France, even beyond the governing élite. The French media, which has not always been known to be friendly to the United States, nonetheless takes a much more kindly view of the *déontologie* of American journalism and of the professionalism of American journalists. French journalists take the view that their American counterparts are more independent, and therefore more professional. The independence from political power allows American journalists to work in a manner that accords with the ethos of the profession. A book of interviews with some 20 French journalists makes this quite clear. A theme that runs through most of the interviews – regardless of the affiliation of the individual journalist – is the dissatisfaction with the journalistic profession and the French journalists' admiration for their American counterparts.[10]

Now, the admiration which the governing élite, the liberal professions and journalists display towards the United States may strike an American observer as somewhat misplaced. American criticism of American business practices or of journalism abound. It matters little that the French élites may admire the 'wrong' things about America. Their perceptions constitute *a* reality.

CONCLUSION

The pro-Americanism raging in France today needs to be seen in perspective. In part, it does not represent a profound transformation since the governing élites, and the public as a whole, had not previously been fundamentally anti-American, though they may have been hostile to American foreign or economic policies. In part, it reflects a changed attitude towards the United States by American and French intellectuals. And, finally, it is in part a reaction to a series of conjonctural events – Reaganism in the United States, Socialism in France, anti-Sovietism on the part of both countries, Poland, Afghanistan, and so on.

Just as what was viewed as anti-Americanism in an earlier period was mostly conjunctural and not ideological anti-Americanism, except for the anti-Americanism of intellectuals, so the pro-Americanism of today is also mostly conjunctural. As the *conjoncture* changes, the 'excessive' pro-Americanism of today will once again find its equilibrium. The governing élites will continue to view America as their ally and admire aspects of American society, even as they object to specific American foreign and economic policies. The public will continue to look to America as the major supplier of popular culture and as a protector. In other words, the élites and the public are likely to display similar attitudes towards the United States as in the past. The intellectuals, on the other hand, are not likely to be able to keep up their current level of pro-American sentiments. Perhaps most significant is the fact that the phenomenon of pro- or anti-Americanism is one that involves a reaction on the part of the French. It has little or no significance for policies.

Notes

1. Daniel Vernet, 'Les Français préfèrent M. Reagan au "reaganisme"', *Le Monde*, 6 November 1984. See also, E. J. Dionne, 'Poll Finds French Support Reagan; Germans and Britons Split', *New York Times*, 31 October, 1984.
2. Not everyone in France agrees that the multifarious activities of French intellectuals which give them several power bases is a healthy development. See Hervé Hamon and Patrick Rotman, *Les Intellocrates* (Paris: Ramsay, 1981); and Régis Debray, *Le pouvoir intellectuel en France* (Paris: Ramsay, 1979).
3. See Michel Winock's ch. 4. in this volume.
4. See Paul Hollander, *Political Pilgrims: Travels of Western Internationals to the Soviet Union, China, and Cuba, 1928–1978* (New York: Oxford University Press, 1981).
5. See Jacques Attali, *et al.*, *L'Opinion européenne face aux multinationales* (Paris: Éditions d'Organisation, 1977).
6. Karl Deutsch, *et al., France, Germany, and the Western Alliance: A Study of Elite Attitudes on European Integration and World Politics* (New York: Charles Scribner's Sons, 1967) p. 69.
7. Ibid., p. 70.
8. Ibid., pp. 70–1.
9. See Stanley Hoffmann, 'West Europe: Wait and Worry', *Foreign Affairs*, Vol. 63 (1985) No. 3. p. 648.
10. Anika Michalowska, *19 Journalistes et leur métier* (Paris: Editions d'Organisation, 1980).

8

Sartre, Beauvoir, Aron: An Ambiguous Affair

Marie-Christine Granjon

Over the 30 years from 1950 to 1980, opposing judgements of the United States were expressed by Jean-Paul Sartre and Simone de Beauvoir, on the one hand, and Raymond Aron, on the other. They reflected two opposing visions of the world, the one generally shared by the left-wing intellectuals, and the other by their right-wing counterparts. The former, who were in the majority, and conscious of the fact, tended to identify with Sartre. The opposing camp, who had long been in the minority and frequently challenged the label of 'right-wing' pinned to them by their opponents, largely subscribed to Aron's positions.

Like Aron's pro-Americanism, the anti-Americanism of Sartre and Simone de Beauvoir is inseparable from the East-West conflict which originated in 1947 and from the sharpening ideological conflict between Marxism-Leninism and liberalism. This conflict continued into the 1960s, when the Third World took over the Soviet Union's special role as a force of progress and revolution. Sartre's attacks on the United States were intended as an onslaught on capitalism, imperialism and exploitation – *la réaction*, in a word. Aron's intention in defending the United States was to protect democracy and freedom against Soviet totalitarianism. Rarely was the United States *per se* at issue in either case. It was almost always chosen simply as the antithesis of the Soviet Union or the Third World, in contrast to which it either represented absolute evil (in the view of Sartre and de Beauvoir) or relative good (Aron). Condemnation or defence of US world power took precedence over study of American realities for their own sake. What turned Raymond Aron into a pro-Atlanticist in 1947 was his anti-Communism. Not having any great inclination to study America's culture or the features of its civilisation, he focused his attention primarily on the political and economic aspects of US diplomacy. By contrast, Sartre and de Beauvoir had both shown a great interest in American culture as such during the 1930s and 1940s and published their assessments of that country's civilisation after their tour of the United States in 1946–47.

How did Jean-Paul Sartre and Simone de Beauvoir perceive the United States before they became anti-American? Did Aron manage to reconcile his pro-NATO stance with the right to criticise the United States? In what respect did the anti-Americanism of de Beauvoir and Sartre and Aron's support for NATO reveal different concepts of the relationship between morality and politics, and between commitment and objectivity?

During the 1930s, Raymond Aron – then a moderate left-winger and friend of Jean-Paul Sartre and Simone de Beauvoir – had a great interest in German culture, philosophy and sociology, which he went to study in Cologne and then Berlin (1930–33). He recounts that particular intellectual journey in his *Mémoires*,[1] which make no mention of the United States prior to 1940. It was a country that seems scarcely to have interested him. Sartre and de Beauvoir, on the other hand – both of them left-wingers with anarchist tendencies (neither of them using their vote nor ever contemplating joining any party) – were enormously interested in American civilisation. Admittedly, their enthusiasm was not entirely qualm-free:

> We regarded America as the country where capitalist oppression had triumphed in the most vile fashion. We detested the exploitation, unemployment, racism and lynch-law there. None the less, leaving aside its good or evil aspects, there was something gigantic and unfettered about life over there that we found fascinating (...) Ironically, we were attracted by America whose government we condemned, whilst the USSR, the scene of an experiment we found admirable, left us cold.[2]

Sartre and de Beauvoir combined a love for jazz and Hollywood films (which they preferred to the products of French cinema) with a burning enthusiasm for the American novel – Dos Passos, Faulkner, Hemingway, Steinbeck, Caldwell – which they saw as revolutionising narrative techniques. Before the war Sartre devoted two essays to Faulkner and one to Dos Passos, whom he regarded as the greatest writer of his day.[3] Sartre and de Beauvoir both acknowledged having been influenced by the literary techniques of these American novelists – frequently regarded as second-rank by well-read Americans of the 1940s. In a lecture which he gave at Yale in 1946, Sartre was to declare à propos French novels written during the Nazi occupation: 'We intend to give you back the techniques that you lent us. We will return them to you in a digested form: intellectualised, less effective and less brutal – deliberately adapted to the French taste'.[4]

In January 1945 Sartre was invited to spend several weeks in the United States as a journalist. Camus asked him to represent *Combat* and he was also to send articles to *Le Figaro*. The 32 articles which appeared alternately in the two dailies are striking for their lack of black-and-white thinking. They were a record of the complexity of American society with all its extremes. The Americans living conditions appeared to him to present a contrasting picture of 'wealth and thrift, pleasure and deep sadness, comfort and anguish'.[5] He noted that 'external signs of class' were 'non-existent' while a 'genuinely human civility' prevailed in relations between classes.[6] However, he also stressed how the automation of the work process was a source of stress and exhaustion among the workers, who went in fear or unemployment, although he did acknowledge their dread of Marxism.

Sartre sought to understand how it was that the Americans managed to reconcile conformism and individualism, those two apparently contradictory mainstays of American society:

> Being conditioned by propaganda which is not State-made but the product of society as a whole and living within a community which trains him to be an "all-American", the individual naturally behaves just like everyone else. The upshot is that he can feel supremely sensible and nationally-minded at one and the same time, so that it is when he is displaying the greatest degree of conformism that he experiences the greatest sense of freedom.[7]

Sartre saw nothing totalitarian about such conditioning, since the accent was on universal reason accessible to all people, whatever their nationality. And the presence of the machine as a factor of universalisation served to accentuate this unsectarian rationalism all the more. Consequently, the first Americans Sartre encountered seemed to him 'conformist because of freedom and depersonalised because of rationalism. They seem to identify Universal Reason with their own particular Nation, within the framework of the same creed'.[8]

While conformism constituted the bedrock of that society, this did not mean, Sartre insisted, that individuality and personality were suppressed. These qualities had a latent existence and could materialise as part of the struggle to survive and in the race for material and social success. Sartre counselled against regarding the drive for success and money as solely the outcome of greed or a taste for luxury. Money was no more than a symbol of success, itself the yardstick of virtue, intelligence and divine protection. Most of all, success enabled the individual 'to stand out from the crowd as a somebody'.[9] The liberal economy meant that each American could aspire after individual success, and assert his independence, initiative and dignity in a job totally free from stale control. 'Personality is something to be won, it is both a social function and the affirmation of success.'[10] It was only through submitting to conformism that the American could assert his individuality. But there was always the possibility of winning back his independence and escaping to 'an almost Nietzschean individualism, symbolised by the skyscraper in the clear sky of New York'.[11] It was this city, so obviously dear to Sartre, which was to symbolise the deep-rooted connection between conformism and individualism in the United States: the streets were all the same, the buildings were all different.

Even in his preface to a special issue of *Les Temps Modernes* on the United States,[12] Sartre did not simplify American reality. He urged readers not to confuse the system with the people who confronted it. The system – *'l'américanisme'* – may have been for him 'a ghastly tangle of myths, values, panaceas, slogans, figures and rituals',[13] but did not determine the thinking and actions of all Americans. They were free to fight against them, being men 'while it [*"l'américanisme"*] is only a thing'.[14] As the 'product of uneasy freedoms' the system sought to combine the need to be American with the desire for individuality. The enormous gap between the myth (equality, liberty, the rule of law, the law of the market, and so on) and reality meant that Americans had quite a lot of scope for independence and inventiveness.

In *L'Amérique au jour le jour* Simone de Beauvoir described the fascination which that country held for her during her four-month speaking tour of the United States at the beginning of 1947. She recalled most significantly that the reality in America was not homogeneous, that it was a living society, swept by diverse and often contradictory currents. More than once she mentioned the American's kindness and warmheartedness. She also pointed out that the democratic ideal was deeply rooted in the American mind: 'Disparities of wealth do not go hand in hand with a class hierarchy. Rich Americans lack affectation, poor Americans lack servility. In everyday life human relations are created on an equal basis'.[15]

However, in her case, social criticism outweighed praise, and her overall judgement was negative rather than positive. Leaving aside capitalism, racism and moral puritanism 'all of which I detest in this America',[16] she declared that the reality contradicted the Jeffersonian ideal. The individual had achieved no more real possibilities of rising in the social scale, and in such a situation freedom was an illusion. The negative aspects on which she focused included the Americans' condescending or arrogant attitude towards Europeans, and the prevailing anti-intellectualism which turned literature into a 'grocery item' and made life hard for writers, while devaluing mental speculation and abstract ideas in favour of positive results and concrete actions. Then there was the apathy of apolitical students incapable of action, the 'pessimistic individualism' of left-wing intellectuals who no longer believed in anything, oversimplification – with Americans preferring reassuring certainties to discursive thought – conformism, the cult of things engendering a climate of abstraction, a psychological malaise that pushed Americans to drink or psychoanalysis ('that vast operation of social therapy'[17]), boredom, which they tried to banish by indulging in hobbies, using gadgets and reading comics, and women's dependence on men despite the apparent victory of feminism.

Having gone to America a year after Sartre, in a climate of mounting anti-Communism, de Beauvoir adopted a much more critical attitude towards US society. However, she shared his reluctance to reject America out of hand. After the first performance of his play *The Respectful Prostitute* in 1946, Sartre found himself accused of anti-Americanism, a charge which he rebutted vigorously in an article in the *New York Herald Tribune*.[18] Not only was he not at all anti-American, he wrote, he did not even know the meaning of the word. He recalled that he had just published two special issues of *Les Temps Modernes* on the United States, which had indicated both the positive and the more questionable features of American society. Two years later, in the preface to the American edition of *The Respectful Prostitute*, Sartre was again to deny the charge of anti-Americanism in virtually the same terms.

Having spent the war years in London with the Gaullists, Raymond Aron found himself rather shocked in 1945 by General de Gaulle's anti-Americanism. Convinced that France had first of all to recover economically if it was to become truly independent, Aron considered that only the United States could assist it, in terms of raw-materials and machinery. 'It was in that sense that I used to say that American friendship was crucial for us.'[19] As a member of the editorial board of *Les Temps Modernes* in 1946 and a journalist on *Combat* (before joining *Le Figaro* in 1947), Aron soon distanced himself from his friends on the Left when the choice had to be made for or against Communism. In *La Force des choses* Simone de Beauvoir notes that the editorial board of *Les Temps Modernes* had split by June 1946 because of Aron's avowed anti-Communism. 'Aron declared that he had no liking for either the United States or the USSR, but in the event of war he would rally to the West. Sartre replied that he had no fondness for either Stalinism or America, but if war broke out he would side with the Communists.' Aron apparently brought the discussion to an end by declaring 'we might make a different choice between two abominations – but in all events, it would be a reluctant one'.[20] In short, Aron opted for the United States only out of his aversion for the Soviet model. In his *Mémoires* he neither confirms nor disclaims the words attributed to him by Simone de Beauvoir.

In Spring 1947 Aron came out categorically in favour of the Western camp, while Sartre espoused neutralism (up to 1952). In the following autumn, the rift between these two former *'petits camarades'* was to become permanent. Aron supported the Marshall Plan and the subsequent North Atlantic Treaty (1947), while Sartre opposed them both. If it was a matter of democracy or totalitarianism, Aron believed that the choice of *'civilisation atlantique'* was a foregone conclusion. Sartre wanted to see an independent Europe, that rejected both of the blocs. In 1950 Aron considered US intervention in Korea to be justified on the grounds that America needed to maintain its credibility in the eyes of its allies. For his part, Sartre laid the blame for the war on the United States. It was an occasion when Sartre's and de Beauvoir's anti-Americanism were to be given free reign. In *La Force des choses*, Simone de

Beauvoir was to recall how she had the impression of being back at the time of the Occupation (sic) when she saw two GIs entering a hotel in Chinon. 'Seven years' earlier we had adored them, those tall peaceful-looking soldiers in their khaki uniforms: they had been our freedom. Now they were the defenders of a country which was supporting dictatorship and corruption from one end of the globe to the other: Syngman Rhee, Chiang Kai-Shek, Franco, Salazar, Batista ... Now those same uniforms were a symbol of our dependency and a mortal threat.'[21]

It was in 1952 that Jean-Paul Sartre and Simone de Beauvoir started to become increasingly anti-American. It was the year when the Communist Party changed its tack and decided to extend the hand of co-operation to Sartre. Up till then he had been the butt of a permanent campaign of slander and vilification waged by Party ideologists and writers from Jean Kanapa to Louis Aragon and even including Marquerite Duras. Sartre, who regarded the Communist Party as the 'great party of the working-class' accepted with alacrity and forsook his neutralism. He was 'beside himself with rage'[22] over the arrest of Jacques Duclos during an evening demonstration organised to protest against the arrival of General Ridgway to take over from Eisenhower as head of SHAPE. His anti-Americanism reached its apogee at the time of the Rosenbergs' execution (19 June 1953). In an extremely violent article in *Libération* (as quoted by Aron in *Mémoires*), he declared: 'It is a legalised lynching which dishonours an entire people and proclaims eloquently once and for all the failure of the Atlantic Treaty and the inability [of the United States] to assume the leadership of the Western world'. After a reference to 'latter-day fascism', he voiced the conclusion that America is a 'mad dog' and it was therefore time to break off all ties with it. Aron's comment (not without a tinge of hyperbole) was that the Americans 'occupy in Sartre's demonology, the place occupied by the Jews in Hitlerite demonology'.[23]

Engrossed in the struggle for Algerian independence, Sartre and de Beauvoir paid little attention to the United States during the period from 1956 to 1960. In 1956 Simone de Beauvoir noted that her aversion to America had not diminished since the Korean War. Her reading of C. Wright Mills, Riesman and Whyte served to confirm her view that – with the exception of certain individuals, groups and journals – the Americans had become a 'nation of sheep', and were now entirely conformist, 'conditioned' and bereft of any critical spirit. Even writers she once admired no longer aroused interest: Hemingway's individualism had turned him into an abettor of capitalist injustice; Dos Passos' talent had waned since his conversion to western values, and Faulkner had come out in support of the Southern Whites. Intolerant, anti-Communist and racist, America had become the foremost reactionary nation, both within and without.[24]

In 1960 Sartre and de Beauvoir made two visits to Cuba (in February and October) and made friends with Castro. They were to support his regime against such US actions as the Bay of Pigs invasion and the blockade, until the Padilla affair of 1971. In April 1965, Sartre expressed the view that the bombing of North Vietnam was the logical outcome of the structures of American society which had to be shaken to their foundations. He turned down an invitation from American academics at Cornell University (Ithaca, New York) for fear of offending his friends in the Third World who would not appreciate his visiting 'the enemy' at such a time.[25] In the summer of 1966 Sartre and de Beauvoir agreed to take part in the Russell Tribunal set up to assess whether or not the United States was guilty of war-crimes in Vietnam. In May 1967 the tribunal accused the United States of engaging in 'terrorist' bombings aimed at breaking the population's morale. In November 1971 the tribunal found the United States guilty of 'genocide' against the Vietnamese people, the purpose of which, in Sartre's eyes, was to prove to the peoples of the Third World that armed rebellion did not pay.[26]

In the 1965–66 period Sartre had also accused the United States as an imperialist military and economic power of Americanising and depersonalising European cultures.[27] It was Sartre's view that the French economy was dependent on the United States. In spite of de Gaulle's anti-American rhetoric, 'France is no more than a rebellious slave still subordinate to the American order'.[28]

Had America been overtaken entirely by conformism and capitalist imperialism? As left-wing intellectuals, how did Sartre and de Beauvoir perceive their American counterparts (ignored by Aron)? *A propos* her 1947 trip, de Beauvoir maintained that it was the progressive and pacifist writers close to Richard Wright – people with a critical allegiance to America – who had taught her to know and appreciate that country.[29] During the Vietnam conflict, in Spring 1965, Sartre acknowledged that there were Americans who fought against racial segregation, and other, even fewer in number, who actively opposed war. However, he rated as 'nil, unfortunately' the influence of the Left which he considered incapable of compelling the administration to negotiate. For him, the American Left exemplified the 'wretched of the earth' – isolated and impotent – to which he rendered tribute nonetheless. At the same time, he believed that there were very few on the American Left who were ready to rock their country's economic and social structures to its fundamentally imperialist foundations.[30] Nevertheless, in a telegram to the organisers of a Vietnam War teach-in at the University of Boston on 31 May 1965, Sartre voiced his support for those who opposed the war and thereby fostered an awareness that their country's 'disgraceful image' was 'erroneous' and that the rising generation was determined 'to dissociate itself entirely from it'.[31]

John (Tito) Gerassi – the son of Fernand and Stepha Gerassi, friends of their youth – was to be their main source of information on the anti-establishment movement in the United States in the 1960. Gerassi – an active opponent of the war and an admirer of the Black Panthers – was soon to lend his support to extreme arguments in favour of armed struggle. He associated with the underground *Weathermen* group, a break-away from the mainstream Students for a Democratic Society (SDS). Between 1965 and 1973, *Les Temps Modernes* was mostly to publish texts by black revolutionaries (Malcolm X, George Jackson, Eldridge Cleaver, the Black Revolutionary League of Detroit – Marxist-Leninist) or their white counterparts (Gerassi and the *Weatherman* manifesto). Little mention was made of the new – and more moderate – student Left or of non-violent thinking. In consequence the – erroneous – idea was fostered that the revolutionaries were in the majority in the movement of the 1960s.

When Aron visited the United States for the first time in Autumn 1950, he did not communicate any of his impressions of American society and culture. For Aron, the United States was the guarantor of those public freedoms which he regarded as all-important. Though an admirer of the American political model, Aron was not an all-out partisan of economic liberalism. He was convinced, however, that by and large the western economies had done more to ensure growth and promote greater prosperity than the so-called Socialist economies. And when it came to American civilisation as such, his assessment was neither harsh nor overindulgent. He shared some of the reservations voiced by intellectuals such as

Marcuse 'on condition that such criticism is not indiscriminate and that the society is not to be rejected out of hand'.[32] While conceding that criticism of the American model is legitimate, his view was that it should not obscure the 'intrinsic wickedness of totalitarian regimes'.[33]

Being very much a favourite of American academics and the US establishment during the 1950s and 1960s, Aron was frequently invited to the United States to take part in strategic debates at the highest level. Between 1960 and 1963, when he was faced with the choice between Kennedy's 'grand design' of preserving America's nuclear monopoly while establishing a vast free-trade zone between the USA and western Europe, and General de Gaulle's *'grand dessein'* of assuring French independence first and foremost, Aron opted for the latter. Nonetheless he endeavoured to convince de Gaulle not to set up the *force de frappe* in opposition to NATO but 'to integrate it, on the contrary, into the Atlantic framework'. He refused to believe that de Gaulle really entertained the idea of an American troop withdrawal from Europe, in spite of the General's anti-American rhetoric. However, Aron did tax de Gaulle with having kindled 'the French people's latent anti-Americanism' and accustomed them to mistake their true adversary, by fostering the belief that the threat to their independence came from the United States, not the USSR.[34]

In *La République impériale* of 1972, as in certain passages of his *Mémoires* of 1983, Aron sought to refute a number of these ideas cherished by Sartre and other French left-wing intellectuals (for example, Claude Julien) as well as by such American 'revisionists' as Gabriel Kolko, Harry Magdoff and William A. Williams. Roughly speaking, these ideas were that American policy was dictated essentially by economic interests; that the USA derived its wealth solely from its plunder of Third World resources; and that the entire western camp lived under the threat of economic colonialism and cultural asphyxiation by the United States.

While conceding that the United States dominated world markets through the strength of its economy and the supremacy of the dollar, Aron rejected the determinist attitude that this policy was the inevitable outcome of America's capitalist structures. In Aron's view, capitalist industrialisation and support for free trade in no way implied political or military imperialism. After all, the Europeans and the Japanese bought raw materials from Third World countries and sold them manufactured products without maintaining garrisons at the four corners of the globe. The United States could just as easily do the same. The Americans maintained troops in Europe and had intervened in South-East Asia and Latin America for reasons that were indissolubly economic, political and strategic. Their goal was to foster a world order favourable 'to their ideas, their products and their capital'. Aron readily admitted that the determination to preserve an international climate favourable to US global interest created a discrepancy between the Americans' attachment to the principle of national self-determination, and Washington's actual policy of limiting the sovereignty of any country that risked going Marxist-Leninist.[35]

Aron rebuffed the idea that the prosperity of the United States was derived from the exploitation of the Third World. It was belied by the fact that by 1914 the USA already had the highest per capita production and living standards in the world at a time when the Americans were net exporters of raw materials and their economy was in debt to the rest of the world. The prices of raw materials were not the main source of American prosperity since they only represented a small fraction (10–15 per cent) of the national product. As a rich and industrialised economy, the United States did not need an empire to buy raw materials in the Latin American countries, who were only too happy to sell them, even when those countries, nationalised the subsidiaries of American conglomerates. It was wrong to maintain that the underdevelopment of the South was a condition for the development of the North: 'Neither Argentina nor Brazil provided the American economy with the raw materials or the markets it needed'. America's 'gunboat diplomacy' in Central America and the Caribbean had far more to do with historical tradition (the Monroe Doctrine) and the desire to contain Communism than with economic interests.[36]

Finally, Aron challenged the idea, supported by Sartre, that European culture was being Americanised while the continent was being colonised by the United States in economic terms. In terms of culture, Aron maintained, Americanisation was no more than the progress of industrial civilisation in the developed countries. Such progress was 'nightmarish in its Soviet version, flawed and vulgar in its American version'. Anti-Americanism consisted in making America bear the blame for abstract rationalism and commercialism (that is everything had a price) which was in fact the lot of all the developed western societies. In economic terms, Aron refused the notion that American investments had somehow been bad for

France. On the contrary, they had assisted the growth of the French economy by making 'lame-ducks' profitable and by improving France's trade balance thanks to the exports of French subsidiaries of American firms.[37]

Aron did acknowledge, admittedly, that dollar hegemony and the behaviour of multinational corporations served to erode national sovereignty in the sense that individual countries found it increasingly difficult to control their own economies. He even went so far as to predict that the hegemony of the dollar as a transnational currency coupled with American investments around the globe – even in the form of lending needed capital to the host countries – would one day lead to a rebellion 'however much economists could prove that the expansion of the dollar meant greater prosperity all round'.[38] This meant that the existence of 'widespread anti-Americanism' in different parts of the world could be explained in objective economic and monetary terms. In Aron's view, Sartre's anti-imperialist diatribes were the product of ideological stereotypes, which made Sartre incapable of analysing the facts without making value judgements.

Aron's attitude to the American intervention in Vietnam was quite different to that of Sartre and de Beauvoir, and their respective reactions say much about their particular prejudices concerning the United States. They also reveal something of the connections they made between ethics and politics, as well as between *l'engagement* and *l'objectivité*.

Sartre denied being the intractable moralist that Aron and others made him out to be. In April 1967 he declared that the Russell Tribunal had no intention of passing a moral judgement on the alleged atrocities committed by the US army. The Tribunal would judge the Americans according to their own laws. The question was whether it was acceptable for the American bourgeoisie, which was conditioned by the historical process of capital and class struggle, to violate its own official code of conduct. Sartre did add, however, that ethics – the 'superstructure' in historical development – had a reactive effect on the latter. It was therefore right to remind the workers of the 'ethical and judicial structure of every historical action'. In an article published in *Tricontinental* of 3 December 1967, Sartre maintained that the masses had a 'simple and revolutionary' spontaneous morality, which antedated all political education and demanded an end to exploitation and oppression. The Tribunal would respond to this instinctive need of the masses for clear-cut ideas and judgements in order to demonstrate the 'universalisation and objectivisation of their moral indignity'. Sartre was to acknowledge in 1975 that the masses had failed to heed the Tribunal's appeal. The fact remains that in his eyes the Vietnam War was a black-and-white conflict between Good – the progressive forces of an exploited Third World that had been bled white – and Evil, in the form of American imperialism, guilty of the 'genocide' of a small nation of heroic peasants. What was at stake in the conflict, Sartre declared, was humanity itself: 'Vietnam's victory will prove that people can stand up to "things", in other words the profit motive and those who serve it'. The Vietnamese were fighting on behalf of mankind as a whole, 'the American troops against everyone'.[39]

Aron's assessment of the Vietnam War was based on a different approach. Sartre identified with the victim, *les masses*, and the Third World, and judged the issue in terms of ethics and revolutionary politics. Aron, on the other hand, put himself in the place of the 'decision-taker' (in other words, the President of the United States): 'For more than half a century now, I have consciously restricted my freedom to criticise by posing myself the question: what would I do in his place?'[40] Sartre, for his part, judged and condemned what was necessarily an unjust and violent policy for being imperialist in the Leninist sense. He implicitly absolved the Vietcong's crimes by refusing to place on the same footing the oppressed – 'a group of poor peasants, hounded and obliged to enforce iron discipline in their own ranks', whose only recourse was terrorism – and the oppressor – 'an immense army supported by a highly industrialised country of 200 million inhabitants'.[41] Aron considered that the atrocities committed by the Vietcong were just as bad as those perpetrated by the Americans.

Although he abominated the use of napalm and torture, these were not sufficient basis for his judgement of the war: 'I am not high-minded (*une belle âme*) ...'[42] Convinced that politics could neither be reduced to ethics nor explained in ethical terms, he refused to be a 'spokesman for the universal conscience'. His intention was not to condone or condemn, but instead to try to understand the United States' *Realpolitik* in terms of the likely motives and intentions of the actors and the logic of different situations. He highlighted the Americans' successive errors, and the inadequacy and inappropriateness of the means they deployed in relation to their goals. He noted the importance of the psychological and cultural factors neglected by the Americans, who had failed to realise that the North Vietnamese would rather be bombed to death than capitulate: 'American opinion, with its tendency to reason in technological terms, was to discover to its amazement and admiration the mystery and grandeur of human nature'.[43]

Aron started to get into deep water, however, when he claimed that *La République impériale* was written as an 'ideologically neutral work', 'lacking, as far as possible, all value judgements'.[44] But in the introduction to *La République impériale*, he denied being cynical or basing his judgements solely on 'expediency or pragmatism'. In fact he did not entirely eschew 'ethical considerations', even though ethics in his view were 'an ill-defined and complex category'. There was no doubt in his mind that the North Vietnamese soldiers were bringing with them totalitarianism and underdevelopment: the Gulag and poverty. Forced to choose between absolute evil and relative virtue, he had chosen – without any sort of enthusiasm – the Republic of South Vietnam, and condoned at the same time the American intervention. What was at stake in the conflict was the credibility of the Americans in the eyes of their allies. Aron approved the American decision not to forsake the South Vietnamese government until the signing of an 'honourable peace' (in January 1973) which gave the latter a chance to survive.

Neither Sartre nor Aron had any desire to judge the Vietnam War on ethical grounds. For Sartre, ethical considerations were a matter for the bourgeois, who were heedless of the meaning of history as revealed through the science of history (Marxism-Leninism). Aron, for his part, left such considerations to those '*belles âmes*' who were incapable of grasping the essence of international relations in which 'cold-blooded monsters' confront each other. Nonetheless the systematic anti-Americanism of the one and the critical pro-Americanism of the other are shot through with ideological choices and value judgements, albeit more subtly so in the case of Aron. The ethical dimension was more pronounced in the case of Sartre who sought – with the help of dialectical contortions, '*langue de bois*', and the mythology of 'the masses' – to reconcile ethical judgements with historical necessity posited *a priori*. Aron's pro-Americanism did not blind him to the strategic errors committed by the Americans in Vietnam. However, his support for the war's objective – the containment of Communism –

made it impossible for him to remain a mere 'spectator of human folly and misfortune',[45] restricted to the objective analysis of *Realpolitik*. From this standpoint 'objectivity' only applies to the means chosen to obtain certain goals, reflecting the fundamental values of the *'spectateur engagé'*.

After 1947 Aron never once abandoned either his pro-NATO stance or his attitude towards the USSR. Looking back with 30 years' hindsight he held to the view that the decisions taken between 1949 and 1955 by the United States and its allies had been justified.[46] After the Vietnam War was over, he continued to support the ends of American foreign policy, while occasionally criticising the means employed. While admiring Kissinger as a 'crisis manager', he regarded détente as 'ambivalent', citing the Yom Kippur War in which the Soviet Union had armed the Arabs and goaded them into action once the battle commenced. Did not Kissinger's talent conceal the 'retreat of American diplomacy and the decline of the Imperial Republic?'[47] President Carter was taxed by Aron over his belief in the compatibility of ethics and diplomacy. The human rights policy would not have lasted even if Carter had been re-elected: 'No "cold-blooded monster" can be expected to obey either people's rights or morality'.[48] Nor did the early period of the Reagan administration put an end to Soviet military superiority in Aron's view. Just prior to his death, Aron continued to regard the East-West conflict – the contest between American freedom and Soviet totalitarianism – as the key issue of the century.

For his part, Jean-Paul Sartre, who had been converted to left-wing extremism in May 1968 and was a friend of *'les maos'*, as the Maoist militants were known, was never to renounce his new-found variety of anti-imperialism which regarded both the USA and the USSR as the adversary. He, nevertheless, considered that Europe was more at threat from the United States than from the USSR. That celebrated occasion in 1979 when Sartre and Aron shook hands in front of the Elysée Palace, where they had come to plead the cause of 'a boat for Vietnam', was by no means the sign of an ideological reconciliation between the erstwhile *'petits camarades'*. Shortly before his death, Sartre was to declare that the international situation from 1975 to 1980 had been characterised by 'the triumph of the Right – among the rulers, at least – in almost all countries' including the USA and the USSR. Unlike Aron, Sartre believed that North-South antagonism was more fundamental than the East-West conflict. The global class struggle between the poor and the rich transcended, in his view, the confrontation between the two superpowers which were objectively in cahoots.[49] As a result of their early fascination with American culture and civilisation, Jean-Paul Sartre's and Simone de Beauvoir's first encounter with America was fairly prejudice-free. Even Sartre's assessment of American conformism was forbearing, not to mention his view of competition, which he considered compatible with the conquest of individual freedom and sovereignty. It was the Cold War and the East-West conflict which turned Sartre and de Beauvoir into virulent anti-Americans. Meanwhile, Aron turned into a supporter of NATO, without any particular affection for the 'American model'. Their respective allegiances to one of the two camps derived from ideological considerations. Sartre saw it as a choice between the forces of progress (the USSR) and those of reaction (the USA). For Aron, the choice was between totalitarianism (the USSR) and democracy (the USA). Their choices reflected the two opposing perceptions of the world characteristic of the French intellectual élite from 1947 to 1975. Sartre typified the behaviour of left-wing intellectuals over the period, having gone from defence of the USSR to support of the (Maoist-oriented) extreme Left, while all the time blaming US imperialism for all the world's ills. From such an angle, intellectuals like Aron, who supported the Atlantic alliance, were inevitably dismissed as 'right-wing', or even condemned as henchmen of reaction and enemies of the proletariat.

Just prior to his death (15 April 1980), Sartre would seem to have been at one with Aron in condemning Soviet imperialism and the violations of human rights which it engendered. But as far as we know, neither Jean-Paul Sartre nor Simone de Beauvoir revised their judgement of the United States. Aron's death on 13 October 1983 came at a moment when many left-wing intellectuals in France were becoming increasingly anti-Soviet, as well as pro-Aronite and pro-American at the same time. While welcoming their abandonment of off-the-peg anti-Americanism, can one feel so happy about their endorsement of American *realpolitik* imperatives – such as support for friendly dictatorships or interference in Central America? Are these born-again Americanophiles prepared to dissociate ethics and politics? (In theory, at least, the practice leaves much to be desired, as could be seen in respect of the Vietnam War.) Is the role of intellectuals to be disrespectful and critical of power, or should they – as Aron believed – trim their freedom to criticise, out of respect for the constraints of power ('What would I do in his place?'). I personally prefer Sartre's response when he was refuting the charge of anti-Americanism, at a time when he was not yet obsessed with the fear of being taken for a petty-bourgeois humanist: 'The task of the writer and his special duty towards the public is to denounce injustice wherever it is to be found, and particularly when he loves the country which allows such injustice to be committed'.[50]

Notes

1. Raymond Aron, *Mémoires* (Paris: Julliard, 1983).
2. Simone de Beauvoir, *La Force de l'âge*, I, p. 160.
3. Jean-Paul Sartre, *Situations*, I (Paris: Gallimard, 1947) p. 24.
4. In Michel Contat and Michel Rybalka, *Les écrits de Sartre* (Paris: Gallimard, 1974) p. 151.
5. Ibid., p. 119.
6. Ibid., p. 122.
7. Jean-Paul Sartre, *Situations*, III (Paris: Gallimard, 1949) (revised 1976), p. 82.
8. Ibid., p. 84.
9. Ibid., p. 96.
10. Ibid., p. 91.
11. Ibid., p. 91.
12. *Les Temps Modernes*, août 1946.
13. Jean-Paul Sartre, *Situations*, III, op. cit., p. 126.
14. Ibid., p. 127.
15. Simone de Beauvoir, *L'Amérique au jour le jour* (Paris: Gallimard, 1954), p. 285.
16. Ibid., p. 55.
17. Ibid., p. 66.
18. *New York Herald Tribune* (European edition), 20 November 1946, cited in Contat and Rybalka, op. cit., p. 137.
19. Raymond Aron, *Mémoires*, op. cit., p. 203.
20. Simone de Beauvoir, *La force des choses*, 2 vols ('Folio' collection) (Paris: Gallimard, 1963) Vol. II, p. 135.
21. Ibid., Vol. I, p. 348.
22. Ibid., Vol. I, p. 358. (Cf. also Introduction by Denis Lacorne and Jacques Rupnik in this present volume).
23. Raymond Aron, *Mémoires*, op. cit., p. 308.
24. Simone de Beauvoir, *La force des choses*, op. cit., Vol. II, pp. 130–3.
25. Jean-Paul Sartre, *Situations* VIII (Paris: Gallimard, 1972) pp. 12–13.
26. Ibid., pp. 100–24.
27. In Contat and Rybalka, op. cit., p. 422.
28. Jean-Paul Sartre, *Situations*, III, op. cit., p. 36.

29. Simone de Beauvoir, *La force des choses*, op. cit., Vol. 1, p. 176.
30. Jean-Paul Sartre, *Situations*, VIII, op. cit. The references are to pp. 16, 12 and 39 respectively.
31. In Contat and Rybalka, op. cit., p. 416.
32. Raymond Aron, *Mémoires*, op. cit., p. 416.
33. Ibid., p. 327.
34. Ibid. The references are to pp. 430, 439, 434 and 448 respectively.
35. Raymond Aron, *La République impériale. Les Etats-Unis dans le monde, 1945–1972* (Paris: Calman-Lévy, 1973). The references are to pp. 184, 187 and 307, respectively.
36. Ibid. The references are to pp. 186–7, 642 and 196–7, respectively.
37. Raymond Aron, *Mémoires*, op. cit., The references are to pp. 331, 679 and 613, respectively.
38. Raymond Aron, *La République impériale*, op. cit., p. 297.
39. Jean-Paul Sartre, *Situations, VIII*, op. cit. References to pp. 28–30, 35, 97, 157, 93 and 124, respectively.
40. Raymond Aron, *Mémoires*, op. cit., p. 632.
41. Jean-Paul Sartre, *Situations, VIII*, op. cit., p. 34.
42. Raymond Aron, *Mémoires*, op. cit., p. 621.
43. Raymond Aron, *La République impériale*, op. cit., pp. 13 and 126, respectively.
44. Raymond Aron, *Mémoires*, op. cit., pp. 637 and 642, respectively.
45. Ibid., p. 619.
46. Ibid., p. 282.
47. Ibid., p. 630.
48. Raymond Aron, *Les Dernières Années du siècle* (Paris: Julliard, 1984) pp. 204–5.
49. Interview with Benny Lévy (Pierre Victor) in *Le Nouvel Observateur*, 24 March 1980.
50. *New York Herald Tribune*, 20 November 1946.

Part III
Economy: Dream of Modernity

9
Managerially Yours
Richard Armand

France's top company in terms of net profits only ranks at 200th place in the American corporate league. In such leading-edge sectors as information technology, communications, aerospace, biotechnologies, and arms manufacture, the USA has an almost unbeatable lead. Dominant and sure of itself, US industry is perfectly capable of arousing the hostility of its competitors. But the fact is that manifestations of anti-Americanism in business circles are few and far between to say the least, since the benefits of good relations far outweigh any temptation to find fault.

The seeds of anti-Americanism come essentially from misrepresentations, which themselves derive from stereotypes, the 'model syndrome', powerlessness and political considerations.

In industry – as elsewhere, no doubt – truth and stereotype frequently go hand in hand. A prevalent managerial style can quickly pass for a national trait. It does not take long for it to become linked with some shortcoming and occasionally the latter is substituted for it in the mind of the outside observer. It would even seem that on each side the Americans and the French alike have a tendency to judge the other in terms of what is antithetical to themselves. In other words one side attributes to the other defects which are the opposite of those which it vaguely feels are its own, while claiming for itself the contrary characteristic. Thus out of a possible fear of being a bit amateurish, you will find the French describing themselves as *cultivé* (cultured) and taking heart at the thought that the Americans suffer from over-specialisation, even if it is also a sign of greater professionalism. This game in which merits and demerits are contrasted mirror-fashion is liable to lead to generalisations, exaggeration and, eventually, misrepresentation.

It is somewhere in this spiral that anti-Americanism can make its appearance. At the very least it is a latent risk.

AN IMAGINARY DIALOGUE

A Frenchman:		An American:	
Je suis	Tu es	I am	You are
cultured	over-specialised	professional	an amateur
imaginative	simplistic	businesslike	unorganised
an individualist	inflexible	team-spirited	undisciplined
subtle	crude	dynamic	indecisive
an old fox	a big baby	an eagle	a frog
a true Frenchman	an ugly American	all-American	very French

In the post-Liberation years French productivity missions discovered management American-style. The resurrected writings of the likes of Taylor and Sloan were used to spread its theory and practice. New disciplines came into being sparked-off by the war and they were taken up by American universities. Firms of American management consultants then exported them overseas. They rejoiced under the names of *marketing, operations research, management science, management by objectives,* and so forth. In the process, American companies were held up as models of good management. The same still applies today. Over 85 per cent of the firms cited in the recent best-seller *In Search of Excellence*[1] are American, European companies representing only 5 per cent of the list – and the Japanese 8 per cent. ... This constant harping on about the 'high flyer' can just as easily inspire envy as it does admiration. It is just as capable of arousing contempt.

The objective might of the American corporations is inclined to have subjective effects on the dominant as much as on the dominated. On the one hand you have American leaders declaring that the French seem to them like people wanting to be basket-ball champions without being six-foot tall, while on the other, there is Enrico Mattei comparing what he calls the 'Big Sisters' of the American petroleum industry to cats sharing a bowl of milk while lashing out to prevent the Italian kitten coming near. Without going to such lengths, it is tempting to find fault with organisations that one has no hope of rivalling, rather like the fox's attitude to the grapes in the fable. Moreover, even when cogent analysis of the state of play leads Europeans to ally themselves with the Americans, it can sometimes feel to them like a loss of liberty.

In all events, the might of America can appear as a challenge, to borrow the title of a once-celebrated essay.[2] And it is but a short step from that to its appearing a threat. The negative repercussions of such feelings become magnified as a result of politics.

What gave rise to the French Electronic Plan *'Plan Calcul'* was the US administration's refusal to sell the French Atomic Energy Agency the biggest scientific computer of the time: the Control Data 3600. France is currently buying the present most powerful computer, the CRAY 2. People still recall the recent American embargo on deliveries to the Soviet Union due to be made by certain French subsidiaries of American corporations under the terms of the Franco-Soviet natural gas contract. Scarcely has a consensus been announced among the Western nations concerning the delivery of sensitive materials to the Eastern European countries that bickering is already breaking out between the French and the Americans over the dispatch of telecommunications materials.

These examples are an indication of the extent to which business can be disrupted by politics. Being more complex and all-embracing, the latter involves far greater risk of misunderstanding and even conflict. Furthermore, public opinion is often influenced by it, and it is good at whipping up confusion and chauvinism.

Industry is concerned by politics and industrialists are part of public opinion. Neither the one nor the other are unaware of these influences. On occasions they are even active participants: one finds captains of industry reviling state intervention while flattering government officials for protectionist ends. Troubled waters like these can help feed anti-Americanism. . . .

The point should be made, however, that these various causes of anti-Americanism are equally capable of fostering pro-American sentiments. The Americans' real or conjectured defects would be less likely to be noticed or conjured up if they were not associated, rightly or wrongly, with their opposites. The American model and American power can excite admiration and respect, just as they can provoke animosity and suspicion, and politics is situated within a framework of alliance. Thus the temptation to criticise and the grounds for affinity have common origins to a great extent.

Alternating competition and partnership, the cautiousness of the multinational companies, shared managerial experiences, the cultural affinity of the captains of industry and the rise of Japan are all factors that help attenuate or even suppress anti-American tendencies.

If you can't beat 'em, join 'em, is what the Americans themselves say. Their might makes them doughty competitors and therefore sought-after partners. For one thing, they are able to supply the latest technology, which is why the European telecommunications giants have all signed agreements with IBM or ITT. For another, they can offer access to the huge US markets as American Motors did for Renault, even though they were not a market leader. In all events such agreements at least eliminate one competitor.

Furthermore, it is easier for a European group to acquire a majority holding in a European subsidiary if its partner is American rather than European. The latter is more likely to demand control or, at the very least, parity, the moment that its own national market is covered by an agreement.

Since markets evolve very quickly and industrial groups are generally diversified, it is not unusual to find French and American firms collaborating in certain of their operations and competing in others, or that their positions are reversed on occasions. As can be seen with the Bull-Honeywell or Framatome-Westinghouse link-ups, industrial marriages are clearly not for ever. Though a competitor once more, yesterday's partner can even remain a client. For all these reasons, a relationship with a powerful competitor needs nurturing. Besides, what use would acrimony or malice be to anyone?

These factors explain why industrialists try to maintain the best of relations with their big competitors and even more so with their major partners, even when – and above all – a separation is on the way. There is no way, therefore, that they could express anti-American sentiments on behalf of their company, nor, if it can be avoided, allow their staff to voice or peddle such views.

It is in the interest of multinational corporations to develop good relations with host countries. It is a way for them to avoid potential areas of friction. By and large they even avoid getting involved in politics, contrary to widespread belief.

These are all good reasons for abstaining from any expression of xenophobia. Moreover, the relative simplicity of management techniques helps ensure that the risk of any such manifestation is very low.

Industrial criteria are fairly straightforward: growth, the market share, profit, and the like. More often than not they are precisely measurable. Since the rules of the game are so simple, there is no great difficulty in steering clear of politics. Besides, communication between businessmen of different nationalities presents no real problems. The latter understand each other all the better in that they too are assessed according to these same criteria. Throughout the life of a joint-venture, from its creation right up to its eventual dissolution, and including the inevitable instances of arbitration on the way, there tends to be a community of interest between the parties involved, and that interest is assessed according to the same indicators. The existence of such a guideline means that many problems can be solved irrespective of personal considerations or feelings.

A community of goals along these lines is even easier to achieve with the Americans, since management techniques were often created on the other side of the Atlantic and many French executives learned them at American business schools. Need one be reminded of the fact that the word 'management' has gained official acceptance in the French language?

Finally, let us recall that French businessmen have frequently spent some time in the United States during their younger years. In the course of various summer training sessions or longer periods of study, not to mention business trips or private holidays, they have gained a real picture of that country. They have since enhanced their vision in the course of many professional contacts and visits. It is very rare for them not to have made trans-Atlantic friends. This first-hand contact with a culture which is different but familiar, fosters close feelings and attitudes while helping to dispel stereotypes and avoid generalisations and animosity.

Agreements are now very common with Japanese, notwithstanding great cultural differences. Japan has thrown stereotypes into disarray and abandoned the single model, according to which targets had to be fixed by central management, dismissals were immediate and budgets were at zero. Now we find that consensus can originate from the shop-floor, there is life-long job-security (in the big conglomerates, at least) and zero applies to breakdowns and scrap. Meanwhile the Americans themselves have replaced the 'one best way' approach to management with 'contingency theory'. This also puts paid to the 'single threat', with cars, and above all video-recorders, nowadays coming from the East.

This shift has not only served to reduce antagonisms, it has also been a boost to joint ventures. The arrival on the scene of a new giant means *ipso facto* confrontation with a fearsome/alluring competitor/partner. This immediate consequence is enhanced by a secondary effect. I refer to the fact that increasing global competition accelerates technological developments and requires speed of manoeuvre. This is what has given rise to the spawning of technological agreements between American, Japanese and European groups which are lending a new dimension to industrial partnerships. These are yet further reasons to get on with each other, as well as opportunities to rub shoulders, not to mention scope for mutual understanding.

In contrast with the seeds of anti-Americanism, which are frequently associated with antidotes, there are many cogent arguments in favour of good relations with the United States. Moreover, the French intelligentsia's renewed interest in the United States over the past years, coupled with its repudiation of the Soviet Union, have been a move in the same direction. It is hardly surprising, therefore, that French industry does not provide fertile soil for the spread of anti-Americanism.

What I have said does not imply that conflicts between American and French partners never arise. It is not uncommon for shareholders of different nationalities to disagree on a company's investment, financing and dividend policies. The relationship between the franchise-holder and the franchisee is not entirely tension-free, such as when the former refuses to allow the latter to modify a product, lest the purity of its brand-image be tarnished. Executives can also differ on their assessment of a particular social context: drawing up contracts is not the sum total of lawyers' involvement in industry.

Admittedly, such disagreements can be exacerbated as a result of differences of education, language or culture, even though they are seldom very serious. However, experience has shown that even in the event of serious financial crises, both the French and the Americans are careful not to inflame any dispute by the use of xenophobic arguments. A worthy practice, if you like, but most certainly a prudent one.

Notes

1. Thomas J. Peters and Robert H. Waterman Jr., *In Search of Excellence* (New York: Harper & Roe, 1982). The French translation, *Le Prix de l'excellence*, (Interéditions, 1983), sold over 80 000 copies, a record for a book about business corporations.
2. Jean-Jacques Servan-Schreiber, *Le Défi américain* (Denoël, 1967).

10
Modernists and Protectionists: The 1970s
Denis Lacorne

The anti-Americanism of the 1970s had none of the virulence of the 1950s and 1960s. The settlement of the Vietnam War and the obvious progress of détente served to demobilise the most militant members of the 'anti-imperialist' Left. The ending of the dollar's convertibility into gold and the creation of a system of floating currencies were not the sort of things to rouse the masses, in spite of the political commentators' impassioned denunciations of the 'American diktat' and the 'brutality' of US diplomacy.

Anti-Americanism continued to exist, for all that, in the spheres of politics, economics and culture. However, a profound change had been wrought in the terms of the debate between the partisans of modernism American-style and the detractors of Yankee capitalism. Since then considerations of economic strategy (*intendance*) would seem to have overshadowed discussion of foreign policy options and cultural concerns. The emphasis on the economic factor is clearly not fortuitous. The oil crises, the fall in growth rates and the collapse of such national trail-blazers as the liner *France*, *Concorde*, and the computerisation project known as *Plan Calcul*, were the most obvious signs of France's decline. Even the President was heard to declare that the country's only remaining goal was 'to fight its way back among the leaders' of the major nations.[1] It was over the issue of crisis that the sharpest, and often acrimonious, debates were to take place between the 'modernists' – free-traders who considered that France's future depended on the 'battle for exports' – and the 'protectionists' who advocated retrenchment within the country's frontiers and the 'reconquest' of domestic markets. Within the latter camp there was to be a strong temptation to seek in the United States the cause of the crisis then affecting all the industrialised countries. Who were the chief protagonists of the economic debate? Did the modernism/ protectionism divide correspond to Left/Right polarisation? Who needed a scapegoat and why were the Americans favourites for the role? What were the political and cultural repercussions of the economic debate?

Before attempting to answer these questions, it should be pointed out that the personality of Valéry Giscard d'Estaing and the inevitable comparison with de Gaulle aroused the anxiety of those nostalgics who deplored the country's lost *grandeur*. The writings of the left-wing Gaullist Philippe de Saint-Robert are fairly typical of that particular reaction. Giscard, he maintained, was the antithesis of Charles de Gaulle, and the incarnation of 'mediocre government'. He had superseded the 'heroism' and 'sanctity' of his great predecessors with a vulgar 'consumerist hedonism'. In common with many other heirs to a philosophical tradition going back to the Renaissance, Saint-Robert called for the kind of historical 'energy' which only 'a man of genius' could impart to France.[2] What the incumbent President lacked was Machiavellian *virtù*: the strength of character that allows the 'new Prince' to impose an order on the chaos of events (*fortuna*).[3]

Confronted with what Saint-Robert called the 'goddess Crisis' Giscard was simply an anti-hero who allowed himself to be buffeted by circumstances, one who, 'confronted by this uncontrolled world ... plays with words but has no original ideas'. An accomplice in the 'plot against France', Giscard's government 'seems to have no other objective than to suppress and marginalise all remnants of vitality and ambition in France'.[4]

What has this to do with anti-Americanism, one may well ask? Did the author blame the United States for the decadence which, in his view, was the chief outcome of a lack of character in a prince of little *virtù*? The answer is simple. According to Saint-Robert, the men of the new régime had been 'programmed' by the Americans, and the 'plot against France' was quite simply a US plot against France carried out by persons interposed. The quadrupling of the price of oil, if one was to believe Saint-Robert, was no more than an enormous practical joke, whose sole aim had been to 'reduce' America's energy dependency, boost the profits of the 'Seven Sisters' and set the Arab world at loggerheads. The Americans were seeking, in fact, to create a 'permanent motive' for their military intervention in the Middle East, to satisfy, in the final analysis, 'what has come to be called the Jewish Lobby'.[5] 'The state which claims to lead the world ... has, in the space of ten years, managed to organise two major rackets: the first involving currency, the second, energy. North America behaves in the contemporary world not as a responsible power, but as a supreme *Mafia*.'[6]

Georges Pompidou's former Foreign Minister, Michel Jobert, denounced with similar emphasis the 'servility' of a government which was hiding from its electors the true cost of oil to the country and failing to take the necessary action. The kind of 'liberalism' proclaimed by the Giscardian ruling clique was simply an elegant and misleading manifestation of a 'spirit of national abdication' whose *modus operandi* was to put up with the laws of the market 'instead of trying to change them'.[7]

For Jobert, these 'laws of the market' had been gravely affected by the United States' dual policy of 'plunder' and 'profligacy'. The plunder was the outcome of the undue proliferation of dollars which were issued for the sole purpose of allowing the Americans to 'live beyond their means'. What was meant by profligacy were the 'orgies of heating and air-conditioning' which forced everyone 'to economize in order to save the planet's wealth': 'everyone', the author added, 'but the Americans themselves'. Overcoming the crisis was clearly something that called for *virtù*. For Jobert, 'fatalism' was out of the question; there was a clear choice between 'the self-determination of the country's citizens and acquiescence to foreign ambitions'.[8]

The collapse of the *Plan Calcul* – a project which had been launched on de Gaulle's initiative in 1966 by a state whose generosity was only matched by its ignorance of the business community's actual needs – was seen as further proof of France's economic humiliation. America was the accepted scapegoat because of the merger, in March 1975, of the *Compagnie Internationale pour l'Information* (CII) with the US-controlled Honeywell-Bull. The day after the merger, *Le Monde*'s headline was 'The American way', while *Les Echos* asked the question: 'Honeywell in CII: partner or American Trojan Horse?'[9]

In this connection also, the critics of government policy were to point the accusing finger at a 'Prince' who preferred an American solution to a European one, such as CII's merger with Siemens and Philips within the Unidata Agreement. By opting for a pro-American solution, declared the authors of a book on the adversities of the *Plan Calcul*, 'sleek' Giscard had become 'Uncle Sam's favourite sub-contractor'.[10]

To argue in terms of *virtù* and *fortuna*, or to identify the prime cause of France's economic decline with the 'new Prince's' lack of heroism would hardly be suitable for a Marxist or would-be Marxist analysis. Marxist circles of the 1970s were happier with abstractions along the lines of 'State monopoly capitalism'. Nonetheless, they were not always able to resist the anthropomorphic pleasure of detecting a face behind the abstraction. The hidden face of state monopoly capitalism in the eyes of the French Communists was the Trilateral Commission, an American think-tank founded by David Rockefeller, which they condemned as a 'super-imperialist' organisation whose goal was the promotion of 'US supremacy'.[11]

Left-wing commentators, such as Claude Julien of *Le Monde Diplomatique* and Communist journalist Maurice Goldring, vented their spleen against the inscrutable power of an organisation that brought together 'the masters of today's capitalist world'. Their attacks focused on a Trilateral Commission report entitled *The Crisis of Democracy*, published jointly by Michel Crozier, Samuel Huntington and Joji Watanuki.[12]

Maurice Goldring worked the ideas of his articles up into a book which combines a laborious paraphrase of the Trilateral Commission's report with the author's incensed commentary. The mock telegram on the cover epitomises the style of the author's thinking and the preposterousness of his 'revelations': 'URGENT COCA-COLA – RAYMOND BARRE – CHIEF EXECUTIVES ESSO – FIAT – PARIBAS – JIMMY CARTER – CHIEF EXECUTIVES *SAINT-GOBAIN* – SHELL – BRZEZINSKI, ETC. AGENDA TOP SECRET stop DEMOCRACY MUST BE CURBED stop'.[13]

Not satisfied with exposing the names and collusion of these 'masters' of world capitalism, Claude Julien, Anicet le Pors, and René Piquet fulminated against a statement which is usually attributed wrongly to French sociologist Michel Crozier, and which – QED – suggests the existence of a capitalist plot against democracy: 'There are potentially desirable limits to the indefinite extension of democracy'. (The adverb 'potentially' and the adjective 'indefinite' are generally omitted when it is requoted.)

The actual sense of the offending expression emerges when it is put back in context, namely a chapter by Samuel Huntington devoted exclusively to the United States. Adopting a characteristic

Tocquevillean approach, the author expresses concern at the frailty of a democratic system whose institutions, he claims, have been weakened by the egalitarian and distempered 'passions' of the majority. He deplores the fact that the 'democratic spirit', as it exists in the United States, cannot be tempered by 'those traditional and aristocratic values' which, he maintains, are 'residual inheritances' in the liberal regimes of Europe and Japan.[14] He ends on the following pessimistic note: ' "Democracy never lasts long", John Adams observed. "It soon wastes, exhausts and murders itself. There never was a democracy yet that did not commit suicide". That suicide is more likely to be the product of overindulgence than of any other cause. A value which is normally good in itself is not necessarily optimized when it is maximised. We have come to recognize that there are potentially desirable limits to economic growth. There are also potentially desirable limits to the indefinite extension of political democracy. Democracy will have a longer life if it has a more balanced existence'.[15]

One may disapprove of the author's pessimistic conservative philosophy. One may, like Claude Julien, detest the 'Harvard professor' who is supposed to have dreamt up the 'strategic hamlets' programme during the Vietnam War.[16] However, there is nothing *in the text itself* that points to a capitalist plot against democracy. Huntington has just one concern, and that is to find the means to extend the life-spans of the democracies, even if the means are clearly debatable. The underlying purpose of those who denounced the 'Trilateralist plot' is obvious. By quoting out of context, they sought to demonstrate that democracy was an illusion, that political and economic liberalism were incompatible, that the only real power was the power of money, and that, in the final analysis, David Rockefeller had the final say. One cannot help being amazed at the capacity for survival of such ancient stereotypes of the anti-plutocratic Left.[17]

The fact that the 'capitalist plot' theory was so much in vogue in the Communist press is easily explained in terms of the political circumstances of the period. 1976 was the year of the French Communist Party's 22nd Congress which rejected the notion of the dictatorship of the proletariat and sought to project the image of a genuinely pluralistic and democratic political party. 1976 was also the year of the conference of Communist parties in East Berlin, in other words, the apogee of the Eurocommunist movement. It was the year chosen by the PCF leadership to preach democracy not just to party members in France, but also to its comrades in the 'brother parties' (such as when Leonid Plyushch was publicly welcomed by Pierre Juquin). The message was simple: now that they had become 'democrats', the French Communists would henceforth be more democratic than the democrats themselves. They needed lessons from no one, and certainly not from the Trilateral Commission – that latterday incarnation of the *200 familles*.

The oil-crises of 1973–74 and the need to improve France's balance of trade served to re-open the recurrent debate between partisans of an open economy and the proponents of protectionist retrenchment. The debate became more heated after Valéry Giscard d'Estaing adopted the notion that the world's advanced economies were interdependent, and started pursuing foreign policies designed to achieve a trade thrust by means of large-scale publicly-subsidised trade packages (*grands contrats*). There was vigorous opposition to such measures from a protectionist front that united beneath the same makeshift banner the Gaullists, the Socialists, the Communists and members of the *nouvelle droite*.

What was interesting about that particular debate is that it reflected a clash between two opposing perceptions of modernism. On the one side were those who believed that free trade was the surest path towards restructuring an economy still labouring beneath the crushing burden of a 'liberal corporatist' state and the costly vestiges of policies of *grandeur*. Ranged against them were those who proclaimed retrenchment within the country's frontiers as the only way of stemming the decline which inevitably resulted from the 'globalisation' of a medium-sized economy such as France's. In the face of the combined onslaught of the leading industrial powers (that is, the USA, Japan and Federal Germany) and the newly industrialised countries of the Third World, France would end up being forced to jettison whole sectors of its industry and accept a situation of chronic unemployment. In addition, the need to be competitive would place in jeopardy the social achievements of the previous 30 years. Deprived of any real sovereignty, France would be no more than a marginal country dependent on subcontracts from the main industrial powers – a sort of 'sub-bloc within the Atlantic orbit'.[18]

Hence opinions were sharply divided. For the one camp, only the external discipline of world markets was capable of stimulating an economy facing the 'third industrial revolution': 'I will never do anything to ease the pressure of international competition since it is the only thing that will allow French industry to get into trim', the then Prime Minister Raymond Barre promised the National Assembly on 16 October 1980.[19] The rival camp believed that modernising the French economy required a new discipline: the 'reconquest of domestic markets'. This was the only way to ensure the nation's political independence and retain progressive social policies.

The positions of the free-traders and the protectionists looked irreconcilable. In fact the differences were less clear-cut than they seemed. The liberalism flaunted by the Giscardian élite was of an extremely circumspect variety which by no means ruled out active state intervention. The free trade thesis was always offset by realistic considerations intended to avoid the jolts caused by too rapid an opening of the frontiers. No *Etat raisonnable* could ignore social problems and the risk of political and economic dependence which would result from a situation of unrestrained competition. There was therefore a tendency to use the expression 'regulated liberalism' rather than 'liberalism' *per se*.[20]

Another important reason why the liberalism of the 1970s was less than full-blooded was that Socialist ideology, which had yet to be put to the test, still retained some credibility. This no doubt explains why Raymond Barre felt obliged to declare that his 'liberalism ... is not very different from the ideas held by the social-democratic governments and the sort of policies they pursue'. By making competition the main priority, the Prime Minister explained, nationalisation was not necessarily ruled out in principle, nor for that matter, was massive state assistance to declining industries, support for innovation and the kind of egalitarianism which was the inevitable corollary of incomes policies ...[21] This was still a far cry from the sort of 'liberal/libertarian' triumphalism of certain currents of opinion in the 1980s.

But to call oneself liberal in the 1970s was anathema to those members of the left-wing opposition who placed a rather different construction on the notions of modernity and social progress. Liberalism in their eyes implied allegiance to 'a multinational order led and dominated by the United States'.[22] Hence the sort of liberalism officially espoused by the Giscardians was no more than the hidden face of a full-blown *dirigisme* which would impose 'foreign decision-making centres' on France.[23]

Such statements by left-wing Gaullists were not very different from the sort of things being said by some leading Socialists who did not flinch from employing explicitly Marxist jargon on this issue. Thus a member of the Socialist Party's Executive Committee was to credit Giscard d'Estaing sarcastically with just one achievement: that of protecting the interests of a 'ruling class' which was 'subservient to multinational power'.[24]

As far as ideological certitudes were concerned, the Socialists differed little from the Communists, who denounced both the 'Americanisation of our technology', the 'foreign enslavement' of the economy, and demanded 'an all-out struggle against the multinational companies and the capitalist states that support them'.[25]

There was thus a consensus about the nature of France's ills that ran from the left-wing Gaullists to the Communists. France was 'subjugated', 'dominated' or 'enslaved' and described variously as a country 'in the process of annexation',[26] a 'neo-colony of the United States and Federal Germany',[27] or quite simply as 'a colony.[28] Back in 1971, Christian Goux and Jean-François Landeau had tried to provide irrefutable proof of that 'colonisation'. Using all sorts of figures, the authors demonstrated that most of the leading industrial countries were in the process of becoming American 'colonies'. Having started out as 'independent' states in 1950, France, Italy and West Germany were 'in the process of annexation' by 1970. For their part, the UK, Belgium and the Netherlands had been annexed on 1 January 1970 and were now simply 'condominiums'. Libya had been reduced to the status of 'protectorate' along the lines of Peru and the Philippines. Canada and Panama were both outright 'colonies'. Only Japan and India remained truly independent.[29]

Goux and Landeau had read their Herman Kahn and Orwell and went so far as to prophesy that in 1999 (sic) the economics best-seller of the year, bearing the hardly remarkable title of *The US economic domination of the world*, would reveal among other things that 'out of the world's six billion population in 1999, the Americans now accounted for 4 billion, while the Chinese numbered only 1.5 billion. In these circumstances, if there was now a "peril" it was not "yellow" but "American"!' The authors' fevered imaginations led them to attribute these odd demographic predictions to a columnist on the *New York Times* who had the ear of the US President.[30]

How was this threatening tide of colonisation to be stemmed?

How were the underhanded schemes of the Trilateral Commission to be halted, along with the dominance of the US multinationals? The Left advocated immediate nationalisations, while both Right and Left agreed on the need for a system of protectionist measures.

Jean-Marcel Jeanneney is undoubtedly the best representative of the French protectionist school of the 1970s. His arguments carried all the more weight in that he belonged to the free-trade camp and had once served as trade and industry minister under de Gaulle. It was he who, in 1959, had ended export/import quotas in order to hasten France's integration into the European Community, despite the 'lamentations' of those in the business world who feared for their survival. Jeanneney explained his change of attitude in the 1970s as the outcome of the threat of 'unbridled' competition from outside the EEC, a threat which was negligible at the beginning of the Fifth Republic. He gave three distinct reasons: increased competition from the newly-industrialised countries of the Third World; too rapid a reduction of extra-community tarrif barriers; and the excessive influence of multinational companies. The conjunction of these factors threatened in the long run to produce a 'virtually total free-trade situation', which would inevitably weaken the political independence of France and jeopardise its social security system and standard of living. If it went too far, such a situation could even give rise to a nationalist backlash, with its implicit risk of a global challenge to market values.[31] No realistic solution could be based on protectionist measures conceived in narrowly nationalistic terms. What was needed, ideally speaking, was a collective system of tariff protection involving all the countries of Western Europe. If the protectionist hypothesis was rejected, the result would be a 'less obvious but far more awesome *de facto* subordination to the commercial, financial and monetary policies of the United States, and subservience to the decisions of multinational firms which were free to sell imported goods in Europe at any price, without any thought to the fact that by ruining whole areas of production they risked disrupting entire national economies'.[32]

These ideas, expounded in 1978, were frequently taken up and publicised – even in exaggerated form – by certain Gaullists, as a means of dissociating themselves from Giscard. Policies for 'reconquering domestic markets' were the subject of one of the debates at the national convention of the Gaullist RPR (Rassemblement Pour la République) in September 1979. One year later, future presidential candidate Michel Debré denounced the 'theologians of unconditional free trade' whose shady intrigues were threatening to transform the Common Market frontiers into 'veritable sieves'. He therefore called for an industrial policy designed to 'reconquer the domestic market'.[33] In similar vein, Philippe de Saint-Robert demanded a return to the 'initial protectionism' of the original Common Market.[34] For his part, Michel Jobert, in his editorials in the *Midi-Libre*, vigorously condemned the Giscardian leadership's 'doctrinaire liberalism' which demonstrated, in his view, 'a spirit of national capitulation'.[35]

The debate on international economic policy did not split along majority/opposition lines. The controversy between partisans of 'regulated free trade' and protectionists cut across party lines, on the left as well as on the right. It divided the trade union movement (*Confédération Générale du Travail* vs. *Confédération Française et Démocratique du Travail*) and in the Socialist Party the supporters of the doctrinaire left CERES (Centre d'Etude, de Recherche et d'Education Socialiste) were ranged against those of Michel Rocard. Only the Communist Party displayed monolithic unity.

What concerns us here is not so much the nature of the debate as what was at stake in strategic and diplomatic terms, namely the status of France within the Common Market and the future of its relations with its major trading partners (particularly the USA and West Germany). The CERES's analysis was quite unambiguous on this point: neither France nor the EEC could claim to be independent so long as they were dominated by 'American capital' and its favoured European agency, 'German capital'. Gaullism's mistake, in the view of the CERES, had been to have limited its quest for national independence solely to the political arena. By doing so, Gaullism had found itself forced to reproduce on a national scale the most advanced forms of 'capitalist domination'. The solution advocated by CERES overtly courted conflict since it was based on a 'strategy of international severance', involving the establishment of a new 'Socialist pole in Southern Europe', separate from the EEC and detached from the 'Atlantic world'.[36]

This strategy for international separation went hand in hand with a strategy for a national partition, intended, among other things, to separate the wheat from the chaff, that is, the 'national bourgeoisie' from 'those sections of the bourgeoisie closely involved in the multinationalisation of capital'. The latter category, in the CERES' view, had just one single goal: 'to work under the protection of American imperialism and on its behalf ... to preserve and police the capitalist order'.[37]

Michel Rocard and his friends were to react sharply to these crude oversimplifications – and ended up being labelled 'the American Left' for their pains (a designation which their detractors no doubt regarded as insulting). Rocard's speech at the Socialists' Nantes congress, summed up well the position of a Left which is at once modernist, realistic, in favour of free trade and which refuses the equations: US = capital of imperialism = Enemy No. 1, and West Germany = the Trojan horse of US imperialism = Enemy No. 2.

Censuring his CERES comrades' anti-German reflexes and warning of the risks of a separatist dynamic, Michel Rocard stressed that in the absence of their own oil or uranium, or other essential raw materials, the French had 'no option but to export', and this precluded any fundamental challenge to the way that international trade was conducted. A refusal to face up to these facts, Rocard declared, was a sign of utopianism. It also meant incurring the risk of 'sinking into protectionism'. For, as Rocard shouted from the platform, 'whoever talks of protectionism means state control, and that inevitably implies centralisation ...'[38]

The protectionist positions defended by the Communists were very close to those of CERES, though not absolutely identical. They were first voiced publicly in 1977 in various PCF documents, including a volume entitled *Changer l'économie* and an article in *Le Monde* with an even more telling title: *Vouloir rompre pour changer*. The latter article, written by Politbureau member Philippe Herzog, was a veritable protectionist manifesto which castigated the 'invasion' of the market by imports from Federal Germany and the USA. That 'invasion' went hand in hand with the 'dismantling' of entire tracts of the French economy with all the misery which that entailed, including higher unemployment, lower purchasing power, and so on. Herzog's solution was 'renewed growth', which implied a whole number of nationalisations coupled with the rapid development of the 'domestic market'. That protectionist programme was part and parcel of the nationalist scenario of 'a battle to win back our sovereignty'. Every effort had to be made to halt France's transformation into 'a neo-colony of the United States and Federal Germany'. What was called for, therefore, in addition to protectionist retrenchment, was a 'diversification' of France's economic relations with the rest of the world.[39]

But what did the Communists mean by 'diversification'? The answer was to be given in a later volume by the same author, where he talks about 'the stepping up of cooperation' and 'a large increase in trade with the Socialist countries and the Third World'.[40] The Communist Party's geo-political strategy was thus aimed at detaching France from the Common Market and integrating it into an 'anti-imperialist' bloc sympathetic to the Soviet Union.[41]

In terms of domestic policy, the Communist scheme was even more ambitious. It sought, quite simply, to 're-unite' a France which the excesses of Giscardian liberalism had 'literally split in two'. On the one hand, there was a France 'globalised by multinational capital and supranational organisations' and controlled by 'rootless men [...] who spend their lives in a global network of air-conditioned offices, international airports and standardised chain-hotels'. On the other there was the 'old-fashioned' France, 'the home of the rejected', which was 'falling apart in a chronic state of underdevelopment, and spending its time redistributing poverty *ad infinitum*, as a penalty for its failure to widen its international frontiers'.[42] For the Communists, the solution was obvious. What was required was a new kind of 'self-centred' growth advertised under the slogan *produire français*. This was the only way of escaping the latterday Trilateralist Leviathan whose 'economic base' was the world network of multinationals and whose 'superstructure' included NATO, the IMF, GATT and the Socialist International.[43]

We ought to put these acerbic judgements in context by pointing out that the condemnation of the multinationals by French left-wing intellectuals had little effect on public opinion between 1974 and 1976. According to IFOP polls, the French tended on average to be more favourably disposed towards the multinationals than their German, Dutch or English counterparts. For instance, 41 per cent of the French were convinced that multinational companies were capable of 'hastening the modernisation of industrial techniques', compared to 36 per cent of the Germans, 28 per cent of the Dutch, 27 per cent of the English and 24 per cent of the Italians. Only 6 per cent of them regarded those companies as 'American' (compared with 22 per cent of the Germans, 14 per cent of the English and 11 per cent of the Dutch). Only 10 per cent of the French labelled them 'imperialist' as against 29 per cent of the West Germans. Furthermore, the French (at 19 per cent) were far less ready to declare the 'US multinationals *immoral*' than the Germans (33 per cent), the Dutch (28 per cent) or the British (27 per cent).[44]

The economic debate of the 1970s was inseparable from the cultural debate. This was confirmed by a whole number of authors, starting with those who favoured 'organised' free-trade. Christian Stoffaës, for example, stressed that the apparent existence of a climate of economic war 'disguised the actual confrontation, which was a war being waged by culture on modernity'. On the one side, there was an 'ailing and defeatist culture' which was calling for protectionist solutions, while on the other, there was a 'technostructure' in which the protagonists were concerned to hasten 'a major transformation of industry' and were therefore open-minded both 'about the world and about the whole question of change'.[45]

It was a confrontation of a completely different order in the eyes of those who maintained, on the contrary, that 'the *génie* of our peoples is already being erased by the cold-blooded calculations of bureaucrats and accountants' or, alternatively, that European societies were under the sway of a 'kind of techno-fascism manipulated by rootless, co-opted officials'.[46] It was a war between culture and anti-culture. Culture in this scenario was viewed as an *asset* to be preserved and protected at all costs, which went under the name of le *génie français* (or elsewhere, as 'the spirit of the Mediterranean peoples').

'*Produire français* goes for culture as well', wrote Communist Party General Secretary Georges Marchais in 1980.[47] 'Economie et culture, même combat!' shouted Jack Lang in Mexico City in July 1982 . . . But what exactly was this 'anti-culture' which was directly threatening the French heritage? It was, said Jack Lang 'that which erodes national cultures'. Michel Jobert saw it as the confusion of 'national values with commodities, and men with things' and even 'poetry with washing-machines'.[48] According to Alain de Benoist, it was 'the levelling of people' and 'the reduction of all cultures to a single "world civilisation" based on the lowest common denominator'. For Henri Gobard, it was a 'profound negation of cultures' which were 'ground to mince by the mass-media so that arts, styles, epochs, religions, countries and everything else emerge as a formless hamburger'.[49] It was the 'opinion polls' and 'TV-induced imbecility' which Jean-Marie Benoist regarded as 'the equivalent of physical aggression by napalming from which Asia has already benefited . . .'[50]

By now it must be obvious who was the agent of this vast 'deculturation' exercise: none other – of course – than 'uncaring American-style liberalism', 'the system of international financial denomination', 'acquisitive mercantile puritanism', or put even more simply 'the American party in France ...' and its 'deliberate scheme of national depersonalisation'.[51]

How was this steady process of colonisation and the imperial tyranny of this latterday Philip of Macedonia to be opposed? 'Resistance' was the watchword of those who stood up for *le génie français* on Right and Left; even 'profligacy', so long as it was 'august and superb'.[52]

The most extreme anti-Americans saw the future as belonging to those who were ready to fight for the primacy of culture. In their view, the 'economic base' – which had been inevitably 'distended' by the supporters of the 'liberalist dogma' – needed to be 'put back in its place', in other words, reduced to a 'sub-system of the overall organic system of society'. Denouncing the 'shop-keeper mentality' and the 'dictatorship of affluence' imported from the United States, the theorists of the *nouvelle droite* called for a new 'circulation of élites' to allow the summit of the state pyramid to be occupied by 'creative minds', – namely an 'economic aristocracy' – who, unlike 'the profit-motivated liberals of Right or Left' would launch 'grand industrial projects' similar to *Concord* in terms of technical prowess. The new anti-liberal economy thus envisaged would operate within a 'semi-autarkical' Europe. As a result trade with the outside world would need to be reduced to a *'maximum of 5%'* of the GNP of the envisaged *nouvelle Europe*.[53]

To sum up, the anti-American positions of the 1970s, with their fundamental stress on economic issues, were bolstered by a coalition of opposites which managed to rally under the same banner the protectionist forces of the *nouvelle droite*, (left-wing) Gaullism, (anti-Rocardian) Socialism and the Communist Party. The cumulative effect of that extraordinary convergence of supposedly antagonistic ideologies contributed directly to the defeat of Valéry Giscard d'Estaing. Incidentally, it is rather surprising that this president failed to exploit the protectionist dimensions of his economic policies which were, in fact, more Colbertian than liberal.

However, this was a President who was a self-confessed 'globalist', one who wanted a France which was *'amie de tout le monde'* and who sought to hasten the demise of ideologies by coming up with the term *'décrispation'*. Was someone like that really in any position to withstand a challenge from opponents who, under the cover of Gaullist or Marxist orthodoxy, actually raided the old arsenal of decadent stereotypes in order to smear in turn the 'trilateralisation' of the French economy, the colonisation of French minds and the clearly disgraceful collaboration of the *'parti américain'*?

Although it threw considerable light on that much older debate about the modernisation of French society, the anti-Americanism of the 1970s – by going to extremes – served to obscure the real issues: namely, how was France to respond to the oil crisis and the challenge of the new technologies without undermining growth, upsetting its allies and jeopardising its cultural identity, and was a 'modern France' inevitably an 'American France'? It is ironic that in the 1980s it is America's admirers who are now obscuring the real issues of the modernisation debate, by overstating their case.

Notes

1. Valéry Giscard d'Estaing, interview with Jean-Louis Servan-Schreiber, TF1, 16 October 1978.
2. Philippe de Saint-Robert, *Dieu que la crise est jolie!*, (Paris: Ramsay, 1979) pp. 13, 22, 143 and 145 respectively.
3. Cf. chapter six of Machiavelli's *Prince* and the excellent commentary by J. G. A. Pocock, *The Machiavellian Moment* (Princeton: Princeton University Press, 1975).
4. Saint-Robert, op. cit., pp. 148, 145 and 143 respectively.
5. Ibid., pp. 68, 77 and 62 respectively.
6. Ibid., p. 91, underlined in the text.
7. Michel Jobert, *Chroniques du Midi Libre* (Paris: Hachette, 1982) pp. 99 and 55 respectively.
8. Ibid., pp. 28, 29, 18 and 67 respectively.
9. *Le Monde*, 13–14 March 1975; *Les Echos*, 13 May 1975 quoted by Jacques Thibau, *La France colonisée* (Paris: Flammarion, 1980) p. 125.
10. Jacques Jublin and Jean-Michel Quatrepoint, *French Ordinateurs* (Paris: Alain Moreau) p. 287, and more generally Alfred Grosser, *Les Occidentaux* (Paris: Fayard, 1978) pp. 381–2.
11. Anicet Le Pors, *Marianne à l'encan* (Paris: Editions Sociales, 1980) p. 92.
12. Cf. Claude Julien, 'Les sociétés libérales victimes d'elles-mêmes?', *Le Monde Diplomatique*, March 1976, p. 14; Idem 'La nouvelle idéologie', *Le Monde Diplomatique*, May 1976, pp. 4–5; Maurice Goldring, 'La démocratie, un mal qui répand la terreur', *France Nouvelle*, 26 April 1976, pp. 28–30. See also 'Dans l'ombre de Jimmy Carter, la Trilatérale, un entretien de Colette Bernas avec Claude Julien', *La Nouvelle Critique*, January 1977, No. 100, pp. 50–5.
13. Maurice Goldring, *Démocratie croissance zéro*, (Paris: Editions Sociales, 1978). According to the testimony of the Managing Director

of Saint-Gobain-Pont-à-Mousson, the activities of one member of the 'French Section of the Trilateral Commission' consisted entirely of meeting twice or three times a year ... nice people and good company'. Roger Martin, *Patron de droit divin* (Paris: Gallimard, 1984) p. 427. He found his membership of the 'international consultative council' of the Morgan Guaranty Trust much more engrossing, stimulating and instructive by comparison. Ibid., pp. 267 and 327–8.

14. Samuel Huntington, 'The United States' in Michel Crozier *et al.*, *The Crisis of Democracy* (New York: New York University Press, 1975) p. 114.
15. Ibid., p. 115.
16. *Le Monde Diplomatique*, March 1976, p. 14.
17. Cf. Bernard-Henri Lévy, *L'idéologie française* (Paris: Grasset, 1981) pp. 271–91. It is ironic, historically speaking, that no pamphleteer ever raised the question of that curious and historic U-turn when the members of the Socialist majority met the founder of the Trilateral Commission: 'To mark the Paris meeting of its international brains-trust, the Chase Manhattan Bank held a grand reception at the Opéra on 13 November, attended by the Minister for Foreign Relations, M. Claude Cheysson and the Mayor of Paris, M. Jacques Chirac. The members of the brains-trust, which is chaired by Mr. David Rockefeller and includes Mr. Henry Kissinger were previously received by the President of the Republic, M. François Mitterrand and the Prime Minister, M. Laurent Fabius', *Le Monde*, 16 November 1984.
18. Saint-Robert, op. cit., p. 126.
19. *Le Monde*, 16 October 1980.
20. Cf. Denis Lacorne, 'La politique giscardienne de promotion des exportations ou le colbertisme dans les moyens en vue du libéralisme comme fin', in Samy Cohen and Marie-Claude Smouts (eds), *La Politique extérieure de Valéry Giscard D'Estaing* (Paris: Presses de la F.N.S.P., 1985) pp. 151–72.
21. Interview with Jean Boissonnat, *L'Expansion*, September 1978.
22. Thibau, op. cit., p. 230.
23. Saint-Robert, op. cit., p. 137.
24. Christian Goux, 'Un échec souhaité', *Le Monde*, 24 August 1979.
25. Georges Marchais, *L'Espoir au présent* (Paris: Editions Sociales, 1980) pp. 152 and 172.
26. Christian Goux and Jean-François Landeau, *Le péril américain* (Paris: Calmann-Lévy, 1971) pp. 40–1.
27. Philippe Herzog, 'Vouloir rompre pour changer', *Le Monde*, 16 December 1977.
28. Thibau, *La France colonisée*, op. cit.
29. Christian Goux and Jean-François Landeau, op. cit., pp. 35–43.
30. Ibid., p. 10.
31. Jean-Marcel Jeanneney, *Pour un nouveau protectionnisme*, (Paris: Seuil, 1978) pp. 10, 62–74, 122.
32. Ibid., p. 85.
33. Michel Debré, *Lettre ouverte aux Français sur la reconquête de la France*

34. (Paris: Albin Michel, 1980) pp. 81 and 74 respectively.
35. Saint-Robert, op. cit.
35. M. Jobert, op. cit., p. 99.
36. Cf. 'Le compromis géographique', 10th CERES symposium, *Repères*, June 1976, No. 33, p. 46 and 'L'indépendance pour quoi faire?' *Repères*, December 1976, No. 38, pp. 16–33
37. *Repères*, June 1976, pp. 52–3.
38. *La Nouvelle Revue socialiste*, June 1977, No. 27 (special issue on the Nantes congress) p. 74.
39. Paul Boccara *et al.*, *Changer l'économie: trois clés et un calendrier* (Paris: Editions Sociales, 1977); Philippe Herzog, 'Vouloir rompre pour changer', *Le Monde*, 16 December 1977.
40. Philippe Herzog, *L'économie à bras-le-corps* (Paris: Editions Sociales, 1982) pp. 297 and 298 respectively.
41. The reference here is to the article by Stéphane Courtois, 'Le P.C.F., l'économie et la révolution', in *L'Express*, 27 May 1983, pp. 144–53.
42. Anicet le Pors, op. cit., pp. 187–8.
43. Ibid., pp. 94–5.
44. Jacques Attali *et al.*, *L'opinion européenne face aux multinationales* (Paris: Editions d'Organisation, 1977) pp. 60, 47 and 69 respectively.
45. C. Stoffaës, *La Grande Menace industrielle* (Paris: Calmann-Lévy, 1978) p. 741.
46. Jean-Marie Benoist, *Pavane pour une Europe défunte* (Paris: Hallier, 1976) p. 17 and Philippe de Saint-Robert, op. cit., p. 130 respectively.
47. *L'espoir au présent*, op. cit., p. 159.
48. *Chroniques du Midi Libre*, op. cit., pp. 53 and 51 respectively.
49. Alain de Benoist, *Vu de droite, Anthologie critique des idées contemporaines* (Paris: Copernic, 1979) p. 25 and Henri Gobard, 'Les Gallo-Ricains sont parmi nous', *Eléments*, No. 23, September 1977 respectively.
50. *Pavane pour une Europe défunte*, op. cit., p. 88.
51. Michel Jobert, op. cit., p. 52 and Jack Lang, speech in Mexico City, 27 July 1982, Jean-Marie Benoist op. cit., p. 144 and A. le Pors, op. cit., pp. 201–2 respectively.
52. Jean-Marie Benoist, ibid., p. 100. The example used here was *Concorde* which is compared to 'those towers which the aristocracy of San Geminiano had built in the *quattrocento*, each one bigger than the last and serving no useful purpose save manifesting the importance of luxury'. In a reaction to this 'rejection of economics which is blossoming into a "literary imbecility"', Raymond Aron adds: 'It is quite in order to admire aristocrats who spend regardless, it is rather more dubious to admire administrators who fail to budget carefully as they are duty-bound to, and mistake a technical exploit for commercial success. Without the support of the tax-payer *Concord* would never take to the air. This is nothing to be proud of'. Raymond Aron, *Mémoires* (Paris: Julliard, 1983) p. 679.
53. Secrétariat études et recherches: 'L'économie organique', *Eléments*, No. 28–29, March 1979. This text is included in Pierre Vial, *Pour une renaissance culturelle* (Paris: Copernic, 1979) pp. 54–66.

11
The Limits of the American Model
Christian Stoffaës

It strikes me that since the Left came to power in 1981, three new factors have appeared which have done much to transform the nature of the postwar debate about the United States. The first was the deepening of the 'world economic crisis'. The second has been 'the Mitterrand experience', and in particular the revision of the Socialist government's economic policies at the end of its first two years in office. The third factor was the implementation of the Reagan administration's programme. As Denis Lacorne suggests elsewhere in this book, the crisis of the 1970s was one of world inflation, the two oil crises, and the shake-up of the world monetary system. Each of these phenomena served to strengthen anti-Americanism, in so far as there was a tendency to make the United States the scapegoat of the crisis. While no one would attribute the world's economic disorders over the past 15 years to disorder in the US economy, it must be said that there has been a trend in this direction for some years now – particularly since the beginning of the 1980s.

To be more precise, the question arises whether the world economic crisis does not actually reflect a decline in US economic power. Undoubtedly this phenomenon has been obscured by the propaganda effect of the Reagan administration's rhetoric, with its emphasis on the rebirth of the United States ('America is back'). But a glance at international economic indicators is enough to show that US economic power has been falling not just in relative terms, but also in absolute terms. The US economy is facing severe competition not only internationally, but even on domestic markets. The challenge comes from Third World – mostly Far Eastern – countries, in several traditional sectors. Over the past decade, the US textile industry has halved its work-force, while American footwear manufacturers have cut theirs by two thirds.

In the past dozen or so years, Japanese competition has eclipsed US consumer electronics and seriously destabilised the automotive and steel industries. Germany is challenging the United States in chemicals and engineering, and has actually overtaken it in some instances. There are even signs of competition in the high-tech sectors where US supremacy was thought to be unchallenged, such as France's bid in aeronautics, space research, arms and the nuclear industry, while Japan, which currently rivals the USA in electronics components, may well take the lead in computers and telecommunications in the near future. The USA has either lost its lead or been overtaken in many industries, from the most traditional to the most modern. The decline in its international competitiveness can be seen above all in the size of the American foreign trade deficit which topped $150 billion in 1984. At all events – although my conclusions may be open to challenge, and the causes of the situation may be regarded not as structural but as inherent in the economic climate – it is nonetheless apparent that a United States which nowadays accounts for only one quarter of the world's GNP against roughly half at the end of World War II (a period when it played the role of laboratory and factory to the entire world) can no longer lay claim to the leadership it once exercised, even if this inescapable fact has been concealed by the dollar's powerful recovery in the early 1980s. It would seem that the latter phenomenon is more a result of the serious financial measures which are finally being taken to curb inflation and the rise in interest rates, than of any industrial upswing.

In other words, one of the main reasons for the decline in anti-Americanism could well be the very fact that the United States is far less the economic superpower and dominant model that it once was. Consequently it does not arouse envy to the same degree. Moreover, a new model has emerged to rival it in the recent period – that of Japan.

Japan's economic rise is no recent phenomenon, however. It started in 1920 and resumed in 1960 when the country had overcome its wartime difficulties. A whole succession of explanations has been trotted out to account for Japan's success. It has been claimed that Japan bent the rules of free trade; that it under-paid its workforce; that it was no more than a lackey of American imperialism; that it was an imitator or a US satellite.

France has suffered from inferiority complexes about the American model since well before World War II. Although the French still believed France to be the model for the whole world which it had been in the seventeenth century thanks to its geo-political power, and remained so in the nineteenth century thanks to the influence of the French Revolution, nonetheless they saw themselves being relentlessly overtaken by the prodigious nation across the Atlantic. After refusing for years to face up to the reality, French public opinion started taking the American challenge seriously in the 1950s and 1960s, along with the other West European countries. It started to adopt the American way of life, American technology and the American model of organisation, particularly *'le management'* and even American cultural models – reflected in a new style of magazines, television, cinema, jeans, hamburgers and so forth. But at the same time, there was a sense in which the French detested what they were forced to revere. Ever since, France – and it was not alone in this – started to cast its gaze in the direction of the Far East. The 'look East' policy started to take over from the 'one best way' strategy of the postwar years. The French started to take an interest in the MITI model, international trading companies, technological planning, and 'quality circles', all of which allowed the Japanese to ride the crisis with remarkable success. It is astonishing that, when looked at more closely, the organisational principles of Japanese industry are almost the contrary of those followed in America: lifelong job security, no rapid turnover of Labour; promotion by seniority, not merit; the primacy of production and quality control, and the supremacy of the engineer as opposed to the rule of the professional executive. Moreover, relations between banks and industry, and the state and industry are also the diametrical opposite of the American model.

Take, for instance, the fact that there are 20 times more lawyers per inhabitant in the United States than in Japan. And even though the organisation of society in Japan still bears the marks of outmoded, feudal practices inherited from a none-too-distant mediaeval period, that country has nevertheless come up with a model which is at the leading edge of economic efficiency and modernity. It is a model which contradicts the lessons of the American experience and consequently extenuates the latter's power of attraction/repulsion. This should provide food for thought! Similarly, the flood of dollars on world markets used to be interpreted in the 1960s and 1970s – such as by leading Gaullist economic theorist Jacques Rueff – as a sign of US economic imperialism. Nowadays, however – and above all since the end of the 1970s – the question is rather whether, on the contrary, the surplus of dollars is not actually a symptom of decline in US economic might, in the sense that the dollars were the result of the inflation which helped to sap America's economic dynamism. Are they not in reality a sign of weakness, the remnants of a spent force: the power to print the world's money?

The second factor which has altered the nature of the debate about anti-Americanism has been the experience of left-wing government. As we have seen, during the 1970s, anti-Americanism was an important issue in the political debate between the Right in power and the Left in opposition. From 1983 onwards, the Left clearly carried out a thoroughgoing *aggiornamento* of its economic policies. It had come to power in 1981 on a protectionist platform of breaking with capitalism and the market economy, reconquering the domestic market, creating industrial networks, and launching a massive programme of nationalisations. What the Left was proposing, in fact, was to jettison the terms of the modernism-versus-protectionism debate. It was going to achieve modernism via protectionism, in other words to overthrow the accepted idea that modernism was synonymous with free trade. Task No. 1, therefore: the reconquest of the domestic market! The needs of industry – regarded as sacred and redemptive – were to be paramount. This meant priority to technology and research funding. The crisis could be beaten by a combination of correct industrial policy, nationalisations and protectionism. The Left was going to create an industrial model that would be Socialist and French at the same time. In the event, this policy was totally revised. The policy changes announced in 1982, 1983 and 1984, resulted in economic and industrial policies diametrically opposed to what had been lauded at the outset. Such a revision of its economic policy was no easy task for the Left to accomplish. It was seen as a disavowal of left-wing principles and provoked major debates, leading to the departure of the Communists and open conflict with the Communist-led unions in the CGT.

For a while, there was hesitation about the basic priorities of the new economic policy. My impression is that this policy was revised largely in terms of foreign policy options, particularly the swing to European and North Atlantic solidarity. The only alternative to a change of course in economic policy would have been a 'competitive' (that is, massive) devaluation of the Franc coupled with protectionist measures and a boost to industry within the country's frontiers. In other words, it would have been a Brazilian solution, which could have turned into the Soviet model. Thus, there is a sense in which the Left renounced its original economic options out of a relative pro-Americanism which was seen as the corollary of its anti-Soviet foreign policies.

The pursuit of an escapist policy of economic recovery and industrial *dirigisme* proved incompatible with France's international commitments. This was the decisive factor in the change of economic policy. The revision had all sorts of consequences, whose long-term implications have yet to be gauged.

There are two possible assessments of the ideological somersault performed by the left-wing government. The first is that the policy change has profoundly disillusioned its electorate, weakened the unions and split the Left, thereby presaging electoral disaster. The second view is that it finally started France along the path of modernity by paving the way for a new consensus in favour of an open economy and industrial modernisation. The future alone will tell which of these interpretations is correct.

The third element of change in the economic debate is the Reagan experience. During the 1970s, and particularly under the Carter administration, the United States started to become aware of its economic decline. It also realised that is geo-political influence was dwindling compared with that of the Third World (Iran and OPEC), particularly in the face of Soviet rearmament. I believe that it was the Americans' feeling of economic decline that brought to power the Reagan administration, which broke with 50 years of development since the New Deal by advancing the idea that America had to become an imperial power once more. It had to win back global respect and credibility and restore its economy by renouncing Keynesianism and welfare economics and getting back to its roots. Reaganism was the model of renewal by a return to the 'good old' American cultural values of 'work, save and invest'. This was incidentally far more than a revolution in economic thinking: it was a veritable ideological and cultural revolution. The Reagan experience has altered the debate in France, because Reaganism now has wide support, even on the Left. In particular, there is the wave of 'neo-liberalism' which the Left now espouses, with the rehabilitation of the market, the profit-motive, enterprise, deregulation ... in short, all the ideas that currently dominate the agenda.

Among conservatives, overt admiration for the American model is now the rule. Reagan's policies have even become an explicit point of reference in their political programmes. These now include action against inflation, combined with liberalisation and deregulation; tax-cuts; less public spending, and so on. What we have now is an American macro-economic model: the supply economy and Reaganomics being specifically advanced as ways of beating the crisis. On the Left, the centre of economic debate has shifted from anti-Americanism to 'industrial policy', with America no longer the chief scapegoat. Industrial policy has undoubtedly become an issue which has split the French Left from top to bottom. Having been the lynch-pin of the Communist/Socialist *Union de la Gauche*, industrial policy was what caused it to collapse. It was largely over industrial issues that the Communists quit the government – officially, at least. In all events, it has now become an internal debate for the Socialists, and there is less of a tendency to treat Reaganomics as the bogeyman.

There are no doubt a number of ardent partisans of the Japanese industrial model on the French Left. However, there are also many left-wing critics of such facets of its disciplinarian ethos as the regimentation of the work-force, the stifling of intellectual debate. There is much more interest in what is happening across the Pacific, such as the Silicon Valley industrial model, Pittsburgh's industrial reconversion through robotics, and the like.

The Reagan experiment will undoubtedly provoke a reaction, especially if it fails and leads to the sudden collapse of the dollar and financial crash that some predict. Nonetheless, the first two factors I cited – the deepening of the crisis and the experience of left-wing government – are more likely to attenuate future anti-Americanism. However, if the Reagan experiment does engender a movement as deep-rooted and lasting as the New Deal, which profoundly altered American policies for half a century, then it is possible that we shall see a revival of anti-Americanism, particularly if the USA starts being accused of its 'splendid isolationism' or of indifference to the crises it provokes elsewhere.

Part IV

The Rhetoric and Reality of Anti-Americanism in Foreign Politics

12

French Anti-Americanism under the Fourth Republic and the Gaullist Solution

Michael M. Harrison

My basic thesis is indeed a simple one, though I hope not simplistic. It is that in the twentieth century French anti-Americanism, based on a mixture of cultural, economic, political and military factors, has been most intensely felt at times of enhanced French dependence on, even subordination to, the United States in the international arena. This phenomenon is, therefore, essentially a response to France's decline as a world and European power: it is a reaction to the loss of independence and autonomy of decision that produced a growing sense of frustration, rancour and hostility to foes and friends alike. The United States was the most natural object of French hostility and resentment, because the decline of France and Europe was accompanied by the rise of the United States – by the increasing influence of American cultural values, economic power and political military leverage – to the point where the United States had to be counted on to save France in one war, liberate it in another, until finally France (like all Western Europe) had to succumb to becoming a formal part of the American protectorate after 1947. This dependence was strongest and most resented during the period of the Cold War – and was often humiliating and costly in real terms, so that anti-Americanism in France reached its height during the 1950s.

The second part of my thesis is that although General Charles de Gaulle and Gaullism shared many of the cultural prejudices of French Americanophobia, de Gaulle's policies and accomplishments under the Fifth Republic actually put an end to endemic, or structural anti-Americanism in France based on a perception of decline and subordination. This is because de Gaulle offered France a successful mixture of reality and myth organised around the concept of independence and based on policies that minimised perceived dependence on the United States. Thus, Gaullism represented a kind of cure-all for the many ills of the Fourth Republic, of which anti-Americanism was one of the most prominent. And, after de Gaulle, France has been able to confront problems it has with the United States without recourse to pathological anti-Americanism.

I might add that because of de Gaulle, Americans have also been cured of their own anti-French biases, and can assess French affairs and French-US problems without the preconception of France as a country in decay and decline, essentially unreliable on all important matters. Just as de Gaulle made the French respect themselves, he also made France a country more respected abroad, even by a naturally arrogant superpower.

It is clear that the anti-Americanism we find in France during the 1950s represents only the most extreme version of attitudes, prejudices and policies – rational and irrational – that developed during the interwar period, when France first came into sustained and problematic contact with the United States on all levels – cultural, economic and political. For, as Jean-Baptiste Duroselle and others have noted, it was during the conflicts of the 1920s and 1930s that the dual terms of anti-American attitudes were established. There was, on the one hand, the broad anti-Americanism of a cultural and ideological nature, which rejected the values and institutions represented by 'Américanisme', often a French synonym for a modernised society and materialistic economy in which traditional French values were less esteemed within France and less valued as a source of status, prestige and power abroad. French intellectuals and political leaders were preoccupied by the spectre of national and European decline during the interwar period, and were just as fearful of the growing prospect that a decaying European civilisation would be overwhelmed by the financial and political might of the United States carrying the germs of an alien and unattractive civilisation.

The second, and more policy-specific kind of anti-Americanism, is related to the first. France's cultural malaise and its anti-American aspects found a natural counterpart in resentment over national political and economic dependence on both the Anglo-

Saxon powers, but especially the United States – so that intellectuals as well as practitioners of foreign affairs such as André Tardieu lamented the consequences of a subordination to American policy aims and asserted that France should try to stand up to American policies rather than succumb in weakness and indecision. The cultural roots of Gaullism are certainly to be found in such ideas proposing a resistance to growing American power that circulated in France before the war and were only intensified after it.

Turning to the Fourth Republic's troubled relations with the United States, an initial observation is that its embrace of an ostensibly pro-American stand after 1947 was made only reluctantly. This move was imbued with so many contradictory and unrealistic expectations about what could be gained from the American connection that the experience was bound to lead to frustration and failure, thereby intensifying French anti-Americanism rather than assuaging it. We know that both de Gaulle and the tripartite governments of the early Fourth Republic preferred a policy of neutrality in the Soviet-American conflict, and, in fact, wanted France to serve as a kind of interlocutor between two camps. 'Neither Ford nor Lenin', as the Comte de Fels once put it. And, when forced to choose the American-led West, the Fourth Republic managed to adapt to unpleasant reality only by creating an outrageous package of expectations about what the US would bring to France. Other chapters of this book deal more specifically with foreign policy failures and their effects on French attitudes towards the United States, but I want to note that Fourth Republic leaders expected to use the Atlantic Alliance and other ties to the US as devices for securing vast quantities of American economic and military aid, for securing an absolute guarantee against the Soviet military threat, for ensuring that Germany remain subordinate to France in Western Europe, and for help in shoring up France's threatened colonial empire. In general, the Fourth Republic expected to recover a kind of status, security and even independence that France had not enjoyed at any time in the twentieth century. It was bound to be disillusioned because a United States that dismissed its Gallic ally as a second-rate and essentially unreliable partner was not about to meet any of these demands – or could not have met them because, for example, absolute security is not available through alliances in this nuclear age.

The Fourth Republic experienced growing difficulties in meeting its foreign policy expectations largely because the goals were beyond France's means, and because the political system of the Fourth Republic was unable to articulate and pursue a coherent set of foreign policy aims. In an immobilist regime where nearly everyone shares responsibility for such a state of affairs, there is a tendency to search for scapegoats – and the natural scapegoat in this case was the United States and the American political connection. The principal anti-American political movement that sprung up in France around 1950 was one that proposed ending or drastically diluting the American connection essentially by opting out of the Cold War and adopting a posture of neutralism in this conflict. There was a variety of positions represented in this heterogeneous movement, ranging from the overtly pro-Russian and not really neutralist stand of the Communists to the more benign attitude of Etienne Gilson and the Catholic left (often published in *Esprit*) which (like de Gaulle in the 1960s) feared American bellicosity, tended to underrate the Soviet menace, and went so far as to advocate benevolent neutrality in the Cold War, partly on the grounds that a neutral France would still benefit from American protection because of geography.

Hubert Beuve-Méry, writing under the pseudonym Sirius in *Le Monde*, did much to popularise the idea that France should side with neither the United States nor the Soviet Union. Beuve-Méry often attacked American moral qualities as reprehensible from a French point of view, and neutralists on the left shared the hope that by opting out of the bi-polar political-military conflict France could find a socio-economic 'third way' between Soviet Communism and American capitalism. The newspaper *Combat* and its editor, Claude Bourdet, launched this campaign early in 1950 and were responsible for reviving the kind of anti-Americanism in France that condemned both the American economy and political system as de-humanising and unable to foster genuine social progress. Franklin Roosevelt's New Deal had partly disarmed critics in previous years, but during the Cold War resentment over the expanding global power of American capitalism renewed fears of American materialism, while McCarthyism and the Rosenberg trial and execution were useful instruments in attacking American liberal democracy both as an inappropriate model and as a system that condemned American leadership of the West as far as France was concerned.

This anti-American neutralism was linked intellectually and politically to a more successful political idea of the Fourth Republic – the 'European idea' or, more specifically, the version of it that proposed a united Europe as a way of escaping both the menace in the East and the polarised reaction in the West which subordinated France and Europe to the United States. This was not the perspective of France's leading 'European' of the period, Jean Monnet, whose prescription for a united Europe was so firmly grounded in the ideal of an integrated Atlantic partnership that he was the natural favourite of Atlanticists and Americanophiles everywhere. But many in France on both sides of the political spectrum – de Gaulle was only the most prominent and outspoken on this subject – rejected Monnet's pro-Americanism and his integrationist ideology in favour of an independent third force in world affairs, subject to neither superpower. For those on the right in France, American support of the fantastic European Defence Community (EDC) scheme confirmed that Monnet's integrated Europe was only a device to perpetuate French dependence – in fact, a kind of double dependence to both the United States and a resurgent Germany. The EDC scheme managed to incite both anti-Americanism and anti-Germanism in an atmosphere of bitterness that marked an important stage in the postwar deterioration of French-American relations.

The kind of French anti-American nationalism stirred up by the EDC debate reached its apogee in the colonialist conflicts between France and America that escalated during the Algerian war and culminated in a profoundly anti-American atmosphere accompanying the demise of the Fourth Republic which brought France's most self-assured and realistic critic of the United States to power – General de Gaulle. France's experience in involving the United States in the Indochina War had taught many Frenchmen that the Washington connection was a double-edged sword, since America was anti-colonialist in wanting to end France's overseas empire, but also imperialist in asserting an indirect financial, political and military control in the Third World at the expense of European powers. Not always an astute observer of public affairs, President Vincent Auriol was nevertheless correct in asserting about Indochina that 'They give us money and we pay with parts of our independence'. Auriol, by the way, certainly qualifies as a leading anti-American of the period, since his view was that 'the Americans are naïve, ignorant and understand nothing'.

France's Algerian trauma inspired an orgy of French anti-Americanism on both left and right, especially after the national humiliation suffered in the Suez affair as a result of American pressure that brought that other Anglo-Saxon power to its knees as well. The Algerian war brought out resentments against the United States from all parts of the French political spectrum, since prominent anti-Americans were found among the Socialists (Lacoste), in the MRP (Bidault), and of course among the Gaullists. The ultra-right-wing Gaullist polemicist Jacques Soustelle may best illustrate the extreme anti-American attitude of the period, since his own virulent mixture of French nationalism, colonialism and hypocrisy managed to condemn American imperialists in Guatemala, claim that aggressive American capitalism was trying to push France out of the Third World, and attack an Atlantic Alliance which was 'rotten with American anti-colonialism'.

Resentment over perceived American efforts to undermine France's position in Algeria was so widespread in leading political, military and intellectual circles that the prospect of settling the Soviet dispute with Tunisia according to the recommendations of an Anglo-American commission (involving the notorious Robert Murphy) helped bring down the government of Félix Gaillard. It is perhaps only a slight exaggeration to claim that the events leading up to the '13 May' and the collapse of the Fourth Republic virtually constituted an anti-American revolt on the part of the French, as they desperately grappled for a national solution rather than one imposed by the Western superpower.

In his press conference of May 18 1958, de Gaulle noted that he, indeed, represented an alternative to the outside world – namely, the United States imposing foreign solutions on a French problem. Thus, in turning to de Gaulle in 1958, France was in an indirect way expressing a profound rejection of the United States and a world in which American power seemed to undermine the national interests of a country like France. At the time, and for much of the following decade, de Gaulle seemed to many in both France and the United States to represent the most obstinate and virulent kind of French anti-Americanism, as conflicts between the two countries escalated into a comprehensive French challenge to the American vision of the Atlantic partnership and, indeed, a world order essentially shaped by American power, interests and values. But can de Gaulle's ideals and policies, really be termed 'anti-

American' in any genuine and profound sense, and are they really similar to the kind of anti-Americanism that took root in the Third Republic and flourished at the end of the Fourth? It seems to me, rather, that de Gaulle was not really much of an anti-American at all and, instead, he pursued policies that in the long run actually cured France of its Americanophobia, just as they helped rid Americans of a deprecating view of France that constituted the American counterpart to French antagonism towards the United States.

Part of de Gaulle's critical stance towards the United States can be traced to sentiments he shared with the Right and Left in France about the dangers of Europe's gradual submission to American cultural, economic and linguistic power at the expense of indigenous continental national identities. De Gaulle's memoirs and his policies after 1958 certainly illustrate his rejection of a certain kind of American or Anglo-Saxon materialist culture and economic system in favour of an idealised French-European system in which human values would take a certain precedence. As de Gaulle once explained to an Arab, he and France hoped to offer the world a model of how to 'build an industrial civilisation which is not derived from the American model and in which man will serve as an end, not a means ...' A certain natural pride in the French language and customs against the onslaught of Anglo-Saxon civilisation led him to stress the defence of the French language and identity around the world, as in the famous incident at Quebec.

De Gaulle also asserted and fostered the development of an independent French and European economic and technological capability as an instrument to defend against American power in this domain. But it is important to note that, unlike many on the right and left who resisted Americanisation because they feared modernisation, de Gaulle was a ruthless moderniser who wanted to confront American economic power on its own terms by fostering the independent development of the French and European industrial economy. Thus, De Gaulle refused to accept the idea that France and Europe were condemned to decline, second-rate status, or to absorption within an Americanised Western sphere dominated by the United States.

The sources of de Gaulle's ideas about the United States and French-American relations came partly from his personal experiences during the war, and partly from his well-known classical ideals of nationalism, independence and power politics as the basis of international relations. The wartime experiences with Roosevelt and others are too familiar to recount in detail. Essentially, de Gaulle learned that Americans, like FDR, had 'a will to power *which* cloaked itself in idealism', and he found out through bitter experience that American insensitivity could lead Washington to attempt to take over France, directly or indirectly, and perhaps even dismember it if possible. The only solution for a country in this situation was to eschew logic and sentiment in favour of power politics, because 'what matters is what one takes and what one can hold on to'. 'France', he concluded in a famous passage of his war memoirs, 'must count only on herself'. It must be stressed that, to de Gaulle, America's tendency towards domination and expansion were not peculiar to that country, but were an inherent characteristic of state behaviour in an international system that happened to throw the United States to the top of the heap in the postwar world.

The basis of de Gaulle's attitudes and policies towards the United States was not essentially determined by a rejection of American values as such, but by a perspective which asserted that France and Europe should not be dependent on either the United States or the Soviet Union. His policies did not depend on a moral or social critique of the United States, as in the case of anti-Americans on the Left and extreme Right in France. De Gaulle had mixed views about Americans like any sensible person – he once said 'The Americans are strong, courageous and — [*expletive*] (but after all, he made worse statements about his own people, the French). But his policies were based on the more simple, yet profound and unsettling idea that France had very different interests than the United States. Thus, from the Gaullist perspective, the emotional, ideological, neurotic and self-deprecating sources of previous French anti-Americanism were as irrelevant as they were wrong, since both France and Europe should determine relations with the United States simply in terms of interests and power politics – which called for neither pro- nor anti-Americanism, but a realistic, carefully controlled relationship of mutual independence and respect.

It was not a specifically American arrogance or will to dominate that de Gaulle identified as a problem for France, Europe and global stability; it was the natural temptation of any powerful state to take advantage of the weakness of dependents that made de

Gaulle such a firm opponent of the United States during the 1960s. The great Gaullist-American conflicts of the period were not intrinsic to the United States itself, but simply a matter of course in an international system in which weak states that somehow find a voice to resist and assert themselves are bound to clash with a strong state. There is nothing very anti-American in this point of view or the policies that follow from it, merely a realistic judgement that a reviving France was bound to challenge the United States. As de Gaulle put it at one press conference, 'the fact that we have resumed independence of judgement and action regarding all problems seems at times to displease a state which might believe that because of its power it is invested with a supreme and universal responsibility . . .'

De Gaulle's formulas for national self-reliance in the face of American power were based on his well-known notions of grandeur and independence – essentially foundations for an assured and activist France to recover its economic, political and military independence and influence in a world where activism was the only guarantee against national decay and an overconfident, overbearing American power that threatened the identity and integrity of European states. This was less anti-American than it was pro-French and pro-European, as de Gaulle astutely (in Alfred Grosser's words) tried to 'replace the nationalism of humiliation by a nationalism of pride'. Rather than the negative and self-defeating image of both France and the United States typical of traditional French anti-Americanism, de Gaulle asserted a positive image of national revival that could restore France's integrity and self-respect, and might even alter the European and international systems. De Gaulle flattered the French by enlisting them in a grand cause that had both a self-serving national dimension and the kind of universal mission that appealed to their national culture.

Practical judgements about de Gaulle's foreign policy accomplishments can be left aside, since that is not the issue here. De Gaulle may not have changed the shape of the East-West system, the Atlantic order, or international policies as such – history's judgements are not yet in, I believe. But he certainly undertook a dramatic and successful cure of France's view of itself and its major partners by creating a new and successful constitutional order, intensifying the process of industrial and technological modernisation, and imposing an independent foreign and defence policy model that was finally accepted at home as well as abroad. De Gaulle announced the end of France's decline, and cleverly tailored French aspirations to the country's means while disguising this retrenchment with an audacious, globalist, and ostensibly anti-American foreign policy. He replaced the myth of American responsibility for French decay with a new, inspired, positive image – part myth and part reality – of an independent and successful France that no longer needed foreign scapegoats.

We have many images of de Gaulle's role in French and Western history. In the case of French anti-Americanism, perhaps we should add another one of de Gaulle the expert psychologist who cured France of pathological anti-Americanism, so that post-Gaullist France can now have 'normal' relations with the United States based on reasonable judgements (or misjudgements) about coincidence or conflicts of interest. That is why, today, despite intellectual vogues here and there, France is probably neither pro- nor anti-American in any profound sense, but faces the always difficult task of working out a mature relationship with the United States based on realistic assessments of interests while looking inside rather than outside for the sources and solutions to many, perhaps most, of its own problems.

13

Unruly France

Alfred Grosser

This topic merits a book all to itself. What other subject has so utterly preoccupied governments, political parties and newspapers whenever the question of France's foreign relations and international role has been on the agenda? Franco-American relations have always been a story of tension and harmony. Suffice it to recall de Gaulle's resentment of a Roosevelt who had engaged in dealings with Vichy while remaining enormously popular with the French, or the more recent difficulties which François Mitterrand – the most 'Atlanticist' President of the Fifth Republic – has had with Ronald Reagan's passion for SDI and agricultural free-trade. And the image of the United States in France has always been as important a political factor in determining French conduct as American operations in Africa or the pressure of the dollar on the franc.

The abruptly changing political climate certainly complicates analysis of this phenomenon. If one takes the last two decades, for example, it is evident that the preservation of national independence was a major issue in the European elections of 1979. Jacques Chirac even used to accuse Giscard D'Estaing of heading 'a foreigners' party' while the Communist Party claimed that François Mitterrand wanted an Americanised Europe. In the run-up to the presidential election, the Socialists came out very strongly against American imperialism. The victorious left-wing at the Socialist Party's congress in Metz believed that it had put the kibosh on the party's 'American left' – as it dubbed those around Michel Rocard. However, while the Socialists' general election victory led to a certain coolness towards the American model, the need was also felt to be rather warmer about alliance with the United States, if for no other reason than to show, after the formation of the second Maurois government, that François Mitterrand's foreign policy was not influenced by his four Communist ministers. Furthermore, the West German peace movement and a large part of the German Social-Democratic Party turned out to have adopted most of the French Socialists' anti-American arguments of the pre-1981 period, but had placed quite a different construction on them, one that was quite unacceptable to the Socialist Party now that it was the President's loyal supporter. All such arguments were therefore out of favour, given that the failure of the government's economic policies and the rise of unemployment in France (concomitant with a fall in the number of jobless in the USA) made the American model rather more attractive to the opposition parties. But such enthusiasm with America was not confined to them: on a visit to Silicon Valley, the Socialist President was to sing the praises of private enterprise, forgetting that without the Pentagon's public money, those particular technological developments would have been rather less prodigious.

The advantage of writing in the late 1980s is that there is not so much of a need to do battle with three myths of unequal importance and substance. In France, the commemoration of the 40th anniversary of Yalta had the effect of virtually putting paid to one myth (at a time when, in Germany, the growth of anti-Americanism has revived it). The emergent consensus is that there was no global carve-up; the Crimean conference was not a cover for growing expansionist designs on the part of America. Though not invited, France had not been sold out: on the contrary this country was the chief beneficiary of Yalta, having been accorded equal rights as one of the four joint custodians of German sovereignty. Yet how heavily that myth used to weigh on the political climate here, particularly after the invasion of Czechoslovakia in 1968, an action perceived by de Gaulle as a logical outcome of Yalta!

Another mythical war-horse to have bitten the dust is the notion, cherished by Communists and left-wing intellectuals, that the Marshall Plan allowed America to dominate the French economy. It has not yet breathed its last, however. For one thing, there is still a reluctance to accept the idea that American aid has attained its goal of creating a Europe just strong enough to rival the United States itself, which (until its change of heart in 1969–71) was prepared to make an economic sacrifice in order to obtain the political advantage of a stable Europe. Furthermore, France – official and unofficial alike – prefers to remember La Fayette rather than Marshall: in both 1976 and 1977 there were bicentenary celebrations to commemorate French assistance to the birth of the United States, while the 30th anniversary of American aid to the rebirth of France went largely ignored.

And ever since the President started exalting the Atlantic alliance, a third myth has been discarded. I refer to the theory that America forced the Europeans to subscribe to the Atlantic Treaty, whereas in point of fact the five signatories of the Brussels Treaty of 1948 were only too relieved when they managed to get the United States to subscribe, the following spring, to a document far less binding than the one the Americans would have liked to see.

A rather more complex and less categorical issue is the acquiescence of the Fourth Republic in American objectives. The fact that France was receiving outside assistance did not oblige the governments of those days to put up with the various kinds of interference in the country's internal affairs, nor to kowtow in the way they did, particularly when seeking financial and military support for French operations in Indochina. Nonetheless, it was Anthony Eden and not Guy Mollet who was the first to bow to Eisenhower's pressure for an end to the Suez expedition: a venture undertaken against America's wishes. And it is fair to say that when it came to decolonisation or Europe, French policies were not always quite what America would have wished them to be! In Indochina France started waging what the United States considered a colonial war. It ended in 1954 at a time when the Americans wanted to see the war continue as an anti-Communist crusade. In response to America's insistence that West Germany should join NATO, French creative genius came up with the European Defence Community (EDC) and made such a good job of convincing John Foster Dulles of its excellence as an invention that it was against America's wishes that the National Assembly buried the Treaty, despite the fact that this meant West German membership of NATO. And as for Algeria, it took de Gaulle's return to power to bring about the policy of self-determination so long demanded by the United States.

Franco-American friction over decolonisation would never have been so marked had it not been for two stumbling blocks. The first of them related solely to Indochina. It so happened that Ho Chi Minh was the only major nationalist leader also to have been a leading member of the Communist International as well. It was no doubt inevitable that between 1945 and 1975 he was either regarded primarily as someone who could ensure his people's liberation, or primarily as the person who had brought about, or would bring about, their enslavement. There was hardly any chance that these perceptions of him would prevail simultaneously in both France and America. The unilateralist sentiments voiced by General de Gaulle at Phnom Penh in 1966 were the counterpart to Dulles' unilateralism of 1953–54.

The second stumbling block relates to America, and Roosevelt's anti-colonial reasoning was a perfect example of it. Basing himself on the American War of Independence, in which internal freedom went hand in hand with external sovereignty, he argued that the same two factors should necessarily figure in the decolonisation process. It is debatable, however, whether 1776 was really a struggle for liberation from a colonial power. As far as the Algerian War was concerned, the George Washington of the piece was not Ben Bella, but General Salan fighting against the seat of the Empire in the name of the colonists.

General de Gaulle might be said to have wrong-footed the previous regime in more ways than one with respect to relations with the United States. The dying Fourth Republic had accumulated an enormous amount of rancour and bitterness against its American ally for supposedly wanting to get the French out of North Africa. As soon as he became President, de Gaulle accorded independence to Algeria and to the French colonies in Black Africa, magnificently substituting in the process the notion of cooperation for that of domination and quickly overcoming the resentment and bitterness of the Algerian defeat. As a result, he restored his compatriots' sense of pride – and their ambition.

However, at the same time, this ambition implied the need for a shift of attitude towards America in terms of France's foreign policy goals. The attitude of the Fourth Republic had not been very different from that of Germany. The great power that needed to be kept constantly in view was the Soviet Union and the threat it posed. Looked at in this way, the United States is seen as a bulwark against the Soviet threat, even if it meant paying a high political price to maintain it. With de Gaulle, the situation was reversed. Naturally, at those moments when the Soviet Union adopted a threatening attitude, it was necessary for France, as a Western power, to behave as a loyal ally of the United States, whether over Berlin or Cuba. But whenever the power of America looked as if it might start outstripping that of the Soviet Union, it was time for France to assert its independence and authority *vis-à-vis* the United States, essentially by using the Soviet Union as a lever to do so.

This was notably the case during his trips to Moscow in December 1944 and in July 1966.

Such an outlook and objectives were by no means shared by Georges Pompidou or Valéry Giscard d'Estaing. Pompidou admittedly had the impression of being treated as more of an equal by Brezhnev than by the Americans, particularly at the time of the Chicago incident, when he was the target of hostile demonstrators. Moreover, at the time of the Afghan crisis, Giscard clearly felt the need to assert his independence *vis-à vis* an unpopular American President. As for François Mitterrand, it was not until the Bonn summit in May 1985 that he felt it necessary for France to go it alone, on the grounds that the critical topics (for example, the French-speaking world and Latin America) were related to an entirely different category of issues.

It was undoubtedly the military dimension of French policies which could be perceived as anti-American. In fact, in most other areas, what was said and what was actually done were two quite different things. There was no such inconsistency, however, about the ultimatum given to the United States which led to the expulsion of American troops and the confiscation of installations. It was not until Giscard's administration that minor compensation was paid for the property confiscated from the American ally. The use of coercion against the US guardian was seen as a way to assert France's independence, even if it did mean that the Americans were obliged to squeeze all their logistical forces onto the territory of the Federal Republic of Germany. There were never any doubts about the need to retain an American protective shield: the expulsion of American units had been possible because the Lord, in his wisdom, had seen fit to place Germany between France and the Soviet Union.

The need for the presence of American troops in Europe was publicly affirmed by Georges Pompidou at a meeting with the US President, although at the same time he reasserted the doctrine that France had to have the final word about the deployment of its forces in the event of conflict and over nuclear deterrence. It was under Giscard's administration in 1974 that the Ottawa Declaration finally brought the doctrinal dispute to an end. On the one hand, the NATO members, including France, asserted that the British and French nuclear weapons played a separate deterrent role and reinforced the alliance's overall deterrence, while on the other, they declared that 'a substantial US military presence' would continue to be an irreplaceable part of the defence of Europe.

Although France did not rejoin NATO's military structures, there was no longer any obstacle to *de facto* co-operation devoid of any anti-American overtones, particularly following the election of François Mitterrand, whose address to the Bundestag in January 1983 was actually to mark a high point in the new spirit of trans-Atlantic solidarity. The justification Mitterrand gave for the basing of Pershing IIs (on German soil, naturally) was not so much the presence of the SS20s but more the need to 'couple' the defence of the United States with that of Europe. As Pershings could be launched against Soviet territory, the counter-threat was necessarily aimed against *American* territory. Consequently, the destiny of the United States would once more be directly linked to the fate of the European countries.

Right up to 1985, French military policies were to give rise to no Franco-American confrontations, only constant difficulties between France and West Germany. However, a new bone of contention emerged in the debate over Ronald Reagan's Strategic Defence Initiative. With Chancellor Kohl appearing to espouse SDI without demur as the head of a German state which showed much more evidence of anti-Americanism than France, it almost felt like being back in the 1960s, when France used to seethe at the way Bonn always carried out Washington's bidding. Since SDI's arrival on the scene, it is not so much prestige that has been at stake as one particular eventuality, albeit one that is still a long way in the future.

It is significant that, in France, the government and the press virtually ignore the initial phase of the 'Star Wars' project, in other words the moment (also well in the future) when US territory would be invulnerable and the Soviet Union would not yet have its own anti-missile curtain. It would be rather like the 1950s when only the United States had the atom bomb to brandish as a threat or counter-threat. As a result, many of the French at the time were extremely wary about possible American aggression or at least concerned about America alone having the final say. There has been a veritable conspiracy of silence about this phase which would be good in terms of European security, but not so favourable in terms of French independence. It is about the subsequent phase – when the USSR will have become invulnerable to missile attack (except from low-flying cruise missiles) and the French defence system will be rendered obsolete overnight – that concern has been aired. A system conceived as being both independent and part of the Western camp – non-involvement as a means of keeping one's distance from the United States – is no longer relevant. Or put another way, it is no longer any time to be asserting a separate role for France, equidistant from the two superpowers. It is easy to gain the impression that anti-Communism and anti-Sovietism are in fact going from strength to strength in France (particularly in comparison with a quite different trend in Federal Germany). This development has put paid to any hopes for the basic aspiration of people like Pompidou's minister of foreign affairs, Michel Jobert. One rarely hears talk these days about the need to combat the Soviet-American 'condominium', though it would still seem to be a desirable aim in the eyes of many political leaders and activists both in the Socialist Party and on the Right.

What one does come across, however, is growing emphasis on two other ideas. The first is the need for Europe to have the technological prowess to challenge both America and Japan. The second is the need for a coherent and principled stand on the notion of an international status quo. If one denies the Soviets' right to do what they like in Poland, can one justify closing one's eyes to the situation in Central America and not equally deny the Americans' right to regard El Salvador and Nicaragua as their own backyard? One is tempted in this connection to look rather more closely not at the – albeit minimal – element of anti-Americanism in projects like the Airbus or *Ariane*, but instead at the vicissitudes in the emotions, attitudes and behaviour aroused by the Latin American issue. As far as Africa is concerned, matters are both simpler and more complicated: simpler because French policy has always been very consistent, and despite appearances to the contrary, very coherent in its underlying objectives. What complicates the issue is that those underlying objectives are contradictory. The fact is that since the end of the Algerian war, France's policy on Africa has comprised two inseparable goals. The first is to maintain Western influence and even, on occasions, to take action in cases where the United States is either unable or unwilling to intervene. And even when such action has not been taken in agreement with the Americans, it has tended to be in their interest. The second is to appear as Africa's spokesman *vis-à-vis* the United States from an extremely moderate pro-Third World stance. All four postwar French Presidents manifestly supported those two objectives, even though they did not constitute the main plank of their African policy.

France's policy on the Middle East has been rather less consistent over the years. De Gaulle maintained that the Six-day War was a direct consequence of the Vietnam War, and hence the responsibility of the United States. First, Pompidou's foreign minister Michel Jobert, and then Valéry Giscard d'Estaing, spent their time criticising American initiatives, from Henry Kissinger's shuttle-diplomacy to the Camp David Agreement. Things eased with the election of François Mitterrand, who had approved the Camp David process when he was leader of the Opposition.

For a whole number of different reasons, most of them to do with internal developments of an economic and ideological order, the anti-American dimension has very much disappeared since the change of government of 1981.

Part V
The US Constitution: Model or Mimic?

14

The Lawyers' Verdict

Marie-France Toinet

There is no way of ignoring the US Constitution. Probably no other constitutional document has given rise to such a wealth of lasting ... international literature.[1] It is indeed astounding to discover just how many studies of American political institutions were published in France at the beginning of the twentieth century, and that a good proportion of them was of a high standard.[2] For my part I found at least two dozen works published on this subject alone between 1900 and 1940.[3]

Clearly there was a fascination for American institutions, as Jacques Lambert pointed out. The question is whether that fascination engendered anti-Americanism, in the sense of an outright rejection or even excessive repudiation of American institutions on false or unjust grounds.

In the particular books I was able to locate, it would be very hard to find any trace of anti-Americanism, if by that one means systematic or unjust – or systematically unjust – anti-American sentiments, least of all in those works dealing with institutions and political society. I was also unable to discover sentiments of that kind in any particular period or in the writings of any one author, though they do occasionally crop up in the writings of the most unlikely people. Emile Boutmy was the writer who most frequently demonstrated such thinking – even though the examples hardly merit the title of anti-Americanism. Boutmy's strictures are more racist than anything else, and his target is not specifically the United States, such as the occasion when he declared: 'Only the Negroes, as an inferior and spineless race – so many docile and timorous cattle – have allowed themselves to be chained to the soil'. Admittedly Negroes were not his only target; he also vented his spleen on whites of inferior race whom he described as the 'reject scum of European society' exported from Europe to the United States.[4]

Was racism specific to that particular generation? Apparently not, to judge by the subsequent generation. Writing about what he described as *'les saturnales de la Reconstruction'*, André Siegfried asked the question: 'Was it not enough for the former masters to have lost everything' Were they to be made to suffer the supreme humiliation of having to accept yesterday's slaves as their rulers? Have you read Wells' *Island of Dr Moreau*, the fantastic story of how animals, transformed into semi-humans by a scientist, then demand the same rights as Man, before finally being slaughtered, every last one of them? If so, you have an idea of the Negro question'.

Anti-semitism was not to be outdone by other forms of racism, by any means: '[Among the Jews] one can find every sort, from aristocratic bankers, formerly of London or Frankfurt, to flea-ridden fugitives from the ghettos of Poland or the Ukraine ... The hirsute immigrant from a far-away ghetto in eastern Europe has been Americanised ... The end-result is anti-semitism, because in spite of the valued assistance of some of the Jews, protestant America behaves on the whole as a self-protecting organism'.[5] But again, that kind of racism does not seem to me to have anything to do with anti-Americanism.

What looks like anti-Americanism can also be put down to French smugness. American chauvinism is matched by European chauvinism, as can be seen in the following example, where the author extolled the merits of two Britons: 'Meanwhile the United States is outstripping all other countries in this respect [namely, that of a synthetic and general political science]. It it not that they have produced any particularly eminent thinkers in this field or any works of especial note. The United States can boast of no author with the breadth of vision of a [Lord] Bryce or a [Harold] Laski ... In Europe ... the scholar ... can count on a rich store of previously acquired precise analytical knowledge which can do much to ensure the depth, significance and value of his synthesis ... And since analysis and synthesis are both operations of reasoning rather than observation, one should not be surprised to find that, in America, both of them lack depth and even transgress against the laws of logic'.[6]

That criticism of Benjamin Akzin's was not entirely groundless. However, it was unjust both because it was overstated and because it went in for comparisons. Edouard Lambert's analysis of the same phenomenon, on the other hand, was both convincing and discriminating – and all the more convincing because of its nuances: 'The *case method* ... was first brought to the attention of French lawyers by M. Nerinex, whose assessment was stringent though clearly hasty and tinged with prejudice, and then by a French doctor who had spent some time at Harvard where he had had the opportunity to grasp the way it worked, and having used it himself spoke of it with rather more enthusiasm than was appropriate for an independent judgement. It certainly merits closer study'.[7]

There has also been a definite temptation to put all the good things in the American tradition down to French influence – and people have easily succumbed to it. For instance, in a study that was otherwise extremely objective and full of admiration for the American legal profession, Roger Pinto declared à propos Oliver Wendell Holmes, 'Does he not owe his perfect sense of moderation, at least partly, to a French influence that is clearly detectable in his conversation, his lectures and his writings?'.[8] And even as he was scorning the error of explaining phenomena in racial terms, he fell into that very trap: 'There is a more modern, though equally mystical notion that those who frame a constitution do not actually have to be prophets, but instead can embody certain racial characteristics. In the opinion of this school of German scholars, the [American] Constitution's virtually miraculous qualities can be ascribed to the Germanic race's particular aptitude for self-government ... Traces of this attitude can still be found, and they partly explain why the American canon so vehemently denies that the French *philosophes* might have had any influence on the drafting of the Constitution'.[9]

'Anti-Americanism' could also be the outcome of a sense of frustration engendered by American self-satisfaction. However, such feelings were never shared unanimously and analysts seldom agreed with each other. There were those who considered American behaviour worthy of imitation – or rather they saw it as a justification of European decisions. Others, however, saw it as proof that there were two different scales of value, since one and the same practice could be regarded as reprehensible here but admirable on the other side of the Atlantic. An illuminating example was the attitude towards the phenomenon variously described as American 'colonialism', 'imperialism' or 'expansionism' (the failure to agree on terminology being symptomatic of the divergences of interpretation). In the view of André Tardieu (who was a great admirer of Theodore Roosevelt), American interventionism was a long overdue sign that the United States had finally realised it was a great power and was beginning to behave accordingly: 'Far more than any of his predecessors, Mr Roosevelt has worked hard to develop America's might ... Wherever American interests have been involved, whether in Puerto Rico, the Philippines, Panama or Cuba, he has reminded his compatriots of their duty to safeguard them ... International competition is growing sharper all the time, as Mr Roosevelt has clearly realised. This is why his political efforts have concentrated on turning the immense corporation of the United States into a premier power'.[10] For Boutmy, on the other hand, 'American imperialism differs from old-fashioned patriotism in two respects: extreme self-importance and untempered greed ... [The nation] feels that power implies obligations. Its might gives it a right; its right turns into pretension and pretension resolves into a duty to take a position on all matters that would formerly have been sorted out by an agreement among the European powers alone'.[11]

That was really what got in Emile Boutmy's hair, that is, the fact that the Americans were trying to muscle in on the great powers' act as the '*parvenus*' they were, instead of standing aside as their lack of historical tradition should have dictated.

Several decades later, this fear that the United States might become the equal of the great powers was transformed into a dread of America imposing its values on other nations, now that it was mightier than them: 'There is no people with less national egoism or with a greater readiness to help other countries ... However, since public opinion there is convinced that there is no other way of building a better world but according to American models, American aid is not always the nicest thing to receive. All those who want it can raise themselves up or get back on their feet again, but the price of being assisted to get up is stimulation, education and retraining. Sometimes a little brutality is called for, as well as a little intolerance'.[12] Clearly it was anti-Americanism of a moderate variety. Jacques Lambert saw a similarity between American 'cultural imperialism' (was he the first to use the term?) and French 'cultural imperialism'. There were those who stressed rather maliciously that the Americans sometimes displayed a tendency to see the mote in their neighbour's eye as a beam: 'Opinion is too often restricted, particularly in the United States, to big business and their press. None the less, the Under-Secretary of State for Foreign Affairs, Mr Castle, has affirmed the independence of the American press (State Dept. *Press Releases* No. 174, 28 January 1933, p. 49). He forgot, for instance, the senate enquiry into the advertising by the Utilities ... On the other hand he went on to add, "It's a well-known fact that some of the big Paris newspapers are owned by the *Comité des Forges* [the iron and steel employers' federation, trans]. which dictates their policies." Longsightedness like this is quite common'.[13] Was Mr Castle anti-French?

Finally, what might appear to be anti-Americanism is the often breathtakingly blunt manner in which some analysts used to express admiration or criticism. Boutmy, for instance, did not flinch from writing: 'The United States appoints only men of inferior moral or intellectual calibre to posts in the bureaucracy and the government'. Elsewhere he wrote that the American nation was shot through with 'an arrogant sense of its superiority'.[14] However, one should not forget that such harsh appraisals can be coupled with almost lyrical admiration: 'On the one side [in Europe] one has states which are historical, mystical and fateful, which embody a powerful national consciousness; states in which individuals must bow their heads. On the other side [in the United States] there is almost no homeland, scarcely a nation, a state lacking a past or prestige, an expedient combination, the voluntary and conscious achievement of free and equal individuals'.[15]

All in all, therefore, one cannot speak of anti-Americanism – even if one does detect certain traces, and no doubt more than in contemporary studies of a similar kind – in the sense of systematic and unjustified opposition to American institutions. Nor, however, can one talk of dumb admiration. Criticism was frequently severe and even devastating at times. But it was never from a negative desire to systematically destroy. American institutions exercised a force of attraction and the various researchers would weigh up the pros and cons of the system with enthusiasm and diligence in tackling the major issues of the day.

The most striking thing about those works is not just the topicality and high level of the debate on centralisation, the relations both between the Federal Government and local communities – as well as between the President and the Congress – but above all on the role of the Supreme Court, particularly as regards economic and social issues. Equally remarkable is the constant effort to compare American realities and the French situation and a concern to discover whether the American experience might not be fruitfully transposed to the French context.

Throughout the period under review, anti-Americanism – insofar as it existed – was both less common and more discreet than expressions of admiration inspired, as in the nineteenth century, by 'a passion for American institutions, an affinity with the people of that country and a desire to see France take the United States as a model'.[16] However, René Rémond commented à propos these writings that, by and large, 'objective information is rarely their strong point. In all events it is not their main concern, which is persuasion rather than information or education'.[17]

When one comes to the twentieth century, one finds the situation has changed entirely. Now whether in antipathy or admiration, fascination or rejection the authors tried – successfully – to be far more rigorous and scrupulous. Feelings had to take second place to 'la méthode'.

Although the practice of dealing with American institutions by reference to French problems continued into the new century, one can detect the beginnings of analysis which was not only more theoretical, it was also more rooted in reality. In Emile Boutmy's view, this desire for neutrality was motivated by two main considerations. For one thing, politics on one side of the Atlantic could not be compared with politics on the other. Hence nothing could be transplanted.

> Politically speaking, the European states and the great American republic belong to two distinct species or genera which developed in quite different conditions. As they have not known the same phases of development there are not points of correspondence. Consequently any transplants, grafts or propagations from one side of the Atlantic to the other are liable to remain sterile. The Constitution of the United States is an individual and indivisible specimen which lends itself neither to piecemeal borrowings nor to full-blown imitation.[18]

Though clearly overstated, that argument was not entirely without foundation at the time. Comparison or even admiration was in order, slavish imitation was out of the question.

Furthermore, and most importantly, a whole new scientific development was getting under way. From then on 'la méthode' (as Emile Boutmy was to entitle the first chapter of his Eléments d'une psychologie du peuple américain) was to assume increasing importance. In the process, de Tocqueville[19] came in for criticism for failing to 'present his evidence'.[20] What is more, 'the sort of general deductions in which de Tocqueville delighted did no more than relate to Universal Man, an individual who is no concern of ours'.[21] Henceforth, basic research and the presentation of evidence were to become indispensable.

Travel and direct observation were not the only means of analysing the American reality: there was also the study of primary and secondary sources. Boutmy, in common with several other observers of the turn of the century, criticised de Tocqueville for being too abstract.[22] In fact, Boutmy scarcely employed such practices, but his successors, particularly the jurists among them, certainly did. The first of these to show due concern about the availability and quality of source material would seem to have been Edouard Lambert. I came across several passages in his writings where he detailed the difficulties he faced and his attempts to remedy them, even involving supplications to the American Bar Association, the Columbia Law Review and the Yale Law Review.[23] Such commitment to scientific rigour went hand in hand with an ambition to foster comparative study, in the process of which Lambert was driven to tax the American legal profession with 'insularity' and a 'narcissistic'[24] tendency. After Lambert, the scientific approach was the order of the day. The process which had commenced at the turn of the century culminated after World War II.

Indeed the point was reached in those postwar years where authors, having mastered the literature America had to offer (to such an extent that they were to cite their compatriots more and more infrequently), were actually to raise the issue – which none of their predecessors had done – of whether there was any more point in such research, in view of the wealth of material on the other side of the Atlantic. It was going to be necessary to justify the usefulness of European study of the United States since one might just as well translate American publications. Had anti-Americanism given way to humility?

In all events, the new situation was a far cry from René Rémond's description of the publications of the early nineteenth century: 'One so rarely comes across a disinterested and perfectly objective assessment, one devoid of any ulterior motives ... There is something disturbing about the American experience which has had a tendency to ruffle the composure of the most objective minds'.[25]

A century later, there was a literature that was as objective as any could ever hope to be. Stretching from Boutmy to Tardieu, from the Lamberts (Edouard or Jacques) to Seurin and taking in Pinto and Tunc, one can truly speak of a French school of research into American institutions which has continued to evolve, even if it has been all too often ignored. It has reflected contemporary debates and served as an inspiration to many authors (such as Carré de Malberg, Hauriou or Burdeau) who were not Americanists but whose interest in more general issues led them necessarily to examine the American example more closely. Were they pro- or anti-American? Such considerations could not have been further from their thoughts; their concern was solely to record reality as a basis for scientific speculation.

There was a fundamental difference between scholarship before and after World War I. Even though pre-war studies had been of a high standard (and far more often so than is usually acknowledged) their analyses nonetheless tended to be defensive, normative, moralistic and even dogmatic. Occasionally authors would sacrifice reality in order to prove a point, such as when Emile Boutmy declared that American imperialism was 'totally bereft of any mystical element ... It was pre-determined and did not have to take into account abstract or sentimental considerations which it regarded as vapid or puerile'.[26] He could hardly have been wider off the mark. The fact was that the United States also believed itself to have a civilising 'mission' even if it did not use that term, and whenever they decided to intervene anywhere it was always in the name of democratic principles.[27]

After the war, on the other hand, the break was complete. First of all, scientific and analytical methods were introduced. Moralising went out the window and in its place came facts, realities and evidence. There was still an intuitive element, but it was more credible than in the past,[28] being backed up by the analysis of situations and texts. Thus, in an analysis of the actual imperial process, Roger Pinto wrote,

> Born out of the very first 'anti-colonial' struggles, the American Union is not made up entirely of communities with equal rights. The Constitution failed to define the status of those communities belonging to the Union which did not have the makings of full member States. It does not seem to have even envisaged such a status. Some went so far as to maintain that it was actually

prohibited ... US intervention ... at the end of the nineteenth century caused a series of very different communities to be brought under American rule, most of which seemed unlikely ever to achieve statehood ... They were quite simply colonial dependencies. But the United States did not want any colonies and loathed the very word.[29]

Greater precision and a better awareness of trans-Atlantic discussions help explain why admiration and criticism alike were no longer the sort of generalities they had been in the nineteenth century. It was a matter of grasping more thoroughly a more clearly circumscribed reality and seeking to analyse processes and assess their significance, rather than political balances which may well have been admirable but in the final analysis were static – and unreal.

What is surprising about the standard of analysis is that, firstly, it denotes enormous familiarity with American realities, and secondly, that it serves to overthrow certain idols and rehabilitate the excellent work of certain long-forgotten authors previously unknown to my own generation. Take the case of Siegfried who is still regarded as the great expert on the United States, in spite of the astonishing superficiality of his works. Meanwhile Edouard or Jacques Lambert remain unknown although their powerful analyses are both concise and subtle, and invariably topical. There is a glaring contrast between the dilettante traveller and the researchers who worked on the texts.

In the final analysis, is the United States boon or bane? As René Rémond showed, during the nineteenth century the American experience was always looked at in terms of the French situation, either as a frame of reference, 'the desire to see France adopting the United States as a model',[30] or to use that country as an object of scorn (with 'a widespread onslaught on the American institutions'[31] around 1832). From the mid-nineteenth century onwards the difference in attitude was political:

> Left and Right alike ceased regarding American politics as a homogeneous reality that could be accepted or rejected *en bloc*. By projecting their own various likes and dislikes on to the American political scene, they formed a distorted impression of the reality, one coloured by considerations related to French politics. Everyone had an America of their own making![32]

Things did not change totally in the new century, though by now analysis of the American scene was not so clouded by political considerations. There was Tardieu with his perceptively rigorous analysis of US institutions expressing the hope that France would follow suit:

> In Washington ... constant criticism of the government is something that is frowned on ... In France the government is always regarded as suspect. And even the exercise of its normal rights is virtually seen as an effrontery. In the United States it is the erosion of government which would perturb public opinion ... In defining how public authority should be apportioned, the French Constitution based itself on the assumption that in conflicts with the executive, the legislative would always be in the right. In America the possibility is accepted that the executive may be in the right.[33]

Boutmy, on the other hand, found far less to admire in the way the American system had evolved. 'Who would have thought that a government in which [executive and legislative] powers were entirely separate would be notorious for the very extent to which they encroached on each other ...? Who could have anticipated ... that in a national government, no one, neither legislators nor the members of the executive branch, would have effective responsibility'.[34] It was precisely that sort of irresponsibility which Tardieu envied the United States. As for the President, 'the source of his mandate ensures his effective independence. He is not elected by Congress but is instead the people's choice. He is not in a subordinate position vis-à-vis Parliament, as is the case when the elected houses appoint the head of the executive branch. He is bound by the Constitution ... The President and his ministers ... are accountable neither to the Senate nor Congress.[35] No one has the right to challenge them'.[36]

In fact it is not so unusual to come across different interpretations of the same reality in two contemporaneous accounts. With his keen eye for political developments, André Tardieu immediately realised the extent of centralisation in the United States: 'The President of the United States of America is more powerful, in several respects, than most constitutional sovereigns in Europe ... The Head of State decides foreign policy'.[37] Emile Boutmy, on the other hand, considered that the federal system had been preserved intact and he only grudgingly acknowledges a limited evolution: 'Anyway, I doubt whether the Federal Government is actually the nearest analogy to our European governments. The government of a particular state would seem to be more analogous in essential respects ... This fact must be grasped before going on to consider the federal domain and the singular government which administers it with limited powers...'[38]

The difference between the teacher and the politician is enhanced by the fact that the former was describing an America which had undoubtedly disappeared by then, that is, the America of Independence and The Constitution, whereas the second described America, if not as it was, then at least as he actually saw it.

Hence Boutmy belonged to the liberal school for which the least government is the best government. Surprising as it may seem three quarters of a century on, in Europe at the turn of the century, Boutmy and others like him already perceived the 'Welfare State' as a threat to 'individualism' and as something that was growing all the time: 'Public opinion everywhere is encouraging government to regard itself as a father or guardian, to think of itself as responsible for people's physical and spiritual welfare, and to take duties upon itself which justify a whole new sphere of activities and powers'.[39] One can almost hear the voice of Ronald Reagan in such sentiments.

It was a situation that Boutmy deplored. He much preferred minimal government, as in the United States which had yet to start down the slippery slope, or at most had taken only certain steps in its direction. For him, 'in America ... freedom thrives. Each citizen can pursue his own activity with nothing to fear from a government with too much power. All the authorities are weak, uncertain of their rights and restricted in what they can do. The nation plays second fiddle to the individual. It does so because it has little to lose and because the freedom and elbow room of every Tom, Dick and Harry are reputedly the supreme concern of the State.'[40] One can feel the old nineteenth-century esteem for American government perceived in this way: a government 'of which one is totally unaware' as René Rémond put it.[41]

To sum up, Boutmy did observe a move towards more powerful centralised government but mourned the past; Tardieu scoffed at the past and discerned in the present features that he would have liked to see adopted in France. In a sense he was a 'presidentialist', while Boutmy remained a 'parliamentarist' to the core and emphasised what he saw of defects in the American system, whereby it was becoming centralised and 'presidentialised'.

However, these elements, catalogued by René Rémond, which the nineteenth century found so admirable, were to become bones of contention in the twentieth century, for example, government 'of which one is totally unaware'. With his sensitivity to the process of centralisation, Boutmy had a perfect grasp of the judiciary's role in impeding this inexorable evolution (notwithstanding his declared unwillingness to discuss the question):

> At state level, as at federal level, legislative activity is no less restricted than administrative activity. The most recent Supreme Court decisions have invariably tended to increase the number of restrictions on the power of legislative bodies ... Such suspicion about the law-makers themselves shows that the Americans are far from regarding them as the main instrument of progress: ... they would sooner be on their guard against the law rather than appeal to it.[42]

He understood and appreciated those developments and was even of the view that the Americans themselves were in favour of the curbs thus placed on legislation.

It is in this respect that he is out of step with his successors. For them, judicial power at the turn of the century failed to respect the popular will, reflecting instead the 'great apprehensions of the propertied classes'.[43] Edouard Lambert actually revealed the consequences of the system for selecting judges:

> By taking sides in the most sensitive issues of economic and social policy, the courts risked appearing to working people as responsible for all the defects of social organisation ... The workers started to adopt a defiant and hostile attitude towards the law, the Constitution and the courts ... At about the same period, the topic of popular dissatisfaction with the law started to crop up with such regularity in the discussions of members of the legal profession, including professors, lawyers and judges, as well as in so many legal reviews and house journals of law schools and state bars, and provoked such concerns and fears that it was clearly becoming one of the most disturbing trends in American public opinion towards the end of the first decade of the century.[44]

To sum up, what represented the break with the nineteenth century was a much more thorough, albeit uneven knowledge of institutional processes. René Rémond stressed that the nineteenth century's esteem for the American system – as the 'highest degree of perfection to which a political society may aspire' – was not based to any real extent on 'the study of institutional mechanisms, which was rarely undertaken. In fact the study of government has usually consisted of no more than summary analyses or trite surveys. And it was not entirely uncommon for such assessments to be erroneous'.[45] Superficial analysis did admittedly carry over into the new century (most frequently in accounts of travel, in which the author neither observed nor saw anything but instead superimposed his own deep-seated prejudices on reality) and errors still survived. However, the latter were increasingly rare and there was now an abundance of top quality scholarship based on a precise knowledge of original texts and interpretations, as well as on the realities themselves.

The second great difference was that praise and criticism seemed to be no longer based to the same extent on generalisations: there was no longer talk of 'better government', writers did not urge 'adopting the spirit' of American institutions.[46] Twentieth-century specialists were to tackle specific problems (in particular the evolution of federalism, relations between the legislative and executive branches, and judicial review) and to study American responses. Curiously enough, the *'américanistes'* – as experts in American studies were known – were very seldom the greatest partisans of American solutions. They even tended to believe that those of their colleagues who advocated their adoption, without having studied the phenomena directly, erred through insufficient knowledge of the facts.[47]

Roger Pinto, for instance, in his study *Des juges qui ne gouvernent pas*, came to the conclusion that judicial review as practised in the United States was 'contrary to the principles of democratic government'.[48]

[It is] a hypocritical process of government, which actually conceals the exercise of political power under cover of the calm and objective implementation of the law. It serves indirectly to restore capricious and secretive authority, which would seem fundamentally alien to the spirit of American democracy. The fact that it has survived would be incredible but for that other trait of the American character: a reverence for myths, particularly the judicial myth, such as 'the rule of law above the rule of Men'.[49]

Incidentally, this is another instance where one might raise the question of anti-Americanism (was it or wasn't it?), but that is not my concern here. One should not be surprised to discover that his precise analysis did not lead Roger Pinto to recommend the introduction of this aspect of the American system into French political organisation; on the contrary. Nor is it surprising that the author of the book's preface, Gilbert Gidel, Professor at the Law School of Paris University and at the School of Political Science (and not an expert on the United States) wrote: 'In his conclusions the author expresses outright opposition to judicial review in America. He is equally opposed to the introduction of that institution in France. Judicial review is held by Mr. Roger Pinto to run counter to the principles of democratic government. Maybe his conclusions will be the subject of debate. For my part I would like to make known formally my own reservations on this point'.[50]

While my perusal of the literature has been too cursory to permit any definitive conclusions, it has nonetheless been sufficiently thorough to provide some food for thought. In all events, I feel that it is totally inappropriate to talk about anti-Americanism with respect to French analysts of American institutions, either as a group (though they are divided on many issues) or individually (not one of them having been systematically antagonistic towards the United States). Admittedly they were capable, on occasions, of being sharply critical of certain aspects of the American political system and scornful of the universalist pretensions of some of its admirers. Can such judgements as theirs – based on analyses of reality that were as 'objective' as possible and underpinned with a framework of quotations which was gradually reinforced in pace with specific progress – truly be put down to anti-Americanism?

Notes

1. Jacques Lambert, *Histoire constitutionnelle de l'Union américaine* (Paris: Sirey, 1930) Vol. I, p. 13.
2. Our choice of dates was totally arbitrary. Our aim was to consider the attitudes of French lawyers and political scientists during the twentieth-century portion of the Third Republic but we had no

hesitation in referring to certain of the authors' works which predated our period or were published later.
3. We do not include either articles or constitutional chronicles on the United States or the many comparative studies.
4. Emile Boutmy, *Eléments d'une psychologie politique du peuple américain* (Paris: Armand Colin, 1902) pp. 127, 26 and 4.
5. André Siegfried, *Les Etats-Unis d'aujourd'hui* (Paris: Armand Colin, 1927) pp. 87–9 and 23–6.
6. Benjamin Akzin, *La Science et l'éducation politiques aux Etats-Unis* (Paris: Sirey, 1938) pp. 66–7.
7. Edouard Lambert, *Le Gouvernement des juges et la lutte contre la législation sociale aux Etats-Unis* (Paris: Marcel Giard, 1924) p. 24.
8. Roger Pinto, *Des Juges qui ne gouvernent pas: opinions dissidentes à la Cour suprême des Etats-Unis (1900–1933)* (Paris: 1934) p. 40.
9. Jacques Lambert, op. cit., Vol. I, p. 44.
10. André Tardieu, *Notes sur les Etats-Unis: la société, la politique et la diplomatie* (Paris: Calmann-Lévy, 1908) pp. 116–17.
11. Emile Boutmy, *Les Etats-Unis et l'impérialisme* (Paris: Félix Alcan, 1902) pp. 2–3.
12. Jacques Lambert, 'La formation des attitudes américaines', in *Les Fondements de la politique extérieure des Etats-Unis*, Cahiers de la F.N.S.P., No. 8 (Paris: Armand Colin, 1949) pp. 78–9.
13. Roger Pinto, op. cit., p. 7.
14. Emile Boutmy, *Eléments . . .* , op. cit., pp. vii and 153.
15. Ibid., p. 137.
16. René Rémond, *Les Etats-Unis devant l'opinion française, 1815–52*, Cahiers de la F.N.S.P., No. 116–17 (Paris: Armand Colin, 1962) Vol. 4, pp. 15 and 416.
17. Ibid., p. 412.
18. Emile Boutmy, *Eléments . . .* , op. cit., p. 108.
19. Boutmy admired de Tocqueville, a view which was scarcely acceptable by the beginning of this century, 'It is now widely accepted that *Democracy in America* is a dated and outmoded work . . . This is no more than a fashionable assessment and will soon pass. [On re-reading it] my impression was one of profound admiration for the entire book.' (Boutmy, *Eléments . . .* , op. cit., pp. 3–4).
20. Ibid., p. 10.
21. Ibid., p. 13.
22. Ibid., p. 10.
23. Edouard Lambert, *Le Gouvernement . . .* , op. cit., pp. 269–74.
24. Ibid., pp. 269–70.
25. René Rémond, op. cit., Vol. I, p. 417.
26. Emile Boutmy, *Les Etats-Unis . . .* , op. cit., p. 2.
27. President McKinley maintained that the United States would not colonise the Philippines, but would pursue a policy of 'benevolent assimilation' to educate, uplift and convert the Philippines. His successor, Theodore Roosevelt, wanted to bring to the Philippines 'Anglo-Saxon decency and progress'.
28. In the course of our own work on problems of federalism, we were

struck by the intuitions and foresight displayed in the 1930s by jurists such as Roger Pinto, Edouard Lambert, Jacques Lambert and Georges Burdeau in their analyses of the centralisation process.

29. Roger Pinto, *La Crise de l'Etat aux Etats-Unis* (Paris: Librairie Générale du Droit et de Jurisprudence, 1951) pp. 32–3.
30. René Rémond, op. cit., Vol. I, p. 416.
31. Ibid., Vol. II, p. 696.
32. Ibid., Vol. II, p. 698.
33. André Tardieu, op. cit., pp. 194–5.
34. Emile Boutmy, *Eléments* . . . , op. cit., p. 22.
35. This is only partly true; even at that period, Secretaries of State could be called to testify before Congress committees and could not refuse to attend.
36. André Tardieu, op. cit., pp. 193–4.
37. Ibid., pp. 192–3.
38. Emile Boutmy, *Eléments* . . . , op. cit., pp. 24–8.
39. Ibid., pp. 107.
40. Ibid., pp. 169–70.
41. René Rémond, op. cit., Vol. II, p. 544.
42. Emile Boutmy, *Eléments* . . . , op. cit., p. 170.
43. Roger Pinto, *Des Juges qui ne gouvernent pas* . . . , op. cit., p. 264.
44. Edouard Lambert, *Le Gouvernement* . . . , op. cit., pp. 92–3.
45. René Rémond, op. cit., Vo. II, p. 543.
46. René Rémond, ibid., Vol. I, p. 542.
47. Edouard Lambert, for instance, regrets that all of Lord Bryce's chapters of the 1913 edition of *American Commonwealth* were not revised. 'The absence of such revisions in the chapters on the relations between judicial and legislative power, whether in the Federal Constitution (chaps. 22–25 and 34–35), or in the State Constitutions (chaps. 37–42), has done much to conceal from the educated French public the transformations that have been taking place over the past three decades in relations between the American Courts and legislatures, even though they have been both thoroughgoing and caused quite a commotion. All too often, the material we have on such matters may seem up-to-date because it mentions recent titles and dates of recent books but it actually goes back to 1888.' (Edouard Lambert, *Le Gouvernement* . . . , op. cit., p. 40.
48. Roger Pinto, *Des Juges qui ne gouvernent pas* . . . , op. cit., p. 272.
49. Ibid., pp. 269–70.
50. Ibid., p. viii.

15
The Fifth Republic and the American Model
Julien Feydy

One of the reasons why the Fifth Republic has always felt ill at ease with the American model is because it resembles it in many respects. This discomfiture might actually be said to antedate it in the sense that the debate about institutions had been revived in 1956. We would be nearer to the terms of those debates were we to employ the expression 'presidential model', then preferred by political observers and politicians alike. However, the reassuring neutrality of the expression merely concealed the fact that there was only one model in existence. All too often it gave rise to some rather blatant rhetorical effects along the lines of 'The presidential model – why not, when all's said and done? ... Imitate the Americans? Saints preserve us!' One can readily understand how a country, whose venerable and complex constitutional tradition had itself been imitated on myriad occasions, might be reluctant to start taking lessons from others. Above all, it is not hard to appreciate that the transposition of a foreign model to a different social and political reality must be achieved by means of an abstraction appropriate to its new environment. Unfortunately, the combination of Gaullism's traditional complexes with the very explicit antipathies of a large section of the Left meant that, by the beginning of the Fifth Republic, the United States could not possibly serve as a neutral reference. In all events, it distorted the debate on the possible transposition of institutions. Besides, that same – very equivocal – 'model' was itself beginning to mutate by then, to the great dismay of its devotees, so as to be almost unrecognisable by the end of the 1970s. Indeed, 1954 marked the beginning of the long period of Democratic domination of Congress during which conflict with Republican Presidents became a virtual constant of American political life. This has given rise to periods of immobility contrasting disconcertingly with the dynamic or 'imperial' Presidencies of the 1960s. Constantly in jeopardy, the balance between Congressional and Presidential powers fluctuated unpredictably in response to an interminable trial of strength ... The American political system seemed to revert from its erstwhile complexity to a state of savagery until, in the wake of Watergate, it became unfit for export.

Most importantly, it was neither the United States nor the 'presidential model' of the constitutional law handbooks which was eventually to spur the revisionists and constitution-framers, but instead the very specific and changing problems of the French political system. Every situation and every political objective evoked, either explicitly or implicitly, some part of the monument of 1787.

Looked at with hindsight, the debate can be seen to have fallen into three main phases before coming to a final conclusion at the Presidential press conference of 31 January 1964. After that, a lengthy period of semi-torpor set in, during which any possible influence of the American system of government was either marginal or indirect.

It was a debate that traced its origins back to the classic controversy between Georges Vedel and Maurice Duverger in the spring of 1956.[1] That particular controversy was sparked off specifically by Pierre Mendès-France's sudden departure into the political wilderness because of party machinations, and more generally by the growing symptoms of deep-seated crisis in the French system of representation. From the outset, therefore, the issue was posed in terms of a restoration of the executive and its legitimacy by means of designation procedures bringing it closer to the electorate. Maurice Duverger was looking for solutions more along the lines of British-style majority parliamentarism, while Georges Vedel was already advocating a fairly faithful transposition of the American presidential model. However, these two political systems, which the authors clearly knew through and through, were examined solely in terms of the stability and legitimacy of executive power. The American model was treated in a purely utilitarian fashion as a means of solving an urgent and profoundly political French problem. The protagonists did not yield to the temptation of an academic debate about the framing of an ideal Constitution.[2]

The drafting and adoption of the 1958 Constitution, which

marked the end of this first *débat des politoloques* about the presidential system, were the Fifth Republic's first abortive encounter with American institutions. The latter have still to be debated seriously in France, as Jean Foyer pointed out at an international conference on constitution writing at the American Enterprise Institute in Washington in 1983.[3] In spite of General de Gaulle's sporadic interest in American institutions,[4] his anti-Americanism undoubtedly remained crucial, and no self-avowed partisan of the American system was included among those who were directly involved in the framing process. (Not only was Michel Debré a well-known champion of the British system, but the French political establishment remained impervious to the logic of presidentialism). Furthermore, the law of 3 June established the principle of the Government's accountability to Parliament and would therefore seem to have blocked any moves in that direction.

The most promising 'window' would seem to have opened in 1961, with General de Gaulle's speech on 11 April of that year when he mooted the possibility of the President being elected by universal suffrage. The debate among political specialists was immediately revived[5] and was to remain very much alive until the revision of 1962 which involved the political actors themselves. In response to Duverger's categorical advocacy of presidential government,[6] François Mitterrand in *l'Express*, argued against it in ambiguous terms, presaging what was to be the third phase of the debate after 1962. 'I believe that the aspirations for a presidential form of government in France are tantamount to abdication ... I have my misgivings about the election of the head of the executive branch by universal suffrage ... I do not believe it is possible in France, any more than in any other Latin country to reconcile the allocation of considerable powers to a single man on the one hand, with serious guarantees for institutions and civil liberties, on the other.'[7]

And not long afterwards, on 17 July 1962, Mitterrand was to declare before the National Assembly, '... while not necessarily being in favour of the presidential system, I would point out that this anyway is not what is at issue, if the proposed reform consists in increasing the powers of the Head of State without any compensatory provisions, of which the first would be to remove from an elected president his main weapon: the dissolution of the National Assembly'.[8] To put it in a nutshell, the 'American system' was by then an Opposition cause, and the only vaguely credible meeting-place was about to be lost, as was confirmed by the very limited nature of the revision. This was confined solely to the conduct of presidential elections. The two systems were never as close or as remote from each other at that moment in time.

By 1963 the debate was beginning to resume, but the actors were no longer the same, and nor were the issues. In fact what it amounted to was a strictly localised rearguard political action, and it too was to receive a resounding political rebuff. At that period, the eminent law professors Paul Coste-Floret and René Capitant were first and foremost parliamentarians and political leaders. The Coste-Floret proposals for constitutional revision debated in the Legislation Committee of the National Assembly in June 1963, were typical of quite a number of centrist proposals along the same lines.[9] They characteristically advocated a 'true' presidential system. The robustly constructed Coste-Floret Report was a splendid display of the best of the 'agrégation' system. It posited, in effect, that (1) the 1958 Constitution marked the end of the parliamentary system, but that (2) it also marked the beginnings of a presidential system. Since (a) the President no longer arbitrated but governed, and the Government no longer governed but executed, besides which Parliament no longer exercised oversight (and only legislated within a very limited framework), all that was needed was (b) to bring the legislation in line with reality by amending precisely 17 articles of the Constitution. Unlike the 'politological' debate of 1956, this logical demonstration – which was to provide the basis for a great deal of course work at the law faculty – was no longer intended to restore the authority of the State and the executive, but instead to re-establish the rights of Parliament. The latter would be separated from the executive, paving the way for a flexible two-party system. In reality it would be a multi-party system, closer, in the final analysis, to the parliamentary alternations of the Third and Fourth Republics. All these proposals implied a very specific, albeit very different, attitude to the realities of American political life. As a whole, they would not seem to have challenged presidential power, which would have been strengthened by the abolition of the post of Prime Minister. The latter proposal was overtly justified as a means of resisting pressure groups, which Maurice Duverger described as 'the equivalent of federalism'. The response to Coste-Floret's proposals given by René Capitant on behalf of the Gaullists[10] was erudite and courteous – but categorical, and clearly spelled their defeat.

In the circumstances, it is not surprising that when the leading protagonists of the 1956–57 debate came together at the 'Saturday talks' of the Association Française de Science Politique on 22 February 1964, they acknowledged that the public were 'rather tired' of the constitutional debate, and that it was by then a 'spent issue'. This was particularly true in the wake of the Presidential press conference of 31 January when de Gaulle brusquely rejected any 'American-style' interpretation or modification of the 1962 institutions, and even lashed out viciously at the 'unexpected champions of presidential government' . . .

It would be no oversimplification to maintain that, by clouding the issue and creating insurmountable obstacles, the episode in question had the effect of ossifying the positions of the French political system *vis-à-vis* its American counterpart. In this respect, it was characteristic that after having himself defended presidential government in December 1962, Socialist leader Gaston Defferre, in the course of his unsuccessful bid for the Presidency, was to go back to advocating the implementation of the 1958–62 Constitution in a more or less refurbished – and in fact more 'parliamentary' – form.[11]

After this, France – or at least its politicians and 'politologists' – spent quite a lengthy period contemplating its own institutional navel. The resulting consensus was that French institutions were at last developing along original lines and becoming an exportable model. The process whereby the new institutional system has progressively entrenched itself was subjected to close scrutiny at a symposium organised by the Association Française de Science Politique on 8 and 9 March 1984, held to mark the 25th anniversary of the Fifth Republic. Paradoxically, the two major areas where the French and American systems were very close served to demonstrate the extent to which too much contact can engender a defensive reflex. Thus, both the development of the Conseil Constitutionnel and the measures taken in 1969 and 1982 in favour of greater regional decentralisation were accompanied by assurances that there was no question of moving in the direction of a Supreme Court with its overtones of 'government by judges'. Similarly there was no intention of introducing into France any seeds of uncontrollable federalism. The fact is, the only areas where American influence has continued to grow are those which are less immediately visible and consequently less emotive, such as local political and civic practices, and, more generally speaking, the attitude of citizens to the State.[12] Can we be said ever to have accepted the American model in France, since the abortive experiment of 1848? A century later, the taboo about Presidential elections has gone but the image of the American republic has yet to be entirely refurbished.

Notes

1. Maurice Duverger, *La République des citoyens* (Paris: Ramsay, 1982) p. 94 and its bibliography. This work is crucial to an understanding of the debates from 1956 to 1963. See also Georges Vedel, 'Rapport général sur les rapports entre l'exécutif et le législatif', *Revue française de science politique*, 1958, pp. 757–78. For a synopsis of the question see also M. Duverger, *Le système politique français* (Paris: PUF, 1985) pp. 183 and 184.
2. Maurice Duverger, *La République des citoyens*, p. 126.
3. Jean Foyer, 'The Drafting of the French Constitution of Oct. 4th, 1958', International Conference on Constitution Writing, American Enterprise Institute, Washington DC, Sept. 1983, mimeograph.
4. Odile Rudelle, 'De Gaulle et l'élection directe du président de la République', symposium on the 25th anniversary of the Constitution, *Revue française de science politique*, August 1984, p. 187 and in that same issue, René Tuxidor, 'L'évolution du révisionnisme', p. 1042.
5. Maurice Duverger, *La République des citoyens*, p. 98.
6. Maurice Duverger, *La Ve République et le régime présidentiel* (Paris: Fayard, 1961).
7. François Mitterrand, *Politique* (Paris: Fayard, 1977) Vol. 1, p. 218.
8. François Mitterrand, Ibid., p. 228.
9. Proposition de Coste-Floret, *Journal officiel de l'Assemblée nationale* 1963, 2e session extraordinaire, document No. 410.
10. René Capitant, same reference, also reprinted in *Ecrits constitutionnels* (Paris: CNRS, 1982) p. 372 onwards.
11. Colette Ysmal, 'Defferre parle', Centre d'étude de la vie politique française, Fondation nationale des sciences politiques, mimeograph, 1966, Chap. 1.
12. This point was made by Yves Mény at the symposium on French perceptions of the United States sponsored by the CERI (Paris: 11, 12 December 1984).

Part VI

Why Anti-Americanism Is Not Always Quite What It Seems, Nor Americanophiles Quite What They Say They Are

16
United States: Model or Bête Noire?
Guy Sorman

The reason the United States divides us is because, in common with the Soviet Union, it embodies an ideological system. Moreover, France has always had a very special relationship with the United States which can be traced to our two countries' shared – and rather immodest – ambition to impose our particular model on the rest of the world. Our two revolutions, the American of 1776 and the French of 1789, both had pretensions to universality. Ronald Reagan's lecturing of the entire Western world and the claim by François Mitterrand (1981 model) that we had the solution to the crisis – not just for ourselves but for everyone else as well, were both demonstrations of this traditional arrogance. The similarity of our ambitions derives largely, in my view, from one major characteristic we both share, and it is one that we share with almost no one else. I refer to the extraordinary ethnic complexity of our populations. Like the Americans, the French are characterised less by ethnic origin than by their determination to constitute a nation. Whereas the English, Germans, Italians and Spanish recognise each other first and foremost in terms of race or language, the French – and this has been true for a long time now – are not so much *born* French as *become* French via culture and education. The same applies to the Americans. Basically, France and the United States are two nations founded on social contracts. A natural outcome of this is that they tend to think in terms of social blueprints. Hence this constant ideological rivalry between our two countries, of which the Reagan craze is simply the most recent metamorphosis.

The United States has been a source of attraction for the French intelligentsia since the eighteenth century. French liberals enthused over the new republic, regarding it as the achievement of the first democratic utopia. It was this utopian aspect that was to provide the focus for anti-Americanism in the course of the nineteenth century, when it became the dominant political attitude, except in the remarkable case of de Tocqueville.

The two main components of anti-Americanism – the accusations of individualism and materialism – emerge clearly from the critical analysis of de Tocqueville's and de Baumont's studies published by Buchez in November 1835 in his review *L'Européen, Journal de morale et de philosophie*. 'America', wrote Buchez, 'is socially organised egotism and systematic and legalised evil. In a nutshell, it is the materialization of the human destiny.' Individualism and materialism were, in his eyes, the product of Protestantism, whose chief canons he paraphrased as follows: 'Man is born for happiness; he enjoys the fruits down here to the extent that God assigns them to him, and after his death he enjoys celestial wealth: such is his goal'. (Hatred of success and antipathy towards the money created by 'that frightful agglomeration of aristocratic bankers and banking aristocrats' were key elements of anti-Americanism.) The Americans, Buchez continued, were 'a nation of ignorant shopkeepers and narrow-minded industrialists whose entire vast continent contains not one single work of art that was not inherited from various tribes which antedated Christianity. Their libraries contain not one scientific work that was not penned by a foreigner'.

As a nation in its infancy, and hence lacking a history, America also lacked culture. Its immaturity explained its brutality. This was another favourite anti-American argument. Europe, a continent with an ancient culture, was superior to that barbarian country which had only just emerged from the savage state. From Baudelaire down to the present day, the criticism has been the same. That same poet described the United States as a 'Gaslit Barbary'. More recently, Georges Duhamel inveighed against American civilisation in *Scènes de la vie future*.[1] In his eyes, gramophone records were 'canned music' and the legs of American women were 'too beautiful . . . as if they had come off an assembly line . . .' The entire onslaught was based on attitudes derived from the superficial sociological notion that all nations are part of a uniform life-cycle. America must *logically* be lagging behind Europe. Still more recently, in her book *Les Années Reagan*, Nicole Bernheim wrote that the United States was 'Europe in its infancy, a country on its way to becoming European, but which is not there yet'.[2] This supposed superiority of European culture has long been a bulwark of anti-Americanism. Having started out as essentially a right-wing phenomenon, with conservatives lambasting America for being a country where respect for money and social success went hand in hand with a lack of culture, anti-Americanism was taken over, after World War II, by the 'anti-imperialist' Left. Under this new patronage, it was initially nourished by the 'M. Perrichon complex', so admirably analysed by Georges Suffert in *Les Nouveaux Cow-boys*.[3] The French, he explained, found it hard to forgive the Americans for having liberated them. So how long should gratitude last, Suffert asks? During the 1950s, that ambivalent attitude was compounded by a bad conscience about '*les pays pauvres*', that was partly to do with decolonisation. The French intellectuals' sense of collective guilt about the poor countries led them to take a stand against the richest country of all: the United States. It even had the gall to consider its model – liberalism – as the only viable one. Solidarity with the poor of the earth combined with a bad conscience is a far better explanation of modern anti-Americanism than the simplistic anti-imperialist notions that were developed out of Communist Party policies.

In fact the Marxist theses strike me as being the least important component of anti-Americanism, and the most ephemeral. The current decrease in the most vocal anti-Americanism in French society owes as much to the fact that we have lost our bad conscience about the Third World as it does to dwindling Communist influence. Now that people in France have an increasingly hazy memory of decolonialisation, all the French want is modernisation, that is, Americanisation. In this respect, America is becoming a possible future.

Pro-Americanism can boast as long a pedigree as anti-Americanism. It originally assumed the form of benevolent condescension towards the United States, which was treated as an infant Europe. The democratic American citizen was regarded as Rousseau's 'noble savage'. De Tocqueville was the first to upset that historical view. For him America was no infant Europe, but instead the Europe of the future. French historian François Furet has analysed perfectly that abrupt change and turning point in French perceptions of the United States.[4]

Now America was seen as the social, economic and ideological laboratory of the future. It was a hypothesis that engendered a tradition of journeys to America in search of clues to France's own future. After de Tocqueville set the ball rolling, it was the turn of the utopian Socialists, followed by a whole troop of writers and journalists, from Jacques Maritain to Bertrand de Jouvenel and including Georges Duhamel, Robert Aron, Arnaud Dandieu, Jean-François Revel, Michel Crozier, and Jean-Jacques Servan-Schreiber. But none of the accounts brought back from the new world provided any convincing explanation of why it was that the United States should be the constitutional laboratory of the future. Anyway that hypothesis presupposes that Western Europe and the United States are fundamentally homogeneous. My theory, on the contrary, is that the United States has divorced itself from Europe and constitutes a civilisation quite different from our own. Consequently, if the United States embodies our future, then it is because the Europeans want to resemble the Americans. America is becoming Europe's 'frontier', in the same way that, for the Americans, the 'Far West' was a frontier that they had to keep pushing back in order to survive.

In spite of the passions aroused by the United States, that society has rarely been adopted as a political model. Federalism and Presidential government are too alien to our own historical traditions to be transplantable. There have been exceptions, of course. The 1848 Constitution, for instance, was influenced by the United States (though far less than de Tocqueville would have hoped). Tardieu regarded the American system of government as a possible cure for the instability of the Third Republic. In fact, the United States most of all inspired those whose thoughts dwelt on the wealth of nations, no doubt because economics played a greater role there than politics. Notwithstanding, French economists (never a particularly liberal constituency) regarded the United States as a *bête noire*. They went to great lengths to stress its most extreme negative features: its monopolistic tendencies, the destruction of 'the small man', and so on. Images of the 'robber barons' alternated with 'the grapes of wrath'. It was not until 1967 and the publication of Jean-Jacques Servan-Schreiber's *Le Défi américain*, that American capitalism was finally to achieve respectability. It was a book that upset established attitudes and inaugurated the lasting mythology of management and creative capitalism, now symbolised by Silicon Valley.

America's economic recovery, which started in 1982 and was acknowledged in France on the occasion of the Williamsburg summit of June 1983, confounded the forecasts of the previous ten years which had regarded strong growth as a thing of the past and predicted lasting stagnation, based on shared poverty and work. The universal conclusion at Williamsburg was that if the Americans could manage it, then it was time to blow the dust off the legendary statistics of the 'glorious' 30 postwar years. The economic upswing legitimised Ronald Reagan in the eyes of the French. Out went the image of the cowboy incapable of chewing gum and thinking at the same time; in came the image of the 'Great Communicator'. Just one year later, in November 1984, a poll conducted for Le Monde revealed that 'Reaganophilia' had taken a deep hold on the population: the French were 'voting Reagan'! It was nonetheless a superficial infatuation, with everyone choosing the aspects that ground their own particular axe. Moreover, it was one fraught with danger for the political and intellectual currents in France which succumbed to it. This was proved by the American elections of 1984. Reagan's momentary hesitation during his television debate with Walter Mondale was enough to strike terror into the hearts of France's 'Reaganettes'. But the fact is that Reagan's electoral defeat would have been no more than the defeat of Ronald Reagan (that is, a candidate enfeebled by old-age), and not of the ideas he represented. The conservative revolution would not have halted for one instant. It was that revolution, dating back to the early 1970s, which brought Reagan to power, not vice versa. Reagan is its supreme exponent, not its author. If liberals over here hitch their convictions to growth-rates and election results over there, then they are at the mercy of every little – inevitable – change in the American *conjoncture*. It is therefore vital to distinguish between those features of the American conservative revolution which are specifically American and those which are of universal significance.

The conservative and liberal theorists of Reaganomics believe that economic techniques are inseparable from their ideological – or even metaphysical – bedrock. Reaganomics means rejection of positivist systems in which the economy is reduced to curves and equations, and the rehabilitation of the work ethic. It is also a curious alliance between the American employers and liberal intellectuals. Chief executives have become latterday adventurers: invincible heroes whose faces monopolise magazine covers and whose memoirs become best-sellers. This idealisation of success, and even of power; the enthusiastic coming to terms with inequality of incomes; garish religiosity extolling material success; the thwarting of feminist, ecological and homosexual demands – these are all phenomena very much in the tradition of American society. As far as we are concerned, these elements of the new puritanism are its most exotic and least applicable aspect.

That is not the lesson of Reaganomics for us in France. When it is stripped of its local colour, what the American conservative revolution boils down to is a restoration of the personal civilisation, a return to a liberal order founded on individual initiative and a sense of responsibility. That is the universal message of this model, after 50 years of State encroachment on Western societies.

Notes

1. *Scènes de la vie future*, (Paris: Mercure de France, 1989; first published in 1930).
2. *Les années Reagan* (Paris: Stock, 1984).
3. *Les Nouveaux Cow-boys* (Paris: Orban, 1984).
4. François Furet, *Penser la Révolution Française* (Paris: Gallimard, 1978), pp. 32–3.

17
Does Anti-Americanism Exist?
Marie-France Toinet

What is anti-Americanism, when all is said and done? Is it a case of every component group of a given society manifesting anti-American attitudes at one moment and reverting *en masse* the next? Is it a unanimous phenomenon in individual fields such as culture or foreign policy? The expression *anti-américanisme* took a long time even to enter the dictionary, although it has been in use since the nineteenth century. The first mention we have managed to trace is in the latest edition (1984) of the *Petit Robert*, which gives 1968 (!) as the date of the world's first appearance.

Right up to 1984, the term was totally ignored by American or French dictionaries. On the other hand, one can find the expression 'Americanism', and it is interesting to note that while the grammatical definition is certainly given (namely, analogous with *anglicisme* or *gallicisme*), it is only given in second place, after the political definition. The conservative columnist William Safire provides what we think is the best definition in his political dictionary[1]: 'Patriotic political philosophy sometimes abused by chauvinists; also an oddly American word or phrase. Theodore Roosevelt popularised the word "Americanism" in 1909'.

It was Roosevelt who coined or propagated the expressions '100% Americanism' and 'hyphenated Americans' and who returned to the subject again and again, for example, 'Americanism signifies the virtues of courage, honour, justice, truth, sincerity and strength – the virtues that made America'. However, Americanism as defined by Theodore Roosevelt, was not unanimously accepted even in his own time, and not even in the United States.

As for the term 'anti-Americanism', we feel that its use is only fully justified if it implies systematic opposition – a sort of allergic reaction – to America as a whole. It is clear that if defined in this very narrow way, anti-Americanism either does not exist or is extremely rare. Nonetheless, accusations of anti-Americanism are bandied about with ease. However, the accusation rarely has anything to do with what is actually said or written about America. It is criticism *per se* that is regarded as anti-American, because, leaving aside praise and admiration, the Americans themselves challenge not only reproach but also any atttempt to observe them objectively. Analysis they regard as an attack. Right back at the beginning of the American republic, de Tocqueville noted that:

> In their relations with foreigners, the Americans seem to have an impatience with the slightest criticism and an insatiable hunger for adulation. The slightest compliment pleases them while even the most fulsome eulogy will not sate them. You will find yourself constantly pestered for praise, and if you resist their entreaties, they will sing their own praises. One gets the impression that they doubt their own merit, and want it confirmed at every possible moment. Their vanity is not just greedy, it is also restless and full of envy.[2]

The basic issue of anti-Americanism would therefore seem to us to be not so much that of criticism of the United States – justified or otherwise, but rather any judgement of America. Take the case of Italy, for example; it is surprising that the most unjust and unjustified criticism of that country – incidentally one of the best policed and most democratic of societies – should be acceptable, and yet the word 'anti-Italianism' does not exist. In contrast, the slightest reservation about the American political system is regarded as proof of virulent anti-Americanism.

Indeed it is astounding that the United States should be the only Western power towards which one cannot have an attitude of frank and loyal opposition without being dubbed an anti-American, whereas analogous attitudes towards Germany, France[3] or Great Britain do not lead to talk of anti-Germanism, anti-Frenchism or anti-Britishism – or hardly at all. One could hypothesise naturally, that the United States is the target of such sentiment because it is a very big power, whose very might arouses jealousy, and that the same applies to 'anti-Sovietism'. However, apart from the fact that it would not occur to us that jealousy might be the root of anti-Sovietism, the latter is rejection of the Soviets, not of Russia. Furthermore, when the European countries were themselves great imperial powers, they do not seem to have been the target of such feelings. It would be interesting to try to find out if, at the time of Napoleon, there was talk of 'anti-Frenchism', on the other side of the Rhine, the Channel and the Alps. At any rate, the word does not exist in France.

So, is there not something specifically American about the phenomenon? This explanation would seem to be suggested by McCarthyism and the struggle against 'un-Americanness'[4] – something that is apparently peculiar to the United States. The fact is that the majority of Americans feel they have succeeded as a nation and are therefore intimately convinced of American superiority. To them it is as plain as a pikestaff and they say as much with varying degrees of openness. Political institutions in America operate more democratically, and the rights and freedoms of the individual command greater respect. Quite simply, Americans are freer than anyone else and comparisons with other countries cannot fail to reflect favourably on the United States. Hand in hand with self-satisfaction, however, there goes an unspoken and vague anxiety about the permanence of what has been achieved. Any suggestion that American society might actually be affected by social struggles, national interests, racism or xenophobia, not to mention religious quarrels or ideological controversy, compromises the founding myth of the American nation, and is un-American.

All criticism, even justified criticism, is regarded as a challenge to the consensus, and potentially destructive of a society that regards itself as fragile and a nation that believes itself to be in a state of precarious balance. From this standpoint, anything but total and utter acceptance of the American system is dangerous and even abhorrent. In the case of America, to point out negative features, to discuss the results of a particular policy and criticise certain aspects – as one does for all other countries – is to commit the sin of opposition: it is to be inwardly 'un-American' and outwardly 'anti-American'.

No doubt our interpretation is a bit far-fetched. But it does reveal two important phenomena. Firstly, anti-Americanism and Americanophilia are both the outcome of a game of mirrors. This needs to be realised if one is to understand that there is no 'anti-Americanism' without American 'un-Americanness'. Secondly, there is no neutral and universally acceptable definition of anti-Americanism.

Each of the texts in this present volume proposes its own definition. There is a sense in which the diversity of definitions reflects the variety of political opinions and the difficulty of achieving general agreement. On the one hand, there is the person who regards as anti-American any criticism that lumps the United States in with the Soviet Union, while on the other, there is the observer who believes that anti-Americanism should be treated as 'pathological', which, in the eyes of someone else again, is a good reason for desisting from any criticism of the United States.

One need look not further than this lack of agreement to appreciate the issues raised in trying to pin down the phenomenon. First of all, any analysis of the United States very quickly degenerates into the sort of moral judgements that are typical of anti-Americanism, and particularly of French anti-Americanism, because both nations lay claim to universality and each of them offers an ethical model to the world. Secondly, this inability to identify what is undeniably a real phenomenon has led certain authors to question the concept's operative value, on the grounds that it is incongruent with French attitudes. In their view, the pro- or anti-American dichotomy is not very useful when it comes to trying to achieve a classification according to different communities defined in social terms. To parody a well-known French saying, everyone has been, is, or will be anti-American or pro-American, and it is something that dates back to the birth of that nation, because the American 'model' has always been a source of fascination. Anyway, the difficulty of using rigidly defined terminology has been amply demonstrated by the constant fluctuation in the meaning of the words 'anti-Americanism' and 'Americanophilia', and the lasting temptation to talk about anti-Americanism and ignore its antithesis.

Nonetheless, even though it is elusive, the phenomenon of anti-Americanism remains a fascinating one because of what it tells us about the development of collective and individual attitudes and their part in the history of ideas. Who, then, is anti-American or pro-American? We should undoubtedly start by asking ourselves the question, because the dichotomy is intrinsically part of us, particularly those of us involved with the United States.

According to Alfred Grosser, 'any judgement that apportions equal moral blame to the United States and the Soviet Union' is anti-American. Many people are or have been anti-American in these terms. However, they refuse to be regarded as anti-American because they see no difference between American policy in Vietnam and Soviet policy in Afghanistan. It is even conceivable that they regard the Americans as more culpable in this respect, on the fundamental grounds that Vietnam, albeit no paragon of virtue, was devastated by democratic America precisely in the name of shared democratic values. 'The United States ... virtually alone among nations, found and to some extent still finds its identity not so much in ethnic community or shared historical experience as in dedication to a value system; and the reiteration of these values, the repeated proclamation of and dedication to the liberal creed, has always been a fundamental element in the cohesion of American society.'[5] It is in the name of that (imperfect) morality that any distinction is refused as amoral and hence anti-American. Was it anti-French to reject *'Algérie française'*? Oddly enough this aspect of the dilemma is ignored. Are all those who are not anti-Soviet *ipso facto* anti-American? On what grounds?

Thus 'pro-American' and 'anti-American' sentiments can coexist within the same individual, and the contradictions and conflict between them can divide his or her judgement at a given moment. At the same time, individuals can change their perceptions. Usually this evolution is from anti-Americanism to pro-American attitudes – people rarely going in the opposite direction. Moreover, those who have made that particular journey are even wont to maintain that it is not themselves but American realities that have changed. It is always a bit difficult for a 'born again' Americanophile to acknowledge his Americanophobic past ...[6]

Are our personal attitudes a reflection of group behaviour? Are our 'idiosyncrasies' the outcome of the many and varied pressures on us? For whereas at first sight it might seem easy enough to establish a spectrum of attitudes from extreme anti-Americanism to extreme pro-Americanism – on the basis of political affiliation, for instance – it rapidly becomes apparent that historical developments are smoothed out and the reality outrageously oversimplified in the process. Roughly speaking, of course, it would seem that the political extremes are anti-American and the centre pro-American – in France, at any rate. On the extreme right, *'L'Action française* used to believe that "Anglo-Saxon" political ideas and practice exhibited every possible fault; after all they gave birth to the French Revolution: that worst of calamities. The governing "plutocracy" of the United States, the rule of money, "the great empires ... natural or artificial amalgams which will always cause wise men to tremble", "the rigorous criticism of Theodore Roosevelt's American imperialism"'[7] were all at the root of the anti-Americanism found in the works of Maurras. There are even traces of them to be found in the writings of the virtual descendants of Maurrasism of the present day, from Alain de Benoist to the Gaullists: 'General de Gaulle's anti-Americanism, based on his experiences of the years from 1940 to 1945, or more precisely on the subjective conviction he formed about American intentions, was characterised by his demand for national independence and French *grandeur*'.[8]

On the Left, it was the Communist Party which made a big thing of defending French interests in the face of American hegemony. In the process they relied on the support of so-called 'neutralist' opinion which wanted to preserve an equal balance between the two superpowers – an aspiration close to the one of the pillars of Gaullism. Here again we have an area of ambiguity.

It is also fair to assume that the centre ground of French politics is more favourable to the United States. Indeed, ever since the end of the war, parties ranging from the Socialists to the Christian Democrats have frequently adopted pro-American positions, so much so, in fact, that they provided easy targets for accusations of '*atlanticisme*' on the part of their ideological opponents: the Communists from one side, and the Gaullists from the other. For the fact is that the actual antithesis of the charge of anti-Americanism – in the scornful sense – is the accusation of '*atlanticisme*' (also used pejoratively).

This is clearly a generalisation. There are, of course, currents within the Socialist Party which are less impressed by American ideas, such as the CERES who even accused Michel Rocard's followers of being ' *la gauche américaine*' – and no compliment was intended. Similarly, the results of a SOFRES poll published in *Le Monde* of 6 November 1984 showed that the RPR was the party which most supported American positions and that the Socialist Party was less enthusiastic about American policies than the parties of the Right. However, are we really talking about pro- or anti-American positions here, or might it not instead be a question of political assessments of particular political decisions? Might it not be a question of mistaking the leadership for the rank-and-file? It is only too obvious, in fact, that there can be enormous divisions between party élites and the rank-and-file, as well as between different élites in the same party, and indeed within the same élite, on occasions.

Occasionally, however, one does find a social group unanimously displaying a rigorously neutral attitude to the American model. As Roger Martin, Richard Armand and Sylvie Serra[9] have shown, industry has adopted a deliberately 'pragmatic' stance. According to Sylvie Serra, 'In business circles one rarely comes across anything that might conceivably be construed as an anti-American reaction'. She adds that any economic difficulties that businessmen might have with American firms are more likely to engender self-criticism than any bitterness towards their trans-Atlantic partners.

On the other hand, one may well pose the question whether there does not actually exist a sort of 'tropism' about the United States among certain sections of the national community. It is certainly evident in the case of many leading personalities in politics, the economy and culture. One comes across traces of it in the most unexpected writings – such as Charles de Gaulle (in 1917!) worrying about judicial review in the United States. But such tropism does not rule out a rejection of the model. Jacques Thibau, for instance, has stressed the exaggerated nature of 'idyllic' representations of the business world, the artificial contrast 'between the actual state of affairs and what is ideological and rhetorical propaganda'. In fact, as he pointed out at the anti-Americanism symposium, one should include 'among the *"exilés"* and *"fantasmatiques"* of the 1970s M. Vincent Auriol, the last President of the 4th Republic, General de Gaulle, the first President, M. Georges Pompidou, the second President and M. Giscard d'Estaing, the third President of the 5th Republic'.[10] A pragmatic acceptance of reality should not therefore be mistaken for anti-Americanism.

The fact is that (almost) anyone can be put down as an anti-American if one starts playing the entertaining (albeit oversimplifying) game of quotations. Who, indeed, wrote: 'I know of no country, where, by and large, there exists less independence of mind or true freedom of discussion than in America'? Who, for that matter, dared to write: 'The Americans of the United States have [exterminated the Indian race and prevented the Indians from sharing their rights] with an amazing ease, without fuss, quite legally and philanthropically, without bloodshed, without violating any one of the great ethical principles in the eyes of the world.

It would be impossible to destroy human beings with any greater respect for human rights'? Who, finally, had the gall to declare: 'I believe that it is the ever increasing effect of the despotism of the majority in the United States which above all accounts for the lack of noteworthy personalities in political life there at the present time'? None other than Alexis de Tocqueville, in all three cases. Notwithstanding, the only de Tocqueville normally presented to us is the one who displayed admiration and respect for the usages and customs of American democracy. Could it be that the other de Tocqueville, the corrosive and sceptical observer, is a bit too *anti-American*?

It would therefore seem hard to find a genuine anti-American. Or have all the anti-Americans since changed their minds and now deny ever having been anti-American? There is one section of society, however, which has been most prone to switch directly from virulent anti-Americanism to America-worship, to be pro-American on one issue and anti-American on another, fascinated one minute and sceptical the next. I refer to that most aware of all social groups, the one which is also the most fickle and inconstant: the intellectuals. Could it be because they are trend-setters? To answer affirmatively one needs to make the distinction suggested by Diana Pinto between various types of intellectuals, and only retain for the purpose of our demonstration that category of media-intellectual whom Diana Pinto[11] describes as the 'gurus'. In an interview given to *L'Evènement du jeudi* (18–24 April 1985), Régis Debray rebuked them gently. Such intellectual circles were 'marvellous at dressing up opportunism as morality, and disguising the support for the strongest side as the defence of universal principles. When, in the fifties, Stalin was the strongest one around, our intellectuals were Stalinist. When everyone thought that Mao was going to make a world revolution, they were for Mao. Now they're for Reagan. They'll always be for the winning side'. And where was Régis Debray when he was mocking the outmoded provincialism of these old-fashioned thinkers, where did he feel he had to go to 'de-Americanise' himself and 'discuss calmly and without hysteria the political and strategic realities of today, and strip down the machinery of the Western Empire'? Why, to the United States, of course, not Paris. Time was when it would have been Latin America. *Autres temps, autres moeurs* . . .

But can weathervane versatility be justly described as intellectual? By following the trend can one be said to be giving thought to the American model or assisting the exploration of reality? Those who shy away from criticism for fear of accusations of anti-Americanism, ridicule and going against the trend or those who – in order to be up-to-date – adopt the opposite position, do no more than skim the froth of the times and play with a superficial America. Convincing analysis can be harsh and critical. It can sometimes even be contradictory or outrageous. What it can never be is the product of fashion or confusion. So does opinion follow the 'gurus', or is it they who reflect the French population's own hesitations, whims and even volte-faces, and merely express them most accurately?

It is no easier to determine the degree of anti-Americanism (or pro-Americanism) in the population as a whole, than it is to do the same for the groups which comprise it. In the absence of texts or declarations, one has to rely on opinion polls, which have been notorious for their lack of continuity, particularly as regards the framing of questions. Nevertheless, an analysis of poll findings does bring out certain trends which serve to demonstrate the flimsiness of the concept.

In so far as it exists, the anti-Americanism of public opinion would seem to us to be partly linked to the Americans' low opinion of the French. In a poll conducted on behalf of President Ford in May 1976 on the eve of his trip to Europe, only 2 per cent of Americans regarded the French as viable partners. Thirty times as many of them trusted the Germans. Such contempt for the French is age-old[12] and still continues. The Americans 'detest the French' the *Financial Times'* Washington correspondent noted in 1984.[13]

In view of this fact, one is bound to wonder what are the root causes of such a mutual lack of understanding. Jean-Baptiste Duroselle recalls in this respect that at the end of the war 'the Americans were obliged by international convention to give their German prisoners-of-war the same rations as their own troops. On the other hand, the scarcity of shipping prevented them providing the 40-million-strong French civilian population with the same sort of supplies. However, the psychological effect of hungry French civilians having to watch German prisoners eating luxury products which they themselves had not seen for four years, such as oranges, chocolate, etc., was to arouse enormous indignation. The rumour swept the country, and was cleverly exploited by the Communists, that the Americans 'prefer the Germans to the French'.[14] There could be no better explanation of how hostility and rancour can take root and grow, and their immediate effect was reflected in the opinion polls of the time.[15]

But let us consider afresh this much-talked-about volte-face of a people who for years were anti-American to the core before suddenly, in Autumn 1984, falling head over heels in love with America. Before analysing the nature of that abrupt swing, it is worth recalling that in November 1984, it was not so much public attitudes towards the United States that changed but feelings about the American President. By 1984, the ageing cowboy of 1980 had become the miraculous job-creator. Thus there is a risk of forgetting that the 'U-turn' of 1945-48 had been far more spectacular. Such amnesia is especially regrettable in that the comparison of the two 'U-turns' does much to challenge the 'communicating vessels' theory: that the degree of popularity of the Soviet Union is inversely proportional to that of the United States. The fact is that the latter achieved popularity in the 1945-48 period without this adversely affecting the fortunes of the Soviet Union in French public opinion.

And recently – in 1982 – the United States was in particular disfavour and its President held in contempt at a time when the Soviet Union's popularity was at its lowest ebb. The 'Solzhenitsyn effect' certainly influenced the USSR's image but not the popularity of the United States. Each image is autonomous and evolves independently in terms of reality. What is important is not whether this is first-hand experience, or whether they are received or even imagined conceptions, but that they are specific realities. There is no cause and effect relationship between anti-Americanism and anti-Sovietism, even though, as perceptions, they are each defined in many different ways in terms of the particular social groups and the specific moment in history. In this respect, the concept of 'anti-Americanism' is no more operative than the concept of 'anti-Sovietism'. In all events, while the inverse ratio theory might be useful in explaining developments within intellectual circles,[16] it is an idea that fails to take into account the feelings of public opinion – which has scarcely ever been pro-Soviet. Suffice it to recall that Victor Kravchenko and Arthur Koestler were the two best-selling authors of the postwar period in France (over half-a-million copies each).

Anti-Americanism/pro-Americanism, fascination/rejection are indissoluble pairs. They can be explained as part of the interplay of intricate, moving mirrors between epochs, nations and social groups, and even within individuals themselves. These changing reflections are the reason why the concept cannot be 'operative', at least in the classic sense of the word. It does not provide a satisfactory basis for clear-cut, stable and well-labelled classifications. On the other hand, it is a marvellous tool for understanding collective mentalities and the historic evolution of ideas – although it is extremely difficult, because of its mobility, to try to explain the attitude of a particular group, within a particular nation, and at a particular moment of time, towards a particular American issue.

This interplay of mirrors is also, and perhaps essentially, related to specific issues. There can be no doubt that the best way of grasping the various connections is to examine individual anti-American themes. There are certain subjects, which, while not actually constituting myths, are nevertheless a constant, such as the myth of 'weightless government' – a less robust state than those elsewhere. Other themes recur and then disappear, only to resurface with even more vigour than ever. This is particularly true in respect of culture, where ideas of *'barbarie'* and *'impérialisme culturel'* abound and mingle. There are others that would seem to be only dictated by intellectual fashion but are actually the most deep-seated attitudes: American 'things' (including – dare one say it? – women reified for the purpose – or food, so dear to the French) form the basis for such judgements of America – and we use this inexact term quite deliberately, since the Americans have actually appropriated the entire continent. American 'things' serve to structure – and perhaps this is the only respect in which the term can be used – the attitudes of fascination and/or rejection from two ideas which constitute the twin pillars of the 'discourse' about America: *modernité* and *domination*.

The three areas which demonstrate most clearly French fascination with American *puissance* and *modernité* are foreign affairs, the economy and culture. It is there that we must also look for the most striking examples of fear of domination and anxiety about the loss of identity. In this respect, Gaullism served to lend French attitudes a unique aspect, and General de Gaulle (whether or not he was an anti-American) created the conditions for the sort of independence which allowed the country to be far less anti-American than it would have been otherwise, far less than it had been previously, and far less than its neighbours are at the present time. It was this different course of development that was reflected, for instance, in the contradictory attitudes to the siting of

Pershing missiles in Europe. Likewise, it seems to us, the institutions which de Gaulle bequeathed to France, and which, moreover, are the most American the country has ever had, allow the French to feel more 'sure of themselves and domineering' – and even condescending on occasions – in their attitudes towards the way that American political institutions themselves operate.[17]

Indeed, the French have insisted on acting as killjoys since the end of the war. From the European Defence Community (EDC) to the Strategic Defence Initiative (SDI), from Phnom Penh to Beirut, from Vietnam to Nicaragua, from the *'force de frappe'* to *Ariane* it has been one long story of challenges, vetoes, critiques or condemnations *vis-à-vis* the United States, even in those periods when America was the flavour of the month in France.

Of course, one should not exaggerate the specifically national character of anti-Americanism, or rather, it would be better to use the term in the plural. France does not have a monopoly of anti-Americanism/pro-Americanism by any means, even if these sentiments assume specific national forms. Moreover, it is possible for one country (such as France in 1984–85) to experience a marked wave of pro-Americanism (or apparently so) at the very moment when another country, even one next door, can be displaying marked anti-American sentiments. Indeed it was the case of Spain during Ronald Reagan's visit of May 1985. As one may expect, the reasons were very different. On that occasion, France was fascinated by and envious of what it saw as an amazing economic revival, while Spain was still smarting from the support that America had given the Franco regime (which knew how to wield the anti-American weapon on occasions) and regarded the presence of American troops on its soil as a military occupation.

However, there is something specifically French about the sort of attitude towards the United States which William Pfaff captured perfectly in a remarkable article written for the *New Yorker*. The French, he said, 'implacably refuse to be backward, "Latin", or patronized. They insistently go their own way, very competently, being rude about it more often than not, evoking impatience, scorn, and sometimes fury from Americans – and from most other Europeans, to whom French intransigence has seemed selfish and often senselessly destructive of European cooperation with the United States.'[18]

Finally, it would be impossible to understand French anti-Americanism/pro-Americanism (is that duality yet another specific characteristic?) without realising that it is part and parcel of an internal French debate that is more or less unrelated to American realities. Reference to the United States, whether in terms of admiration or rejection, is no more than a device in a discussion which actually concerns national affairs alone. Subpoenaed as witnesses, the Americans are not actually called to the stand, even if the polemic is fuelled essentially by arguments culled in the United States. The journey of initiation to the other side of the Atlantic is only a pretext for references to America. However, for sycophants and detractors alike, the United States is no more than a pseudo-target. What they actually have their sights on is domestic opinion. The United States is used only as an image, and the accuracy of perceptions is actually neither here nor there. In this respect variations in the anti-Americanism/pro-Americanism syndrome have very little to do with American decisions. American policies are used as a cover for domestic quarrels. They are not their root cause. Once this is realised, it is easier to understand certain trends which at first sight seem incongruous. They reflect and amplify both American and French realities and the complexity of their interaction – not to mention our own personal perplexities, as Guy Sorman demonstrates (see ch. 16).

In the final analysis, the anti-Americanism/pro-Americanism phenomenon is a complex sum of multifarious contradictions: within the individual, within a nation, between the United States and the rest of the world. The fact remains that these contradictions are not solely a reflection of American realities, but the outcome of the American mirage. It is not actually the United States but a representation of the United States which underlies the pro- and anti-American debate. But the United States itself is on show and it consciously tries to project a certain image of itself.

However, setting aside specifically French characteristics, the domestic political debate, and individual or group manifestations of anti-Americanism, it is clear that the phenomenon is partly rooted in the behaviour of the Americans themselves. Indeed it is the 'imperial' role of the United States which has motivated outside reactions. There is evidence for this in foreign policy, evidence too in cultural and economic matters. There is a connection between the image that the Americans seek to project of themselves and the image that the French are prepared to accept, criticise or reject. It is very obvious, for instance, that the Americans' smugness about the economic recovery (particularly evident in the more or less chauvinistic demonstrations which punctuated the reactions of the American public at the Los Angeles Olympics) was matched by pessimism on the part of the Europeans, who were just as convinced of their own shortcomings – which the Americans never tired of pointing out to them, such as during Mr Reagan's official trip to Europe in May 1985. Similarly, America's universal and universalist vision is rivalled by that of the French. This point is worth closer attention as being one of the likely sources of misunderstanding. It also happens to be the area where a 'communicating vessels' effect can be most clearly seen – via a rivalry which, though denied, is certainly real, albeit unequal.

What is often remarkable about American declarations is the systematic attempt to prove that France is engaged in cultural imperialism, as a way of proving how wrong the French are to accuse the United States of this dreadful sin. For instance, they mock France's defence of its national language as 'the greatest proof of national insularity' (*Wall Street Journal*, 13 February 1985). The French, it is claimed, are obsessed by the thought that their culture and language are being outstripped. They are apparently seeking to make up for these setbacks by a deliberate official policy of cultural assistance abroad. Nothing of the kind allegedly exists in the United States, according to such American authors.

Wall Street Journal columnist Raymond Sokolov found *Le Monde*'s satisfaction that 300 000 pupils abroad were able to learn French at schools run by the *Alliance française* (incidentally, a *private* association), a trifle ludicrous: there existed nothing of the kind in the United States to assist the promotion of the English language.[19] Yet the USIS (a governmental body whose 1983 budget was $588 million) organises the teaching of English to some 450 000 young foreigners, particularly in Latin America, in its specialised centres.[20] Moreover, is it not actually part of a more global strategy which profits from the far more extensive activities of the British in this sphere (in the shape of the British Council), while greatly diversifying the forms of US aid? Since 1983, for instance, the United States assisted the publication of some 24 000 titles in 57 languages and a total of 183 million copies.[21] France lags far behind in this respect and simply donates some tens of thousands of books each year.

Voice of America (which is sponsored by USIS) was assigned $1.5 billion to modernise its broadcasting capacity over the five years 1984–88.[22] Over three years (1982–84), *Radio-France Interna-*

tionale received $13 million for the same brief. Nevertheless, 'The US Disarms in the International Competition of Ideas' lamented a headline in the *Wall Street Journal* (European edition) of 10 August 1984, whereas the same (anti-French?) newspaper had reported earlier that year (13 February 1984) that the Socialist government had invested 'huge sums of money' to ensure that French remained 'a major world language', and became in the words of François Mitterrand 'the preferred vehicle of universal values'.

Is it that the Americans do not consider their civilisation to be a vehicle of universal values? In fact the way that American cultural action has developed abroad is entirely in line with the concerns expressed by President Reagan in a speech given to the House of Commons on 8 June 1982, which had been announced by the American authorities as the 'most important Presidential address since World War II'. President Reagan made no bones about it: 'The objective I propose is quite simple to state: to foster the infrastructure of democracy ... which allows people to choose their own way to develop their own culture, to reconcile their own differences through peaceful means. This is not cultural imperialism; it is providing the means for genuine self-determination and protection for diversity ... the ultimate determinant in the struggle that's now going on in the world will not be bombs and rockets, but a test of wills and ideas'.[23] In other words, it was a matter of promoting universal values as these are understood or defined by the biggest world power.

In the United States, it goes under the name of 'democracy'. In France they call it 'civilisation'. But although the names may differ, the roots of the rivalry and of the consequent misunderstandings are to be found in a common craving for universalism; in the temptation to believe that 'one's own' values are superior and more universal (superior because they are universal); and in the determination to export them, and even impose them on the rest of the world. This would seem to be the only sentiment truly worthy of the title 'anti-Americanism' – or 'anti-Gallicanism'. It is the feeling of having something unique to offer the world, something that is challenged by one's rival. It can be the Americanisation of France – whether real or conjectured – perceived as something prejudicial to the country's underlying values. Or it can be French criticism of America's behaviour in Vietnam, felt by the Americans as being prejudicial to the democratic mission of the United States. The rivalry between France and the United States, in so far as it can exist between two such mismatched opponents, is actually grounded on an eminently ethical view of national society. In this respect it is implacable. Fascination and rejection will continue to colour French judgements of the United States. To a lesser extent (since the Americans are not particularly interested in France) this dual sentiment will also continue to colour American judgements of France.

Notes

1. William Safire, *Safire's Political Dictionary* (New York: Random House, 1978) p. 19.
2. Alexis de Tocquevillle, *De la Démocratie en Amerique* (Paris: Gallimard, 1961), vol. 2, p. 233.
3. However, the *Trésor de la langue française*, published by the National Centre for Scientific Research (CNRS), does include the word anti-français which it defines as 'hostile to the interests and ideals of France and the French', giving as its main illustration, a quotation from Barrès where he refers to 'a spiteful, anti-French teacher'. But this is the only reference we have traced of it.
4. I use the neologism *in-américanité* to translate 'un-American' since the usual translation of *'anti-américain'* is virtually a contradiction in terms, particularly as it is used to translate two different American words (anti-American and un-American) which express two different concepts.
5. Timothy Garton Ash, 'Backyards', *New York Review of Books*, 22 November 1984, p. 3.
6. Thus, for instance, Jean-Marie Benoist, a reaganite in the 1980s, published in the mid-1970s a strongly anti-American article entitled 'L'épuisement d'un modèle: le mythe anglo-saxon' in *Les Conditions de l'indépendance nationale dans le monde moderne* (Paris: Cujas, 1977).
7. Jacques Thibau, *La France colonisée* (Paris: Flammarion, 1980) p. 33.
8. Jean-Baptiste Duroselle, *La France et les Etats-Unis des origines à nos jours* (Paris: Seuil, 1976) p. 212.
9. These personalities took part in the symposium on French perceptions of the United States, sponsored by the CERI (Paris, 11–12 December 1984).
10. This was Jacques Thibau's argument at 'CERI' symposium.
11. See her contribution to the present volume.
12. Jean-Baptiste Duroselle, op. cit., pp. 39–40 and 86.
13. Reginald Dale, 'L'Amérique fatiguée de l'Europe?', *Trente jours d'Europe*, Sept.-Oct. 1984, p. 5.
14. Jean-Baptiste Duroselle, op. cit., p. 208.
15. See Chap. 5 by Jacques Rupnik and Muriel Humbertjean in this present volume.
16. See the contribution by Marie-Christine Granjon, chap. 8.
17. The reference here is to chaps. 12 and 15 by Michael Harrison and Julien Feydy, respectively, in this present volume.

18. William Pfaff, 'The French exception', *New Yorker*, 24 January 1977.
19. References to *Wall Street Journal* (European edition) 18 January 1985 and *Le Monde*, 12 December 1984.
20. *U.S. News and World Report*, 18 February 1985.
21. *Wall Street Journal* (European edition) 10 August 1985.
22. *New York Times*, 26 December 1984.
23. As reported in *Historical documents of 1982*, Congressional Quarterly Inc., pp. 485 and 487.

18
By Way of Conclusion
André Kaspi

What if anti-Americanism did not exist? After reading the various texts in this volume, which reflect the widest range of viewpoints, such a question must seem pointless to say the least. It must exist because it is spoken about so frequently. Admittedly it is difficult to define. The *Grand Larousse de la Langue française* supplies 32 notorious antis which people the French mind, such as anti-Christian, anti-masonic, anti-racist, anti-spiritualist, and so on and so on. But 'anti-American' is not among them! On the other hand the definition of 'Americanism' dates back to 1866: 'Life-style imitating that of the Americans, especially the inhabitants of the USA'. The entry quotes a sentence by Ernest Renan as an illustration: 'The world moves with a kind of Americanism that injures our refined ways of thinking'. The concept has always been rather too vague to be properly understood.

And yet anti-Americanism is a style of thinking that has resurfaced at various times in recent French history. Take, for instance, the following letter from Pablo de La Higuera published in *Le Monde* shortly after Kissinger voiced his fears and reservations at the prospect of Italian and French Communists participating in the government of their countries: 'Are France and Italy intending to warn the United States against the possibility of an undesirable result in the American presidential election? And one is not talking about the risk of electing a Communist, or even a left-winger, of course. That kind of danger does not exist over there, and even if it did, one can be sure that American democracy would do the necessary to prevent it'. It's all in there: the appeal to the readers' nationalism, the suggestion of a repressive regime, disdain for a political system that prevents a left-wing victory. But having got his teeth into it, the journalist was not going to leave it there and he went on to work himself up to the following conclusion: 'Can one be really sure that the future leader of the greatest economic, scientific and military power of the planet will have the requisite level of intelligence to perform such a function?' Here the aggressive tone reaches new heights, with the suggestion that the statesmen who govern the United States have a low IQ and that the country's strength resides solely in the economy, science and military power. Anti-Americanism is out in the open. The target of the offence can no longer be denied. We have the culprit at last.

In the final analysis, anti- and pro-Americanism often sail in convoy. According to circumstances, they can either be vague feelings or powerful sentiments. They sound quite different if voiced by a politician, by an intellectual or by an industrialist. They constitute a discourse which can be related to everyday reality, or not, as the case may be. In other words, they form part of a backcloth against which similar or totally different acts are played out. Depending on the situation, anti-Americanism can take the form of malice, resentment, hatred or condescension, all of them passions or states of mind. Anti-Americanism is not a rational attitude but a question of passion, instinct and the irrational. Should one conclude, therefore, that it resembles other attitudes such as anti-semitism? Certainly not. One need hardly stress the difference between the situation of the Americans and the Jews in different countries. Moreover, there is no comparing the origins of the two 'antis' or their consequences. Possibly the only thing they have in common is that they are both a matter of imaginations run riot, whereby the image becomes wildly divorced from the reality. One does not need to know the United States to voice anti-American sentiments. It is almost better never to have been there and to have only the vaguest notions of the country, since such attitudes belong to the realm of fantasy and imagination. I would cite as corroboration the excellent little book published by Sorbonne professor Henri Hauser, under the title *L'Amérique vivante*, on his return from a trip to America. On page 12 he makes a point which is so simple that it is almost ingenuous. It may sound trite but it is nonetheless convincing: 'One can like the United States without admiring the Ku Klux Klan'. As far as anti-Americanism is concerned, the USA and the Ku Klux Klan are one and the same, since it refuses to acknowledge any diversity or complexity. It reinforces generally accepted ideas and sets them in concrete. It has nothing in common with critical analysis since the latter takes into account the acceptable and the unacceptable, and seeks to make balanced and sensitive judgements. The anti-American behaves like a bull in a china shop. But this case has an aggravating circumstance: the bull draws the conclusion that the reason the china is fragile is because it is of poor quality.

It remains a mystery for all that. If anti-Americanism belongs to the realm of psychopathology, how are we to explain that the French and the Americans alike revel in it to such a degree that they never tire of asking what it is and what it signifies. On the American side, the question never changes and can even become obsessive, as all foreign observers have noticed. Americans simply love to be loved. They are amazed that anyone could detest them. They are fascinated by the antipathy which they arouse. For the Americans, anti-Americanism is a means for self-contemplation as a nation. 'What have we done to justify such hostility? What can we do to allay it? Are we really Evil incarnate or is it that our opponents are also enemies of Good?' Anti-Americanism is a typically American topic. It does not indicate any real interest in the foreign world; it is a reflection of American preoccupations, a way of staying at home, a kind of narcissism. But it is also typically French. The theme underlies much of the national discourse. The French have always had a tendency to perceive American society either as model or *bête noire*. From top to bottom of the intellectual scale, the same question is being asked all the time: Is what is happening over there a premonition of what will happen over here? Is California now what France will be like in 20 or 30 years time? There is something genuine both about the question and the concern. There is also a lot of amateur guesswork, in the sense that mutual interactions between the two societies need to be taken into account. What matters, in spite of everything, is that the Americans constructed a universal model – just like the French. The two models end up being compared with each other. They cannot co-exist. If one of them weakens, it ceases to inspire the men and women of the planet, and that can only benefit the other. The French love recalling that famous remark of de Tocqueville's: 'I admit that in America I saw more than just America'. So what do we have – two kinds of universalism or two varieties of narcissism?

The debates and controversies analysed in this present volume have given us deeper insights into anti-Americanism, of which we had a rather hazy and intuitive notion until then. For a long time there was a need to distinguish between the different varieties of anti-Americanism, as well as to analyse their arguments and detect which have survived or not. The scope of the phenomenon has changed over the years, of course. Areas of concern at the time of the Cold War are no longer topical three decades on. Georges Duhamel's objections seem antiquated nowadays, as well as ineffectual. The topic of multinational companies had a notable airing in the 1970s which reflected some of the main preoccupations of a particular historical epoch. The classification and chronology of the phenomenon have therefore been as enlightening as they were necessary. The links between the spheres of politics and culture that emerge are most significant. How can one possibly talk about the anti-Americanism of the 1920s without some reference to the painful and traumatic debates about the war debts? The atmosphere of those days is extremely illuminating. Similarly, one should not underestimate the influence of Gaullist attitudes, even if the rhetoric of General de Gaulle did not entirely match what he did in practice. The analysis of thinking in the business world has also proved fascinating. It has shown that even when competition has been particularly harsh and American domination has been indisputable, French businessmen have tended to display admiration or understanding, but never hostility. This is further proof that anti-Americanism is a product of people's imaginations and is not rooted in actual experience. And obviously there are other areas of French national life that still require analysis. It truly is an inexhaustible and instructive field of study.

There are three areas, however, that have scarcely been examined. The role of the media merits wider study. One recalls the fuss over Canadian journalist Denise Bombardier's diagnosis of French TV news broadcasts published under the title *La Voix de la France* – an expression dear to a certain late French President. It is a subject that ought not to be neglected, even if it is not the easiest to tackle. Television news broadcasts offer a mine of information, and detailed study is required of reportage, films and interviews. And, as for the press, I recall on one occasion studying the Parisian dailies to see how they covered the American primaries of 1984. One particular newspaper, which prides itself on providing matter for intellectual debate, clearly did not have a good grasp of what happens in primaries and caucuses. I caught it in the very act of fostering illusions about the American system, and actually creating and promoting stereotypes. Meanwhile, another daily newspaper, which one might have thought to be motivated by a fundamental hostility towards the United States, turned out to display an unshakeable sympathy for that country and to be remarkably informed about its people and their way of thinking. In short, from *Le Monde* to *Libération*, the influence of the daily press merits closer attention.

There is also a need to assess the influence of a phenomenon which is fairly new. Until recently, very few French tourists visited the United States. During the years from Nixon to Reagan, travel to the United States was both possible and profitable, even though the rise in the value of the dollar since 1981 would seem to have halted the trend which was turning the Far West, the Great Lakes and New York City into favourite destinations for French tourists. Previously only the privileged used to cross the Atlantic, to return loaded with memories and impressions about which they would eventually publish the inevitable account reflecting reality with varying degrees of fidelity. There was another possible source of information: American tourists in France. However, these were normally only passing through and had very little contact with the French population. It would therefore be worthwhile studying the impact of tourism on French perceptions of the United States. Has it merely reinforced existing prejudices or actually broadened people's outlooks? It is a question which the present authors fail to answer. Maybe they were too interested in the intellectuals. The latter admittedly produce the literature, but they do not necessarily reflect the feelings of the majority.

Finally, there is no mention of education. This is a regrettable omission. In an article published in the journal *Historien et Géographes*, Diana Pinto has dissected the content of history and geography text-books for the top years of secondary-level education. Her conclusions make fascinating reading. What she has done is to contrast the presentation of the United States and the Soviet Union, and compare what the geographers say with the historians' treatment of the subject-matter. It emerges that the historians have changed their tune over the recent period, so that there is now a greater sympathy for the United States and less for the Soviet Union, whereas at the beginning of the 1980s, the geographers were using the same language they had used a decade earlier. These differences are fundamental. They serve to colour education, and it is education that moulds people's thinking – let us never forget. This is particularly important in view of the fact that many students will never again have the opportunity, in their subsequent course of study, to return to the subject of the United States.

In every case, it boils down to the same question: Where does anti-Americanism come from? What is its main source? The atmosphere of the times, political circumstances, the media, contacts between our peoples (or the lack of them), educational curricula – these are all factors whose influence we seek to measure. It is difficult to come to any hard and fast conclusions, partly because, as we have already said, the subject itself is not easy to fit into very rigid frameworks or categories, and partly because history has more than one trick up its sleeve. Moreover, it proceeds zig-zag fashion as if trying to dodge all attempts to grasp or apprehend it.

There are other avenues of research that come to mind in addition to the subjects dealt with in the present book, or the controversies touched on here. The first is the question of interactions. It is impossible to treat the subject solely in terms of politics, or of economics, or of culture. All three areas belong to an overall picture that has still to be assembled. Studies of separate areas are vital, so long as they are linked to the rest. The same could be said of the different contexts and influences. As an example, we can take the case of the Rosenbergs – a dramatic episode in the history of the United States that gave rise at the time to a mighty explosion of anti-Americanism, particularly in France. The Communist Party was not entirely to blame for this, since such figures as Vincent Auriol, then President of France, and Pope Pius XII also protested against the death sentences and executions. Even so, there were many other issues at the time that affected Franco-American relations, from the rebuilding of Europe (and we have in mind, above all, the European Defence Community), to the German revival and the role of the Communists in the political life of France. Outside the Western European framework, still other events were confusing the picture, such as the death of Stalin and the first signs of a thaw, as well as the consequences of the purges in Czechoslovakia, Hungary and Poland. All those factors interacted, so it is fair to ask what anti-Americanism we are talking about. Which America was the target? Which France was so sharply critical of the United States? Over-hastiness could botch the job. The details are still far from clear. In view of this, is it hasty general conclusions that we need or painstaking comparative study?

The fact is that the French do little by way of comparative study and the Americans are extremely half-hearted about it. Nonetheless it is an extremely promising field, and one which we would be wrong to ignore. A comparison of anti-Americanism and anti-Sovietism is a natural further step: two superpowers, two conflicting models of society, two different concepts of the world and the future. However, France belongs to the Western World, and its relationship with the United States cannot be treated in the same terms as its relationship with the Soviet Union, even if, until recently, the Communist Party exercised an influence over as much as a fifth to one quarter of the population. Comparisons are worthwhile so long as they are not taken to extremes, and make nonsense of the situation. The same goes, in fact, as far as all other 'antis' of our century are concerned, each of which displays its own specific characteristics. We have to observe the same caution when we compare anti-Americanism with the Anglophobia of our grandfathers and the anti-Germanism of our fathers. These are not phenomena of the same order. A long history of wars with England was succeeded by a period of tension and, at the very least, rivalry. After 1870, Germany became our hereditary enemy, before becoming our ally and main trading partner. None of this can be said of the United States. There is nothing humdrum or hackneyed about anti-Americanism. It continues to be a special category.

On the other hand, France is not the only country in the world where anti-Americanism has had its moments of glory. While the French may be more pro- than anti-American at the present time, the same cannot be said of the Germans or the English. But when it comes to comparisons, the least said the better about other parts of the world like Latin America or the Middle East. It would be interesting to weigh French anti-Americanism and German anti-Americanism on the same scale. Do they share the same origins, the same content and the same evolution? If they are different, why are they different? Comparisons help to bring out peculiarities, and provide a basis for forecasts. There is still one important question that has yet to be raised: Has French anti-Americanism finally ceased to exist? Observers of present events who are too close to what is going on have a tendency to react as if they were standing at a historical terminus, as if history was capable of reaching conclusion. At the risk of jarring with this chorus of optimism, I ought to say that I do not believe that anti-Americanism has yet given up the ghost. Admittedly if has suffered a battering in recent years and been given the last rites – albeit rather hastily. But it would not take much for it to revive, fill out and make a successful return to centre stage, to the astonishment of more than one observer. The proof of what I say is to be found in West Germany. For years, that country was the Americanised country *par excellence*, a kind of unshakeable ally of the United States – some would have happily described it as the Americans' Trojan Horse. Public opinion there has changed. Not to the point that the 'antis' are now in the majority, but sufficiently for France now to be regarded as a refuge for positive feelings towards the United States

Finally, my third suggestion brings us back to the United States itself. There has always been a tendency to ignore American anti-Americanism. It is superflous to recall that unlike all other nations the Americans do not belong to a homogeneous community. The most diverse opinions are aired and published there. What one can hear on the university campus has nothing to do with what is said in the Deep America of Peyton Place. Many Americans loathe their government, their economic system and their social structures. They proclaim their views both at home and abroad. And there is no reason why they should not. But foreigners then join in a chorus of which they do not understand all the words – with understandable results. McCarthyism, for instance, caused intellectuals and film-makers to flee the United States and they rightly alerted the people of Europe to the dangers then facing America. On occasions, they even managed to create or foster stereotypes. The American played by Jules Dassin in his film *Never on Sunday* is friendly and stupid. He wants to do too much and ends up producing the opposite result. He lacks the least refinement. When the canny Greeks take him to the cleaners, he has no one but himself to blame. As we all know, the Vietnam War gave rise to demonstrations, first in the United States and then abroad. This was another case where the most violent accusations against US government policy came from the mouths of Johnson's and Nixon's political opponents. They were taken up either innocently or otherwise – in Europe. The list of examples is endless, from Watergate, which in spite of everything shocked the French less than the Americans, to Jimmy Carter's presidency, to what has come to be called Reaganism. The influence of American anti-Americanism on French anti-Americanism – this is an avenue that urgently needs exploring if we are to get to the bottom of a phenomenon which so eludes our understanding.

Index

L'Action française 223–4
Adam, Paul, Le Trust 48
Adams, John 147
Afghanistan 20, 183, 223
Africa, French policy 185–6
agrégation system 208
Akzin, Benjamin, criticism by 190
Albert, Michel 104
Algerian independence
  gained 182
Algerian Independence
  struggle 122
Algerian War 173, 174
America, see USA
American adventurism 87
American anti-Americanism 108–10, 238, 242
  influence on French anti-Americanism 242
American characters,
  stereotyped 43
American cinema 50, 69
  invasion by 71
American civilisation
  seen as anti-French and anti-humanistic 67
  seen as non-aesthetic 20–1
American corporations 138
American cultural action
  abroad 233
American cultural imperialism 25
American cultural influence
  (1984) 93–4
'American Dream' 1
American economy 104
  expansion of 25
American embargoes 139
American flexibility/French
  rigidity 113–14
American foreign policy,
  commitment to Europe 112
American foreign trade
  deficit 104, 161
American imperialism 11

American insensitivity 176
American institutional processes
  20th-century French
  specialists 201
  a more thorough knowledge
  of 201
American institutions
  attractive to researchers 193
  French school of research
  into 196
  political, French
  publications 189–202
American intellectuals
  positions of 110
  pro-Americanism of 110
American investment, assisted in
  growth of French
  economy 126–7
American left, view of Sartre 124
American macro-economic
  model 165
American might, a challenge or a
  threat 138
American model
  attractiveness of 180
  change in 205–6
American neutrality, and
  Vichy 55–6
American novel, enthusiasm of
  Sartre and de Beauvoir 117–18
American people, seen as puerile
  and arrogant 93
American policies, image of 86–8
American radicals 100
American smugness, about
  economic recovery 231–2
American society
  capacity for innovation, mobility
  and professionalism
  admired 113–14
  and culture, attractiveness
  of 93–4
American tourists in France 240

244

Index

American tradition, supposedly influenced by French 191
American troops
  expulsion of 183
  need for in Europe 183–4
American Universities, intellectual activities 100–1
American Way of Life 20–1, 94
  aversion or fascination 74–5
American wealth, resentment of 12
'américanisation' 46
Americanisation
  defined 236
  only the progress of industrial civilisation 126
  reversal of to make France strong again 58
'Americanism(e)' 170
  defined 219
Americanisms
  complaints about invasion of English language 36
  invading the French language 22–3
Americans
  behaviour of, and anti-Americanism 231–2
  as competitors and partners 139–40
  convinced of American superiority 221
  cured of anti-French biases 170
  in French fiction (1870–1914) 43
  love to be loved 238
  low opinion of French 227
  reconciling conformism and individualism 118
  seen as conformist 122–3
  seen as perpetual adolescents 59
anti-American criticism, in the 1930s 71–2
anti-Americanism 42, 190, 202, 228
  in the 1970s 143, 156–7
  accusations of individualism and materialism 214
  American 108–10, 238, 242
  and anti-imperialist left 215
  causes of in business 138–9
  Communist 17
  conjoncturel and *conjecturel* 111
  declining, USA no longer a dominant model 161–2
  definitions of 219–20, 222; no universally accepted definition 221
  distinction between cultural and political 52
  epidemiology 39–40
  an expression of anti-German feeling 15
  Gaullist 16–17
  immunology 40–1
  interwar period 170
  and left-wing French government 163–4
  not rational 237
  nothing in common with critical analysis 237–8
  in other countries 242–3
  political and cultural 70–1
  of population as a whole 227
  posology 38
  predisposition 35–7
  rarely found in business 137
  resentment over dependence on USA 170–1
  in the resistance 62–3
  result of American self-satisfaction 191
  result of France's decline as a major power 169–70
  resurgence of in cultural field 20
  where does it come from? 240–1
anti-Americanism/pro-Americanism 230–1
  interplay of specific issues 228–9
anti-Americans, and primacy of culture 155–6
anti-colonialism, American 173, 174
anti-Communism 185
anti-culture 155
anti-Reagan feelings 4–5

anti-semitism 99–100, 190
anti-Sovietism 70, 80, 81, 185, 220, 228
Aron, Raymond 116
　anti-communist 116–17, 121
　assessment of Vietnam War 128–9
　attitude to American intervention in Vietnam 127
　comment on Sartre 122
　defence of USA 116
　felt that Western economies had succeeded better than Socialist economies 124
　La République impériale 125, 129
　Mémoires 101, 117, 121
　opposed *force de frappe* 125
　shocked by General de Gaulle's anti-Americanism 121
　supported US foreign policy 130
　views on the USA 124–5
Aron, Robert 48
arrogance, traditional 213
Association Française de Science Politique, Saturday talks 209
Atlantic Alliance, movement in favour of 88–9
Atlantic Treaty myth 181
atlanticisme 224
Auriol, President Vincent 225, 241
　on Indochina 173
Aveline, Claude, *Lettres Françaises* 68
aversion and fascination, French attitude to USA 83

Barre, Prime Minister Raymond, on international competition 148–9
Barrès, Maurice 48
Baudelaire, Charles P. 46
　describing USA 214
Baudet, Claude, and anti-Americanism 172
Baudrillard, Jean 1
Beave-Méry, Hubert 70
　suggested neutralism 172
Beauvoir, Simone de 116

　interest in American civilisation 117
　La Force des choses 121–2
　L'Amérique au jour le jour 119–20
　Les Mandarins, quoted 69–70
　praise and social criticism of USA 120
　saw America as reactionary 122–3
　took part in Russell Tribunal 123
　view of American intellectuals 123
Benoist, Alain de, on totalitarianism 21
Benoist, Jean-Marie
　and American cultural imperialism 21
　and anti-culture 155
　on twin monolithic tyrannies of uniformity 19
Benoist-Méchin, Jaques, rejection of USA 61
Bernanos, Georges, *La France contre les robots* 75
Bernheim, Nicole, *Les Années Reagan* 214–15
Bloch, Jean-Richard, *Destin du siècle* 48
Blum-Byrnes agreements 69, 71
book titles published, France and USA 73
Boris, Georges 51
Boutmy, Emile 51, 199–200
　on American imperialism 192, 196
　blunt manner of analysis 193
　criticised de Tocqueville 195
　Eléments d'une psychologie du peuple américain 194
　expressing racism 189
　on the federal system 198–9
　on legislative activity in USA 200
　perceived Welfare State as bad for individualism 199
　recognised Europe and America as different 194
Britain, attitude to USA 36–7

British Council 232
Bryce, Viscount, *American Commonwealth* 36
Buchez, Philippe B. J., critical analysis of de Tocqueville and de Baumont studies 214
business, disrupted by politics 139

Canu, Jean, *Villes et paysages d'Amérique* 48–9
capitalism 68
capitalist industrialisation 125
capitalist plot theory 146–8
Capitant, René 208
Carter administration 4
Carter, President Jimmy 5, 86, 130
Central America, American policies 88
centralisation 193, 198
CERES (Centre d'Etude, de Recherche et d'Education Socialiste) 224
solution offered 152–3
Chastellux, Marquis de 47
chauvinism
American and European 190
good and bad 45–6
Chevènement, Jean-Pierre 9, 81
Chirac government 26
Chirac, Jacques 179
civilisation 233
class struggle, global 131
'classe dirigeante', consistency of 110–13
Closets, François de, *Toujours Plus!* 114
Cobol-Kabul coups 18–19
Coca-Cola, symbol of American colonisation 18
Cold War 110, 131, 169, 172
and anti-Americanism 67–75
effect on French attitudes 83
colonialism, conflict between France and USA 173
'colonisation' of France 150–1
Communist factor (de Gaulle) 17
Communist influence 14

Communist Party
protectionist position 153
and Sartre 122
Communist Party and press, during the Cold War 68–9
Communist/Socialist rift (1947) 67
Communists, and cultural criticism 71
comparative studies, little tried by French or Americans 241–2
conformism 131
American 118–19
Conseil Constitution 209
conservative revolution 217
Coste-Floret proposals for constitutional revision 208
Courtin, René 70
crisis issues 143
criticism of USA 193
Cuba, visited by Sartre and de Beauvoir 123
Cuban missile crisis 86
cultural and economic debates inseparable (1970s) 155
cultural imperialism 192
culture
American, French fascination with *puissance* and *modernité* of 229
and anti-culture 155
French: of the 1960s 98–9; politics of being transformed 26
Czechoslovakia, invasion of 81

Dallington, Sir Robert, comment on the French 38
Dandieu, Arnaud, *Le Cancer américain* 48
Darlan, Admiral
France as maritime and colonial arm of 'new Europe' 59–60
sought bargain with Germany 57
de Gaulle, *see* Gaulle, President Charles de 229
de Tocqueville, *see* Tocqueville, Alexis de
Debray, Régis 9, 226

Debré, Michel 207
  against free trade 151–2
  decentralisation 209
  decolonisation 215
  Franco-American friction 181–2
  deculturation, product of
    American-style liberalism 156
defence, French perceptions 85
Defferre, Gaston 209
défi americain 111, 112
democracy 233
détente, improvement in Soviet
  image 83–4
deterrence, of British and French
  nuclear weapons 183–4
diversification of economic
  relations, Communist
  idea 153
Domenach, Jean-Marie, on
  disinformation about
  Reagan 4
Dos Passos, John 117, 123
Doyen, General Paul 60
Drujon, François, *L'Amérique et
  l'avenir* 48
du Bellay, Joachim, *Deffence et
  illustration de la langue
  Françoyse* 24
Duhamel, Georges 239
  on America 49–51
  Scènes de la vie future 45, 49, 71,
    214
  Voyage á Moscou 50
Duhamel, Georges and Blanche, *Le
  Livre de l'amertume* 49
Dulles, Foster 70
Duroselle, Jean-Baptiste 170
  causes of mutual lack of
    understanding 227–8
Duverger, Maurice 206, 207, 208

East-West conflict 116, 131
  seen as key issue of century by
    Aron 130
economic aid, food and fuel for N.
  Africa (1941) 56
economic crisis
  lowered French image of
    America 91
  now overcome 92
economic recovery, USA 216–17
economic rivalry, seen by Vichy
  government 59
economic strategy considerations,
  importance of 143
economics, French perceptions 85
economy, the, French fascination
  with American *puissance* and
  modernité 229
education 240
emancipated woman 48
ethical models, offered both by
  France and USA 222
ethnic complexity 213
'Eurafrique' 59–60
Eurocommunist movement 147
Europe
  American attitudes towards x–
    xi
  danger in gradual submission to
    American cultural, economic
    and linguistic power 175
  need for technical prowess 185
European culture, seen as
  superior 214–15
European Defence Community
  (EDC) 173, 181, 230, 241
European idea 173

Faulkner, William H. 117, 123
federalism 209, 216
Fifth Republic
  anti-Americanism 169–70
  not at ease with American
    model 205
Finkielkraut, A., *La Défaite de la
  Pensée* 22
floating currencies 143
force de frappe 89, 125
foreign affairs, French fascination
  with American *puissance* and
  modernité 229
foreign domination, fear and
  rejection of 45
foreign policy changes, fostered
  pro-American sympathies 6–
  7

Fourth and Fifth Republics,
continuity between 16–17
Fourth Republic
acquiescence in American
objectives 181
expectations of USA 171
foreign policy goals beyond
country's means 172
pro-American feelings 15
relations with USA 171–4
France
attitudes towards USA xi;
correlation with attitudes to
Soviet Union 79–80; deeply
divided 1940–44 55; left-
wing ambiguity 5–6
behaviour as top-ranking
power 44
clash between economic
ambitions and cultural
identity 1
closed in upon itself 106
'colonisation' of 150
cultural identity threatened by
use of Americanisms 23
Declaration of the Rights of
Man 26
dislike of the Americans 35
effect of international
commitments 163–4
a history of 'antis' 242
an industrial competitor 161
inferiority complex: about
American model 161–2; at
time of liberation 83
interests differed from those of
USA 176
modernisation of 106–7
a more realistic view of French
power today 82–3
political extremes 223–4
preference for distant
strangers 38
salvation through internal revival
(Vichy) 58
saw itself as loser in global
economic war 13
and SDI 184–5
status within the Common

Market 152
strategic and military
independence 7
USA: little emigration to 44;
perceptions of 2; spread of
enthusiasm for 39; support
for economic policy 91
wished to be a world power 82
France, Anatole, L'île des
pingouins 48
'France éternelle, la' 1–2
Franco-American relations
a history of opinion swings 9–
18
a story of tension and
harmony 179
Franco/American rivalry 233–4
Franklin, Benjamin, Way to
Wealth 39
free trade, restructuring the
economy 148, 149
free trade/protectionism
controversy 152
French
acting as killjoys 230
admiration for foreigners 38
becoming French 213
entertaining illusions of
grandeur 82
in favour of less state
intervention 91–2
felt disappointment over
American economic aid 15
obsessed by thought of French
language and culture being
outstripped 232
opinions of USA's strengths and
weaknesses (1962) 93
prefer Reagan-style America 79
views of American society 238
wanting modernisation
(Americanisation) 215
French business community 112,
239
French civilisation, survival of 75
French Communist Party 179
22nd Congress, changes at 147–
8
anti-Americanism 17, 224

French Communist Party – *cont.*
  domestic policy 154
  economic policies 153–4
  electoral decline of 20
French Constitution (1958) 206–7
French decline 143, 145
  consensus about nature of ills 150
  temptation to blame USA 143–4
French economists, view of USA 216
French executives, trained in American business schools 141
French governing élite
  little attempt to import American practices 113
  perceptions dominated by political realities 112–13
French industry, pragmatic view of USA 225
French institutional system, new, American influence not obvious 209–10
French intellectual élite, opposing perceptions of the world 131
French intellectuals/intelligentsia
  1970s, turned away from realities of public life 7–8
  and American Universities 100–1
  anti-Americanism 97; became marginalised 9
  attachment of 109
  and Central Europe 101
  collective guilt about poor countries 215
  conversion to Western liberal democracy 101–2
  crisis of 106–7
  importance of 109
  left and right wing 116
  media-based 102
  neutralist 69–70
  new, pro-Americanism 98
  postwar political world-view 97–8
  rethink of national past 99–100
  struggled against capitalism and imperialism 99
  switching views of America 226
  USA: inconsistency towards 110–11; renewed interest in 101–2, 142; view of 98, 109
French internal debate, and anti-Americanism/pro-Americanism 231
French language 22–5
  defence of 232; by de Gaulle 175
  preserving purity of 2–3
French life, seen as backward 104
French literature, and anti-Americanism 43
French masses, and American mass culture 94
French media, and American journalism 114
French military policies 184
  seen as anti-American 183
French perceptions
  bipolarity of 81
  of Soviet Union 80, 84, 85
  of USA 80, 85, 86; decoupled 92–3
French political life, politicisation of 105
French political system, changing problems of 206
French public, saw Americans as liberators 60–1
French public opinion: somersault in opinions (1982–84) 87–8, 228; swing in after 1914–18 war 12
French society, diminished role of intellectuals 97
French system of representation, crisis in 206
French tourists in USA 240
Frigidares 17–18
Furet, François 215
future described 48

Gaillard, Félix 174
Gattaz, Ivon, inspired by American millionaires 39

Gaulle, Charles de, writings 225
Gaulle, President Charles de 81, 125, 174–8
  against Presidential government 209
  attitudes to USA 182–3
  basis of attitudes and policies towards USA 176–7
  concept of relations between Europe and USA 16
  conjectural anti-Americanism 111
  created an anti-American consensus 111–12
  created conditions for France to be less anti-American 229–30
  cured France of pathological anti-Americanism 178
  formula for national self-reliance 177
  ideas about the USA 175–6
  independence to Algeria and African colonies 182
  policies cured France of Americanophobia 175
  a ruthless moderniser 175
  stands against America 16–17
  suggested election of President by universal suffrage 207
  vision of Europe 17
Gaullism 7, 14, 229
  anti-Americanism 14
  and capitalist domination 152
  cultural roots 171
  ended structural anti-Americanism 169–70
  mistrust of USA 17
Gaullist RPR (Rassemblement Pour la République) 224
  adopted Jeanneney's ideas 151
Gaullists, left-wing 149–50
'géni français, le' 74
Gerassi, John (Tito), informed Sartre and de Beauvoir of the anti-establishment movement in USA 124
Germany
  demanded French assistance 60
  an industrial competitor 161
Gilson, Etienne 172
Europe, pro-American or neutral 15–16
Giscard d'Estaing, President Valéry 179, 183, 186, 225
  defeat of 156
  foreign policies of 148
  personality of 144
  seen as an anti-hero 144–5
  seen as subservient to USA 145–6
Gobard, Henri, and anti-culture 155
Goldring, Maurice, attacked Trilateral Commission Report 146
Gorbachev, modification of French intelligentsia's perceptions of USSR 20
Gorbachev effect 90
Goux, Christian 150
governing élites, consistent attitude to USA 110–13
GRECE (Groupes de Recherches et Etudes pour la Civilisation Européenne), and American perversions 9
Grosser, Alfred, on anti-Americanism 222
Gulags 19, 84, 99

Hassner, Pierre 19
  levels of analysis for international relations 83
Hauser, Henri, L'Amérique vivante 237
Heidegger, Martin, teachings 22
Helsinki Agreements 84
Hemingway, Ernest 123
Henri-Haye, Gaston, Vichy ambassador to Washington 56
Herriot, Edouard 50
Herzog, Philippe, a protectionist manifesto 153
Ho Chi Minh 181–2
human rights 101

Hungary, Soviet intervention 80–1
Huntington, Samuel, on frailty of American system 146–7

images, projected and accepted 231–2
individualism 214
 American 119
 new 103
individuals
 attitudes to USA 40–1
 growth of immunities 40
 pro- and anti-American sentiments 223
individuality and personality, not suppressed in USA 119
Indochina 173, 181
industrial criteria 140–1
industrial marriages 140
industrial models 165
industrial policy, and French left 165
industrialisation 47–8
INF Treaty 26
inflation 163
intellectual élite, cultural and political anti-Americanism of 94
intellectual gurus 8, 103, 226
intellectual ideologues 104–6
 view of the USA 104–5
intellectual indifference to USA 7
international crises, confidence in USA's ability to act wisely 86
international separation 152
international status quo, need for stand on 185
interventionism 139
 American 191–2
Irangate 26
Italian economic miracle 104

Japan 104
 differing French and British attitudes 36
 economic rise of 161
 an industrial competitor 161
 as an industrial model 141
 industrial organisation 162
Japanese model 162–3
jazz 49, 50
 Vichy campaign against 59
Jeanneney, Jean-Marcel, converted from free-trade 151
Jobert, Michel 81, 185, 186
 and anti-culture 155
 attacking both imperialisms 18–19
 considered French language at risk 21
 on Giscard government 145
joint ventures, boosted 141–2
journalists, and anti-Americanism 68–71
judgement of America, regarded as anti-American 220
judicial review 201–2
Julien, Claude, attacked Trilateral Commission Report 146, 147
July monarchy 11

Kabul factor 18–19, 81, 84–5
Koestler, Arthur 228
Korea, US intervention 121
Kravchenko, Victor 228

La Fayette 180
La Higuera, Pablo de, anti-Americanism 236–7
la méthode 194
Labiche, Eugène, *Trente millions de Gladiator* 43
Lambert, Edouard 190–1, 197
 on the American system for selecting judges 200
 scientific approach 195
Lambert, Jacques 197
 cultural imperialism 192
Landeau, Jean-François 150
Lang, Jack 155
 anti-American outbursts 106
 Mexico City statements 22
Larousse, Pierre, definition of *américanisme* 46
Latin American issue 185
Laval, Pierre 56–7
law of the many 47

law of the multitude 47
le Pors, Anicet 146
  on campaign of national
    depersonalisation 21–2
left-wing government 163–4
  revision of economic and foreign
    policies 163–4
Lehideux, François 59
Leninist theory of imperialism 67
liberalism
  an anathema to the left
    wing 149
  Giscardian 149
  of intellectual ideologues 104–5

McCarthyism 18, 70, 110, 172, 221, 242
Malherbe, Henri, on the American novel 73
Malmaison, André, *Terre d'Amérique* 49
management, American style 93, 138
management techniques, simplicity of 140–1
managerial styles, seen as national traits 137
Marchais, Georges 155
Marshall Plan 15, 71, 121
Marshall Plan myth 180–1
Marxism
  in 1970s 146
  and anti-Americanism 215
mass culture 71, 75
  American 94
  application of marketing techniques 25
  élitist approach to 24–5
  and high culture 47
mass media, and the French language 24–5
mass-consumption 71–2
mass-production 71–2, 73
masses, having a spontaneous morality (Sartre) 127–8
materialism 214
Mauriac, François, representative of French literary ideas about USA 74

Maurrasism, anti-Americanism 224
media, role of 239–40
media intellectuals 102–6
Mendès-France, Pierre 206
Middle East, French policy 186
Minc, Alain 104
Mitterrand experience 160
Mitterrand, President
  François 88–9, 179, 183, 184, 186, 213
  American tour 5–6
  doubts about a Presidential system 207–8
  foreign policy not influenced by communist ministers 179–80
modernisation, authoritarian 59
modernism, via protectionism 163
modernists (free traders) 143
'modernité' 93
  fear and rejection of 45
modernity 2, and the USA 1
Monde, Le, anti-American but favouring European construction 15–16
'mongrelisation' theories 61
Monnet, Jean
  concept of relations between Europe and USA 16
  integrated Atlantic partnership 173
Montherlant, Henri de 48
Morand, Paul 51
Morès, Marquis de 48
Morin, Edgar, *Le Journal de Californie* 8, 100
multi-party system 208
multinationals 112, 140, 239
  condemnation by left wing intellectuals ineffective 154
  excessive influence of 151
Murphy-Weygand agreement 56, 57

national independence 85
  a balancing act 81–2
  French concern for 80
  preservation of 179

national language = national identity 23–4
national partition 152
national sovereignty, erosion of 127
nationalisation, not necessary 149
nationalism, and protectionism 139
nations, problems need seeing in global context 35–7
NATO 181
  and presence of American troops in France 68
  seen to be weakening 89
negative faiths 42
neo-liberalism 91–2
neutralism 15, 81
  anti-American 172–3
  in Soviet-American conflict 171
New Deal 52, 172
newspapers 239–40
Noël, Professor Octave, *Le péril américain* 45–6
  on the influence of Duhamel 51
Noguès, General 62
North Atlantic Treaty 121
nuclear weapons, British and French, deterrence value 183–4

oil crises 148, 160
oil price increases 144
opinion polls 227
Ottawa Declaration (1974) 183

Paris collaborators, attacks on USA anti-capitalist and anti-racist 61
Paxton, Robert 101
PCF (Partie Communiste Française), *see* French Communist Party 148
peace movement, failure of in France 88
period influence 43–4
Pétain, Marshall 56, 58, 60
Pfaff, William, on the French 230
pin-up girls, Communist warnings against 73

Pinto, Roger
  analysis of actual imperial process 196–7
  on judicial review 201–2
Piquet, René 146
Plan Calcul (French Electronic Plan) 139, 143
  collapse of 145
politics of culture, French 20
Pompidou, Georges 183, 225
Popper, Karl 101
positive independence concept, waning of 83
Pozner, Vladimir, on American cultural influence 71
pragmatic intellectuals, wish to renovate France 104
pragmatism in French view of America 225
Presidential government 216
presidential model 205
pro-Americanism 102, 139, 215–16
  conjonctural 114–15
  and taste 39
pro-Sovietism 14
professionalism 137
protectionism 152, 153
  left-wing government 163
protectionists (favoured retrenchment) 143
public opinion 2

racism 189–90
Radio-France International 232–3
Ramadier government 67
Reagan administration 160
Reagan experience, effect of 164–5
Reagan foreign policy, European view 85–6
Reagan, President Ronald 86–7, 179, 213, 233
  a perfect anti-Mitterrand 105
  projected right image 5
  seen as lame-duck president 90
  superficial popularity of 217
Reagan-Gorbachev talks 26
Reaganism 242
  return to old American values 164

Index

Reaganomania 3–4
  decline in 90
Reaganomics 3, 217–18
regulated liberalism 149
Rémond, René 11, 194, 200
  on 19th-century literature 195
  on the American political scene 197
Resistance, anti-Americanism in 62–3
Resistance planning for post-war reconstruction 62–3
retrenchment, to stem France's decline 148, 149
revolutions, American and French 213
Rhine left bank issue 12
Rocard, Michel 179
  modernist position 153
Roosevelt, Franklin D.
  anti-colonial reasoning 182
  refusal to recognise Free French until 1944 55, 63
  social experiments 52
  Vichy Gamble 55, 63
Roosevelt, Theodore, popularised 'Americanism' 219
Rosenberg solidarity campaign 18
Rosenberg Trial and execution 70, 122, 172
  explosion of anti-Americanism 241
Russell Tribunal 123, 127–8
Russian factor (de Gaulle) 17

Sacco and Vanzetti affair 51–2
Safire, William, best definition of 'Americanism' 219
Saint-Robert, Philippe de
  comparing de Gaulle and Giscard d'Estaing 144
  wanted return of protectionism 152
Salacrou, Armand, on America 72
Sardou, Victorien, L'Oncle Sam 43
Sarre question 12
Sartre, Jean-Paul 70, 101, 116, 132
  á propos French novels written during the occupation 118
  anti-Americanism of 121, 122
  attacks on USA 116
  believed in fundamental importance of North-South antagonism 131
  finally condemned Soviet imperialism 131
  friend of the Maoists 130
  interest in American civilisation 117
  joined Communist Party 122
  Les Temps Modernes 119
  as a neutralist 121
  Russell Tribunal: speaking about 127–8; took part in 123
  The Respectful Prostitute, accused of anti-Americanism 120–1
  in USA as journalist (1945) 118–19
  view of American intellectuals 123–4
scholarship, pre and post-World War I 196
scientific and analytic methods 195, 196–7
Second Empire 47
Second Republic, and America 11–12
Sée, Paul, and the 'American Peril' 44–5
Serra, Sylvie 225
Servan-Schreiber, Jean-Jacques, *Le Défi américain* 216
Shaw, G. B. 41
Siegfried, André 51, 197
  Les Etats-Unis d'aujoud'hui 45
  on the Negro question 190
Six-Day War 186
social contracts 213
socialism 68
Socialist Party 224
Socialists, against American Imperialism 179
Solzhenitsyn effect 19, 81, 84, 85, 228
Sormon, Guy
  La Revolution Conservatrice Americaine 3
  La Solution Libérale 3

Soustelle, Jacques, extreme anti-Americanism 174
Soviet imperialism 84–5
Soviet Union 109
  fear of 88
  French perceptions at time of liberation 83
  image 83–4; collapse of (1970s-1980s) 19–20
  little criticised by Resistance 63
  no longer seen as model society 85
  seen as land of the future 98
  seen as totalitarian 99
Spain, anti-Americanism 230
stereotypes 137
Stoffaës, Christian, on cultural-economic debate 155
Strategic Defence Initiative (SDI) 184–5
Suez 81, 174, 181
Suffert, Georges
  Les Nouveaux Cowboys 215
  on Reaganomania 4
superpower images, alteration of in France 80
superpowers, French attitudes towards 82
Supreme Court 209
  role of 193

Tardieu, André 171, 199
  on American interventionism 191–2
  on centralisation in USA 198
  hoped France would follow American political pattern 198
  possibilities of American system of government 216
technological agreements 141–2
technology 112
  appealed to French left-wing government 5–6
  growing importance of 47
Tel Quel group 8
television news broadcasts 239–40
Thibau, Jacques 225
  on cultural homogenisation 21

thinking, open-style 101
Third World 126
  challenge to US industry 160–1
  taking over Soviet role 116
  USA influence indirect 173
Thorez, Maurice, denounced American expansionism 67
Tocqueville, Alexis de 40, 47, 101, 215, 225–6, 233, 238
  on American institutions 10–11
  in American relations with foreigners 220
  criticised 194–5
  De La Démocratie 36
totalitarianism 21, 101
  Soviet, new evil for Paris intelligentsia 19–20
tourism, impact on French perceptions of USA 240
trans-Atlantic solidarity 183–4
Trilateral Commission (American think-tank) 146

un-Americanness 221
unilateralism 182
Universal Exhibition, first 46
universal models 233, 238
US economic power, falling 160
US industry 137
  challenges to 160–1
US markets, access to 140
US nuclear missile deployment 92
US President
  image of 85
  influence of personal image 86–7, 88
  position of 198
USA
  accused by Sartre of Americanising and depersonalising Europe 123
  affected laws of the market (Jobert) 145
  believed it had a civilising mission 196
  the case against 49
  the Constitution 26–7
  cultural imperialism 192–3

cultural picture of 103
desire to contain
  Communism 126
domination of world
  markets 125
economic dynamism 44
emerging as a great power
  (1900s) 45
European knowledge of x
fascinates and exasperates
  French 1
finds identity in dedication to a
  value system 223
French criticisms never
  obsessive 42
French perceptions
  unchanged 25–6
historically regarded
  suspiciously by British 36–7
images of (1953 and 1962) 93
lacking in culture 214
little status for intellectuals 71
modernité and domination 229
negative French view 99
a new look at 100
non-intervention in European
  political disputes 44
not exploiters of Third
  World 126
pictured as warmongering 70
a pseudo-target 231
recognised as dynamic and
  creative 100
refusal to compromise over
  French debt 13
seen as antithesis of Soviet Union
  or Third World 116
seen as bulwark against Soviet
  threat 182
seen by French as political and
  social barometer 26
seen as imposing its values on
  others 192
seen as scapegoat 160, 172
seen as willing to support
  France 89
seldom adopted as political
  model 216

source of attraction to French
  intelligentsia 213–14
warmongering image 87
warned that French would
  defend N. Africa 62

Vailland, Roger, on need for
  Frigidaires 17–18
Vedel, Georges 206
Vedel/Duverger controversy 206
Verne, Jules 43
Vichy
  American threats 58–60
  limits of American
    usefulness 55–8
  problem of allied invasion 61–2
  saw America as militarily
    incapable 57–8
  strategies of internal revival 58–60
  variations in space and time 60–2
Vichy coalition
  friends of USA gradually forced
    out 60
  other extreme wished for
    coalition with Axis 61
Vichy government 55
  fought against American cultural
    infiltration 59
Vichy leaders
  did not want American armed
    liberation 57
  tried to use American tie against
    German impositions 57
  used non-Socialist anti-American
    arguments 58–9
Vietcong 128
Vietnam 223
Vietnam War 81, 86, 99, 110, 123,
  127–9, 186, 242
  American defeat 100
  not judged on ethical
    grounds 129–30
Voice of America 232

Wall Street crash 49
war debts, and anti-
  Americanism 239

Watergate 100, 242
Weygand, General 60, 62
Williamsburg summit 216–17
Winock, Michel 109
women
   differing attitudes of 40
   a recurrent theme in image of USA 48–9
work ethic, rehabilitation of 217
world economic crisis 160
world monetary system 160

World War I, swings in French feelings for America 12–13
World War II, ambivalent French attitude to USA 13–15

Yalta myth 14, 180
Yom Kippur War 130

Zeldin, Theodore 94
Zhdanov Report 17